Lonely Planet Publications
Melbourne | Oakland | London | Paris

Simone Egger &
David McClymont

Melbourne

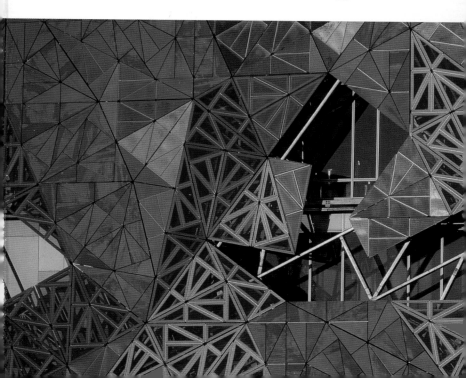

The Top Five

1 St Kilda
Go beachside then venture inland to the beckoning cake shops, boutiques and cafés (p75)

2 Yarra River Cruise
Gain a special perspective of Melbourne (p53)

3 Melbourne Museum
Explore the wonders of the dynamic Melbourne Museum (p66)

4 Federation Square
Experience this striking public space and all its attractions (p62)

5 Royal Botanic Gardens
Take time out in Melbourne's stunning backyard (p60)

Contents

Published by Lonely Planet Publications Pty Ltd
ABN 36 005 607 983

Australia Head Office, Locked Bag 1, Footscray,
Victoria 3011, ☎ 03 8379 8000, fax 03 8379 8111,
talk2us@lonelyplanet.com.au

USA 150 Linden St, Oakland, CA 94607,
☎ 510 893 8555, toll free 800 275 8555,
fax 510 893 8572, info@lonelyplanet.com

UK 72–82 Rosebery Ave, Clerkenwell, London,
EC1R 4RW, ☎ 020 7841 9000, fax 020 7841 9001,
go@lonelyplanet.co.uk

France 1 rue du Dahomey, 75011 Paris,
☎ 01 55 25 33 00, fax 01 55 25 33 01,
bip@lonelyplanet.fr, www.lonelyplanet.fr

The Authors

SIMONE EGGER

Simone Egger lives in Melbourne and works as a freelance photojournalist. She worked with Lonely Planet as an editor before crossing over to authoring. Travel has always been in her bio; she has traversed the globe, which has given her a special appreciation for cities, none more than her home town.

Simone's freelance work has led to investigations of the city's cultural habits, including what motivates people to collect miniature things, and how comfortable city-folk are eating native wildlife, such as possums. Photographic assignments have included documenting everything from muesli bars to the production and installation of public-art projects.

Simone supplemented university studies by working in bars, which proved to be a hard habit to break. Being the world s worst cook, she eats out most nights. Her network of friends, which includes avid shoppers, chefs, actors and artists, are experts in many fields and all contributed invaluable on-the-ground advice (see p190) to Simone as she worked on this edition of *Melbourne*.

DAVID McCLYMONT

David McClymont grew up in a small fishing village on the western coast of Scotland, moving to Australia in 1989. He wrote the previous two editions of *Melbourne* and was a major contributor to Lonely Planet s *Out to Eat – Melbourne* 2001 and 2002, *Australia* 11 and *Unpacked Again*. David lives in Melbourne with his wife and two grey cats.

CONTRIBUTING AUTHORS

Geraldine Barlow

Geraldine Barlow is a curator and project manager of Irish, English and Maori (Ngapuhi) descent who is based in Melbourne. She has developed projects with Australian and international artists at the Australian Centre for Contemporary Art and for the Visual Arts programme of the Melbourne International Festival of the Arts. She was a key member of the team that organised the Melbourne International Biennial in 1999. In this new edition of *Melbourne* Geraldine wrote the Visual Arts section of the Arts chapter.

Jeff Sparrow

Jeff Sparrow is the coauthor of *Radical Melbourne* I and II. He is the Reviews Editor at *Overland* magazine, and a member of Socialist Alternative. Jeff wrote the Radical Melbourne walking tour for this edition of *Melbourne*.

PHOTOGRAPHER

James Braund

James Braund is a self-taught photographer specialising in environmental portraits and stylistic reportage. His work has featured in a variety of publications, both in Australia and internationally, in the corporate, arts and charity fields.

After a brief stint in the UK, and having survived one too many London winters, James returned to Australia in 1994, making Melbourne his base. Initially armed with only a Melways map and a camera, he worked for a daily newspaper. Now, having enjoyed Melbourne's rich and diverse cultural offerings, its legendary restaurants and laneway cafés, James wholeheartedly agrees that Melbourne is the world's most livable city. He lives in the inner city with his wife and baby son, and always makes time for his daily fix of the essential Melbourne ingredient – coffee!

Introducing Melbourne

Melbourne is lush: every facet of its nature is abundant and generous. Its denizens have connections to all parts of the world – nurturing the metropolis of ideas that Melbourne generates and celebrates with gusto. It's a city with wit, style and energy, yet it's demure about its assets. Cobbled alleys and modest doorways conceal an astonishing array of world-class arts, cuisines, design, music, bars and shops. Serendipity is this city's middle name.

The cityscape is fringed by rivers with wide promenades and grassy banks, and endowed with large pockets of garden and parkland. Melbourne's newest park, Birrarung Marr, is another notch in the city's green belt. Bordering the Yarra River, it provides the perfect upriver vantage of downtown. On the opposite river bank, the Royal Botanic Gardens live up to their regal title: grand in both scale and constitution, they form a staggeringly beautiful oasis.

Melbourne celebrates its diversity with a festival or event every other week, where the only door policy is a desire to join in. The city is discerning and conscious, yet not too proud to don a multicoloured beanie and cheer a beloved sporting team to victory. International events hosted around town include the Festival of the Arts, Grand Prix, Comedy Festival and Film Festival. Several Melbourne-specific events attract the nation's attention, particularly the Melbourne Cup horse race and the Australian Rules football grand final. This city officially celebrates the themes of food and wine, ethnicity, youth arts, writers, sexuality and music, to name a few. Local community events extend the list, from sci-fi conventions to kite-flying displays.

Trams, trains, riverboats and signature yellow taxis maintain Melbourne's pace, providing a comprehensive network to move people through the city and surrounding suburbs.

Melbourne's inner neighbourhoods are thriving minicities (minus the office towers). Each has a distinctive character, with a colourful infrastructure to support the city's residents and guests. Bustling markets, eclectic cafés, specialist shops and corner pubs typify life here. No visit to Melbourne is complete without a stop in seaside St Kilda, where the giant face of Luna Park smiles approvingly at the surrounding revelry. Brunswick St, Fitzroy's audacious assortment of cafés, restaurants, boutiques and bars will entice you out of the CBD. Lygon St (Carlton), on the other hand, will seduce you with its

Lowdown

Population 3.21 million
Time zone Eastern Standard Time (GMT + 10 hours)
Daylight saving From the last Sunday in October to the first Sunday in March
Hotel room Around $150
Coffee $2.80
Tram ticket $3
Pot of beer $2.80
Conversation topic The weather – it's a fickle thing

Italian chic, and you'll drift over to Victoria St (Richmond) lured by the aromas emanating from its Vietnamese kitchens. You may even flit down Chapel St (Prahran), drawn to the designer clothing stores by day, and the dimly lit bars and clubs after dusk.

Everyday life looks good in Melbourne, literally, where day-to-day items are not merely functional, but stylish too. From tram shelters to tea strainers, serious thought has gone into ensuring their design is imbued with beauty and meaning. Melbourne's built environment is the city's most conspicuous display of design: vertical layers of architectural styles reflect the changing needs and self-image of this continuously updating metropolis. Ornate grey Victorian architecture dominates the skyline; like a good-humoured parent, it tolerates the modern minimalist styles moving into town.

The city's newest iconic structure, Federation Square, is both revered and reviled for its aesthetic, but there's no doubt that it has become the cultural heart of the city. It's a public gathering place, and houses two main cultural institutions – the Australian Centre for the Moving Image and the National Gallery of Victoria's Australian art collection – as well as other cultural outlets such as shops and restaurants.

More than the populace of any other Australian city, Melburnians eat at restaurants and cafés. The range of quality eating establishments is deservedly world-renowned. Melbourne is a city blessed with flavour influences from around the globe and chefs bold enough to experiment with them. Whether it's blintz for breakfast, noodles about noon or kangaroo fillet for dinner, Melbourne has it covered. Equal consideration is given to ambience as to preparation and produce. Eating out in Melbourne is a memorable experience.

Café culture dominates by day, and coffee rules the café. Drinking excellent espresso is as common as breathing. This caffeine-savvy society is accustomed to being greeted by waiters with a lilted 'coffee?' instead of a 'hello'.

By night, Melburnians slip into a svelte, comfortable bar. Lively and laid-back drinking dens are tucked away in every nook and cranny around town. Step off the main street and venture down a city laneway. These hidden narrow hinterlands are a vital part of the city, containing Melbourne's hippest bars and cafés, and embellished with public art works commissioned annually by the city council.

Melbourne tends to be modest about its treasures, but there's a riot of activity going on behind the ordered city grid. It's as surprising as its weather and as diverse as its people. You have only to come to it to be richly rewarded; the city won't come to you.

Essential Melbourne

- Australian Centre for the Moving Image (ACMI) at Federation Square (p62)
- Royal Botanic Gardens (p60)
- Immigration Museum (p65)
- Queen Victoria Market (p65)
- Rialto Towers observation deck (p65)

SIMONE'S TOP MELBOURNE DAY

I love that instant when the fog of sleep clears and there's the realisation that it's a nonwork day; I have no plans so am free to choose how to spend each moment just before it happens.

I don't really want to swim, but want to have swum, so I get out of bed and out of my head. I follow the black line at the bottom of Fitzroy pool (p143), where the 'Aqua Profonda' sign reminds me how profoundly good water is. Still with goggle marks around my eyes, I buy a Danish pastry at Babka Bakery (p107), and eat it while walking up Brunswick St to Newtown SC, where Kate makes a killer coffee.

I might head into town to buy produce at the Queen Victoria Market (p65), trying to show some restraint in the deli section, then squeeze in a squiz at the Centre for Contemporary Photography (p66) before going west for a cruise along the Maribyrnong River (p53) among the Legolike industry of Melbourne's working docklands. Lunch is a steaming bowl of wonton soup from Bo De Trai (p115), in Footscray.

Over to Prahran to mooch through Chapel Bazaar (p152) looking for that scratchy second-hand Sergio Mendes record. Then I'll just feel the fabrics in my favourite clothes shop, Scanlan & Theodore (p148); some time later…emerge with carry bag and guilty expression.

There's just enough time to catch a movie before dinner at Ladro (p106), then a fabulously big Polish beer and nip of vodka at Borsch, Vodka & Tears (p122), where I'm slowly working my way through the menu of 103 vodkas.

City Life

City Life

MELBOURNE TODAY

Melbourne is intrinsically clever without being brash about it and finds itself quite suddenly thrust onto the world stage. The city has been softly generating ideas and hosting international events for as long as it can remember, but recent major building developments and international marketing campaigns have pushed it into the limelight. It's still blinking with all the bright lights and shiny new surfaces, unused to the hoopla associated with being centre stage.

The past five years have seen a complete overhaul of Melbourne's public institutions, as well as the construction of major new ones. The Melbourne Museum, National Gallery of Victoria (NGV), Melbourne Cricket Ground (MCG) and Australian Centre for Contemporary Art (ACCA) have all experienced a sleek, minimalist rebirth. New arrivals include Federation Square, the Docklands development and Telstra Dome.

The apparent aim of all this development has been to redefine Melbourne as an international city. To attract more overseas visitors and business, a higher degree of visibility and accessibility in the city's institutions has been necessary. To appeal to the broadest possible market, there also needs to be a sense of familiarity in a place. International environments (think airports) are by nature devoid of warmth and character, so as not to offend and to facilitate an easy transition. The debate continues as to whether Melbourne has been so successful in creating an international environment that it has overlooked the people it's meant to serve – the city's residents. Like anything new, it takes time for things to settle. After tentative beginnings, Melbourne is settling into its new institutions, forming a history and a relationship with them. Developments such as Federation Square have been bold enough to

Victorian terraces

take the risk of being unique, making a clear statement that Melbourne will not be diluted into international cultural obscurity.

Melbourne is careful, too, to preserve the icons of its history. Physical markers of the city's rich heritage are stridently protected. Dismissed by its critics as conservative, Melbourne's reverence for its history guards it from the threat of a cultural whitewash inherent in the single focus of a global push. Melburnians welcome the new, but not at the expense of compromising the city's diversity. The Melbourne Central shopping centre, though not particularly graceful, is a prime example. This complex swallowed a 50m-high lead shot tower built in 1889; the Art Nouveau brick tower was preserved inside, dwarfed by three storeys of retail outlets and capped by an enormous glass dome.

The city's development is not limited to the commercial sphere. New apartments have mushroomed throughout town in what has proved to be something of a cargo culture. A build-it-and-they-will-come mentality has been deflated, with many empty apartments generating a nail-biting habit among investors.

With more than 1.5 million cars in Melbourne (more than one per household), road-use issues provide frequent fodder for discussion. There's a constant fracas over delivery of services and tolls. Concerns range from speed limits, the intermittent closure of the Burnley Tunnel due to cracks, and the efficacy of speed cameras, to the eTag shemozzle when users of the toll-collecting unit received fines for nonuse of the units – the battery life had been overlooked.

Many of Melbourne's facilities were privatised during the 1990s in a state sell off instituted by the then government. Public transport, prisons, emergency-call operators and utilities were decommissioned in an attempt to rescue the mired. Many of the private operators have since come under scrutiny, resulting in frequent and costly Royal Commissions. Melbourne was most prominently affected a few years back when tram conductors were replaced with machines. Hundreds of conductors joined the unemployment queue, as passengers grappled with a flawed ticketing system undergoing serious teething problems.

Conversation Starters

- 'Who makes the best coffee in town?'
- Anything to do with sport. For the uninitiated try, 'Who do you barrack for?' or 'Why is it called the Melbourne Cricket Ground if footy is the game predominantly played there?'
- 'Is there a sporting facility that isn't being refurbished for the Commonwealth Games in 2006?'
- To smokers clustered outside cafés: 'Did you hear that some restaurants in NYC serve tobacco as an ingredient with meals?'
- 'Where'd you get that fabulous bag/pair of shoes/tattoo/haircut?'

City Life – City Calendar

CITY CALENDAR

Melbourne's fervour for a festival has earned it the moniker of 'Events Capital'. It's a crammed calendar, with city streets and venues turned over to the public to celebrate everything from fashion to anti-fashion, film and food. Following is a selection; check local press for comprehensive listings or grab a copy of Me!bourne Events – updated monthly – from the Melbourne Visitor Information Centre, Federation Square. For a list of public holidays see p185.

JANUARY
AUSTRALIAN OPEN
www.australianopen.com; Melbourne Park
Come January, the National Tennis Centre is filled the 'oohs' and 'aahs' of Australia's Grand Slam tennis championship. It attracts the world's top players and provides occasion for adult spectators to paint their faces – in national colours.

CHINESE NEW YEAR
www.melbournechinatown.com.au; Chinatown, Little Bourke St
Amid bells, incense and drumming, huge crowds gather for this festival, which culminates in a frenetic dragon parade. For more on the dragon see p54

MIDSUMMA FESTIVAL
www.midsumma.org.au
Melbourne's annual gay and lesbian arts festival comprises over 100 events across the city. All rainbow-coloured streams of the arts are represented.

9

Top Ethnic Events

- **Lunar New Year Festival** (☎ 9428 1060) In January, Victoria St (Richmond) celebrates Vietnamese New Year, with lanterns, moon cakes and dance.
- **Antipodes Festival** (☎ 9662 3307; www.antipodesfestival.com.au) March sees the city's Greek quarter in Lonsdale St (between Swanston and Russell Sts) celebrate film, music and visual art, which crescendoes to the Glendi street festival on the weekend nearest 25 March.
- **Irish Festival and St Patrick's Day** Yep, there's green beer flowing at Irish pubs all over the city. Dancing, singing and food stalls also feature at various venues for several days up to and including 17 March. Check at the **Melbourne Visitor Information Centre** (Map pp202–04; Federation Sq) for venues.
- **Lygon Street Festa** (☎ 9654 0999; www.festagroup.com.au) Since 1978, this late-October Italian festival has brought out the *scopa* cards and bocce balls. Celebrations include community soccer matches, the famous waiters' race, music and, of course, food.
- **Hispanic Community Fiesta** (☎ 8307 2743) In November, Johnston St (Fitzroy) celebrates all things Latin, with song and dance, food and stalls.

FEBRUARY
ST KILDA FESTIVAL
www.stkildafestival.com.au; Acland & Fitzroy Sts, St Kilda

Held on the second weekend in February, this festival justifies St Kilda's reputation for housing a disproportionate number of artists, musicians and writers. Acland St is closed to vehicular traffic and opened to pedestrians, food stalls, street parties, parades and concerts. Restaurants take over the Fitzroy St footpaths. Buff bods, trippers and day-trippers revel at the festival's finale concert and fireworks display over the beach.

MARCH
AUSTRALIAN FORMULA ONE GRAND PRIX
www.grandprix.com.au; Albert Park

Tranquil Albert Park becomes a world-class racing venue as drivers compete on a 5.3km loop around **Albert Park Lake** (p78). For four days, spectators cram the verges of the lake hoping for a fleeting glimpse as the Formula Ones flash by.

MELBOURNE FASHION FESTIVAL
www.mff.com.au

This week-long fashion festival features parades of ready-to-wear garments from hundreds of designers, and hosts fashion forums and exhibitions.

MELBOURNE FOOD & WINE FESTIVAL
www.melbfoodwinefest.com.au

Recently listed among the top 10 international 'hot tickets', Australia's largest food and wine festival has a minted reputation for accessible culinary excellence. Events take place at venues across the city and include market tours, wine tastings, cooking classes and presentations by celebrity chefs.

MOOMBA FESTIVAL
www.melbourne.vic.gov.au; Yarra River

Moomba features 10 days of carnival atmosphere helped along by fireworks, an outdoor art show, a world-class water-skiing event and a Dragon Boat Festival. Back by popular demand is the Birdman Rally, where competitors launch into the Yarra in handmade flying machines. There is some contention over just what 'moomba' means. Organisers will tell you it's an Aboriginal word meaning 'let's get together and have fun'. Others contend that it translates to something more like 'stick your festival'.

APRIL
ANZAC DAY PARADE
Shrine of Remembrance

With a dawn service at the Shrine in King's Domain and a parade along St Kilda Rd, Anzac Day (25 April) is a moving tribute to those who fought and died for Australia.

BELLS BEACH SURFING CLASSIC
www.ripcurl.com.au; Bells Beach

Officially known as the Rip Curl Pro, this event, held over five days (up to and including Easter Sunday), sees the world's top surfers ride the wave of success and celebrity on some of Australia's largest breakers. Nature is a fickle thing, so the competition is sometimes moved along the coast to wherever the waves are.

INTERNATIONAL COMEDY FESTIVAL
www.comedyfestival.com.au

Held at various venues across the city from late March to mid-April, when Melbourne becomes one big laughing stock. One of the three largest comedy festivals in the world, this event brings together Australia's finest comedians and some first-rate international performers, including stand-up and cabaret.

INTERNATIONAL FLOWER & GARDEN SHOW
www.melbflowershow.com.au;
Royal Exhibition Bldg & Carlton Gardens

It's spring every autumn at the Flower & Garden Show. This colourful exhibition is an indoor and outdoor extravaganza, and is considered Australia's leading flower and garden show.

MAY
NEXT WAVE FESTIVAL
www.nextwave.org.au

Celebrating unpopular culture from the city's young, emerging artists, Next Wave runs for two weeks at several venues across town.

ST KILDA FILM FESTIVAL
www.stkildafilmfestival.com.au

This is Australia's longest-running short-film festival, showcasing fiction, animation, documentaries, music video and experimental films. It's held at various venues across town and highlights 35mm film and, to a lesser extent, video. The competition has around 20 category awards sharing a prize pool of over $40,000.

JULY
MELBOURNE INTERNATIONAL FILM FESTIVAL
www.melbournefilmfestival.com.au

This celebration of celluloid showcases some of the best in international and local film making. It's held over two weeks at various cinemas across the city. The programme includes guests, Q&As, forums and the ever-popular Festival Club for heady debriefing discussions after film screenings.

AUGUST
MELBOURNE WRITERS' FESTIVAL
www.mwf.com.au; CUB Malthouse, South Melbourne

Meet the author of that book you fell in love with, or learn how not to be left on the shelf at a writing workshop. Beginning in the last week of August, the writers' festival features 10 days of forums and events celebrating, investigating and popularising reading, writing, books and ideas.

SEPTEMBER
AFL GRAND FINAL
www.afl.com.au; MCG

Unless you're willing to camp out by the ticket booth for a few days, you may have to settle for spending the final day of the Australian Football League (AFL) season in front of the telly. Choose a public TV, such as at Federation Square or in a pub, to experience finals fever. This is Melbourne's beloved game, so you can expect a fair amount of hubbub at finals time.

MELBOURNE FRINGE FESTIVAL
www.melbournefringe.org.au

One of Melbourne's most interesting festivals, the Fringe Festival is devoted to all that is innovative and experimental in the local arts scene. You name it, it's on the bill: theatre, music, performance art, visual art and design. It runs from late September until mid-October – pick up a copy of the schedule and make your way around town from one spectacle to the next.

ROYAL MELBOURNE SHOW
www.royalshow.com.au;
Royal Melbourne Showgrounds, Flemington

The country comes to town for this large agricultural fair. Find out who's the best in show, and judge for yourself how much a dog can resemble its owner (or vice versa) at the dog show. Other events include a rodeo, showjumping, rides and show bags full of goodies. The showgrounds are pegged for a major redevelopment; a theme park has been suggested.

OCTOBER
AUSTRALIAN MOTORCYCLE GRAND PRIX
www.grandprix.com.au; Phillip Island

Held midmonth on Phillip Island, the motorcycle grand prix is dedicated to really fast riding.

MELBOURNE INTERNATIONAL ARTS FESTIVAL
www.melbournefestival.com.au

The Melbourne Festival is a highlight of Melbourne's festival calendar. Held at various venues around the city, the festival features a programme of visual art, as well as Australian and international performers of theatre, opera, dance and music. After three years of directing the festival, Robyn Archer hands over to Kristy Edmunds for 2005.

OKTOBERFEST
www.melboctfest.com;
Royal Melbourne Showgrounds, Flemington
A three-day event styled on the Bavarian festival of the same name, this is your chance to sample Bavarian food, beer and music. Don your best lederhosen and drinking cap; beer goggles are provided.

NOVEMBER
SPRING RACING CARNIVAL
www.racingvictoria.net.au

This series of horse races is one of the highlights of the Victorian sporting and social calendar. The culmination of the Spring Racing Carnival is the Melbourne Cup, known as the 'horse race that stops the nation'. It's held at Flemington Racecourse on the first Tuesday in November, a public holiday in Victoria. You can just about feel the entire nation hold its breath as the horses are reined into the starting boxes. Even if you can't make it to the racecourse, it's worth going to a race party or a pub to catch the action.

DECEMBER
BOXING DAY TEST
www.mcg.org.au; MCG
The post-Christmas slump is traditionally deferred with day one of the Boxing Day cricket Test, which draws around 70,000 people.

CULTURE
IDENTITY
Melbourne's most defining characteristic is its cultural diversity. Around 40% of the city's population was born outside Australia, with over 130 countries recorded as Melburnians' places of birth. There are distinct pockets of ethnic grouping throughout Melbourne and its suburbs, with shops and food outlets providing imported goods.

Melbourne's crosscurrents of ethnicity greatly influence the way people live and play. There's an outlet, celebration, support group and activity for every taste and preference. In one night in Melbourne you could see *butoh* (modern Japanese performance art) and take a salsa lesson before heading to a late-night jazz club. Melburnians are accustomed to a wide variety of influences and opportunities; it's a city that, overall, lives harmoniously as the sum of all its disparate parts. Racism, as a symptom of fear, does exist. It's most prevalent in the 'us and them' mentality adopted by individuals to dismiss practices and beliefs they don't fully understand and therefore see as a threat. Publicly, though, the city's institutions and bylaws are nondiscriminatory and encourage residents to retain their cultural practices. The numerous public festivals and arts projects with a specific ethnic focus encourage participation from the broader community, which promotes understanding and acceptance, while providing a forum for ethnic communities to celebrate their beliefs.

Of all the countries of origin represented in Melbourne, those with the highest number of residents include the UK, Malaysia, Vietnam, China and Singapore. Melbourne is currently experiencing a new wave of immigration from the Middle East. You'll see, or rather taste, Middle Eastern influences in restaurants about town. Since the mid-1970s, immigrants have come from Southeast Asia and the Pacific, many as refugees from Vietnam and Cambodia. In the aftermath of WWII, thousands migrated from Europe. Melbourne's large numbers of Greek, Italian and Jewish people date back to this time, with others coming from places such as Turkey, Lebanon, Malta, Poland and

Top Five Souvenir Books

- **Architecture** *Guide to Melbourne Architecture* by Philip Goad – one for architecture buffs.
- **Art** *lux et nox* by Bill Henson – an urban-adolescent narrative by Melbourne's pre-eminent art photographer.
- **Chronicle** *The Melbourne Book: A History of Now* by Maree Coote – a pictorial ode to this superb city.
- **Cooking** *The Cook's Companion* by Stephanie Alexander – the bible of Melbourne kitchens.
- **Culture** *Car Wars* by Graeme Davison – Melbourne's dominant car culture has shaped its mental and physical environment.

the former Yugoslavia. During the gold rush in the 19th century, people came from all over the world, particularly from China, to join the first white settlers, who were predominantly Anglo-Celtic.

Around 25,000 to 35,000 Koories (indigenous Australians) and Torres Strait Islanders live in Victoria, more than half of whom live in Melbourne's inner suburbs. They work patiently for self-determinism, slowly breaking down stereotypes. The federal government pulled funding from the troubled Aboriginal and Torres Strait Islander Commission (ATSIC) in 2004. The loss of ATSIC has dissolved the indigenous Australian voice in the political arena – further dispossessing the community from the imposed system they are expected to live by.

It's been said that Melbourne's laid-back character stems from its beginnings, with European settlement. Whereas Sydney was settled with convicts, Melbourne's first settlers were pastoralists – explaining the hackneyed comparison between the two cities, with Sydney as the showy sibling needing to prove itself, and Melbourne as its practical counterpart, happy to get on in a productive manner without the fanfare.

Melbourne may not trumpet its assets to the world, but it certainly likes a celebration. Festivals and commemorations are centred on the arts and sport, but are also inspired by religious beliefs, with a range of faiths practised in Melbourne. A shrinking majority of people in Victoria are at least nominally Christian. The Catholic Church accounts for about 30% of Christians in the state, with the original Irish adherents boosted by the large number of Mediterranean immigrants. Non-Christian minorities also abound in Melbourne; the main faiths are Buddhism, Judaism and Islam. Melbourne's religious leaders promote productive interfaith relations with a show of mutual respect and a readiness to listen.

Some would argue that sport is the dominant religion. It's the city's most conspicuous activity, with hundreds of thousands of devotees. Australian football is the main denomination, but anything goes. Sport's importance in Melbourne is reflected by the amount of media coverage it receives. Sport coverage on commercial TV news is approximately one-third of total airtime (advertising comprising another third), and it's fairly common for a sports-related story to make the front page of newspapers.

Equal support exists for the arts, though it's less of a spectacle, being hardly televised and attracting fewer crowds to one place. Melbourne's artistic population is dispersed around the innumerable public and private galleries. Recently over 4500 Melburnians descended on the city at 5am in cold, drizzly conditions to get their gear off for New York photographer Spencer Tunick. He described Melburnians as 'absolute freedom lovers with thick skins'.

LIFESTYLE

The city's diversity makes it nearly impossible to present a typical profile of a Melburnian. Melbourne's blend of lifestyles is influenced by so many variable factors, which is precisely what makes the city so rich and appealing. Melburnians have relatively few restrictions on how they choose to live. The one common guiding influence would have to be money, and the pursuit of it.

According to Australian Bureau of Statistics data, the average full-time wage in Victoria exceeded $1000 a week in May 2004. To increase their opportunities for employment and remuneration, more than 53% of city residents have some form of tertiary qualification. Melbourne's increasing number of university graduates surpasses the national average.

There's a determined work ethic in the city, with many Melburnians working harder and longer to afford a lifestyle that includes luxuries such as travel. Domestic and overseas travel is enjoyed by many in Melbourne…Lonely Planet's home town. And while disposable incomes allow many Melburnians to buy into the city's chichi design aesthetic, there's an increasing awareness of where things come from, in terms of environmental sustainability. Items that are produced in a sustainable manner are highly valued, with Melburnians prepared to pay a premium for such products.

Despite there being a hundred options for a Melburnian to choose from on any given day, the majority of people know what they like and like what they know. The city moves at a moderate pace and has a high level of relatively sedentary participation. Coffee is a verb here and Melburnians do it at a huge number of cafés across the city. More than the

Steering Slogans

Melburnians love their cars. Apart from being a mere mode of transport, the car embodies a sense of personal freedom. So, it's in keeping that car owners use their much-loved 'mobiles' to also express their personality and status. But with 1.5 million cars on Melbourne's roads, it's increasingly difficult to stand out in the traffic. On closer inspection, Melbourne's vehicles reveal a lot about what drivers think of themselves and their city, as well as what their city thinks of them.

Many cars carry clues to a driver's beliefs and preferences. Bumper stickers tell you everything from what radio station drivers prefer to the activities they do in their spare time. Then, there are those yellow suction-signs that don't say much at all, such as 'Baby on Board'. So? Rear-view mirror jewellery is another preferred car decoration. What a pair of fluffy dice or a dancing Elvis tells you about the driver though, is entirely at your discretion. Personalised number plates are clinchers. Not so much the ones that bear the driver's initials, but those that bear the driver's philosophy (condensed to the required six characters): ENVOUS, FANCME, 2HOT4U and GDAYM8.

The state government has personalised number plates as well, imprinting a slogan that appears underneath the registration number. In 1977 all cars carried 'Victoria – The Garden State'. While it's true that there are a large number of gardens in Victoria, boasting the fact on a car – nemesis of gardens everywhere – seems ironic. Perhaps 'Park State' would have been more appropriate, given the double meaning of the word. Nevertheless, it endured for 17 years, until being replaced with 'Victoria – On the Move', an initiative of the Kennett government in 1994. This was also the year when the city's major developments began and, with them, the push for Melbourne to become a more global, business-oriented city. That lasted six years, after which Victoria was in a state of shock, uncertain of what it had become. The state settled for 'Victoria' while it scratched its head. In 2000, Premier Bracks decided on 'Victoria – The Place to Be'. There's still a slight hint of hedging by the government, however, as it prompts the question: The place to be…what?

residents of any other Australian city, Melburnians eat out at restaurants and cafés. Most Melburnians will have seen a film or visited an exhibition or museum in the last month. And despite there being a high level of participation in sports, it's mostly from a spectator's perspective. Victorians aren't the most active bunch, with childhood obesity rates tripling in Australia over the last decade, second only to the US.

Melbourne's changeable weather has created a city of sun worshippers: when the sun's out, so is the city. The population seems to double on a sunny day, with people soaking it up in every available public space. Don't be surprised to see folk lolling in an inner-city park wearing not much more than what equates to Lycra undies. Etiquette seems to be that as long as one is lying down in said undies, it's acceptable. Walking about derobed is ill-advised and will attract unwarranted attention.

There's a dominant car culture in Melbourne. More than 76% of employed people drive to work, despite the available public transport. The car is a person's private sanctuary, seemingly removing them from public accountability. From a car, people exhibit uncharacteristically unsociable behaviour: they shout abuse at their fellow drivers and pick their noses with unusual abandon. People's transport bubbles are equipped with coffee-cup holders, climate control, CD players and decoration.

We all recognise the clichéd outdoorsy, she'll-be-right Aussie. But a narrower focus on the Melburnian reveals a very different stereotype. Peer through the wooden Venetian blinds of the modern apartment dweller and you'll most likely find them either not home or in front of the computer. If they are home, they're probably Googling someone they fancy, scouring the Web incognito for that special someone's achievements. Not home? You'll be able to reach him/her on the mobile, unless they're at the footy, dinner or seeing a film – no-one answers the phone then.

Mr and Ms Middle Melbourne work professionally, administrating some aspect of an arts organisation. Just because they wear black doesn't mean they're not 'individual'. *Au contraire*, it's in the little things – the jewellery, haircut, tattoo, shoes and glasses. They drive a small Japanese car with a mini disco ball dangling from the rear-view mirror. They work out at a gym that has floor-to-ceiling windows that also act as mirrors – they can see themselves reflected in the glass, and outsiders can see in. One or both parents were born overseas, and not necessarily from the same country: that's why they speak a little Spanish and a little Mandarin! Who knows which side of the family the musical talent comes from.

Melbourne Gateway on Tullamarine Freeway (see 'Angling for a Future City', p34)

FASHION

Eminent Melbourne fashion designers often can't sew, knit or even make a pattern. Chances are, they've had no formal fashion training. Designers behind Melbourne's über-cool clothes have very likely crossed over from a fine-arts discipline and are driven by ideas rather than motivated by sales. Seasonal lines may follow a theme, inspired by anything from a Swedish fairy-tale to a fox. If you're looking for a label that says 'Melbourne', check the neck for Ess.Hoshika (who frequently collaborates with visual artists and a composer), and Jain and Claude Maus (both self-taught). Pieces start at around $200.

It wasn't until the 1980s that Melbourne fashion began to define itself, eschewing its habit for reproducing European trends. A flexible and creative approach was instituted in response to Melbourne's ever-changing climate. A style developed that communicated the city's inward-looking nature, which is less body conscious and more contemplative. There's a tailored profile here, often embellished with a modern twist. Melbourne designers consistently receive international kudos for fashions that are well constructed and functional – easily crossing the day/night divide. Labels include Scanlan & Theodore and Bettina Liano.

There's a special attention to detail here that's not always immediately obvious. Take a closer look at one of the suit brigade, for example, and you'll probably find some stellar cuff links, a discreet tattoo and some spiffy shoes and socks. Hair styling goes way beyond the salon; it's a sticky subject with beauticians, where body hair is better off, basically. Facial hair is OK, but no full beards such as a possum could nest in. Facial hair is more likely to manifest as a trimmed goatee or lamb-chop sideburns – harking back to the '70s. Vintage is vanguard in Melbourne, and many pieces recall the halcyon days of yore with a '50s fabric or classic cut.

Enduring Melbourne Essentials

- **Beach Hair** (www.kuscomurphy.com.au) This local product, by Kusco-Murphy, condenses a day at the beach into a jar, complete with grit and scent. Also available: Rockster Hair and Bedroom Hair.
- **Bonds T-shirt** (www.bonds.com.au) Classic Australian cotton Ts, singlets and undies.
- **Crumpler bag** (www.crumpler.com.au) Excellent range of locally conceived bags to carry your things; brassy and street (see p149).
- **Footy scarf** (www.afl.com.au) Where the same colours are fashionable year round.
- **Moleskine notebook** (www.modoemodo.com) Range of elegant Italian notebooks flaunted as the 'symbol of contemporary nomadism'.

Cardigan Culture

Why do Melburnians have a cardigan concealed in their bags on a 34-degree day? No, not because they're ashamed of owning cardigans. That 34°C can drop to 20°C in less than an hour. Changeable weather is part of Melbourne life, so grabbing a cardy on the way out the door is as unconscious an act as reaching for the car keys.

Offices, shops and cinemas can also be uncomfortably air-conditioned. No problem. The humble cardigan is designed to put on and take off easily.

Government statistics on household expenditure reveal that Melburnians top the Australian spending chart for men's coats. That either means men are afraid to admit to wearing cardigans – preferring the euphemism 'men's coat' – or they feel the cold more. Household spending statistics in Sydney reveal a penchant for suits, while in Darwin lawn mowers factored highly on the shopping list.

The Shopping chapter (p146) lists outlets representing Melbourne's independent and local designers, including clothes and accessories. See the City Calendar (p10) for details of the Melbourne Fashion Festival held each March.

SPORT

Sport is a cultural obsession in Australia, with Melbourne recognised as the sporting capital. It's the birthplace of Australian Rules football and hosts a disproportionate number of international events, including the Australian Open, Australian Formula One Grand Prix and Melbourne Cup. Melbourne's sporting precinct has recently undergone a nip-and-tuck in preparation for the Commonwealth Games (2006). The city's arenas, tracks, grounds and courts are regarded as the world's best-developed and well-situated cluster of facilities.

Sport is promoted and followed with such fervour in this city that the attendant surge of humanity is a spectacle in itself. And that's exactly why people love it: sporting attendance brings Melbourne's disparate communities together for the single resounding purpose of following their team. It provides for unending postgame analysis and discussion around the water cooler, and is a favoured family outing.

Australians are frequently perceived as 'armchair experts', and experts they invariably are: there are few cultural pursuits where the audience is as knowledgeable and discriminating. And while spectating may be perceived as an entirely passive pastime, think about the intense concentration and outpouring of emotion expended. There may not be too many muscles moving but a good game is sure to raise a heart rate, and the brain muscle will be working overtime to scrutinise every nuance, decision, kick, call and turn.

The media, in all its forms, is chock-a-block with sporting news and something as seemingly trifling as a star footballer's strained groin makes front-page headlines in the daily newspapers. Media attention fuels the culture of celebrity surrounding Melbourne's sporting heroes. There's an incessant hunger for snippets of players' private lives, and sports people are often used to endorse commercial products. Sporting heroes have sung the praises of products ranging from milk to watches and hair-replacement therapy. A few years ago, the then captain of Geelong Football Club (also known as the Cats), changed his name by deed poll from Garry Hocking to Whiskas – a tinned cat food – to attract sponsorship for his club.

The nation's most-watched sport, Australian Rules football, was given the nod in 1858 by the then dominant cricket faculty. Football was to keep cricketers fit in the off-season, and hence was admitted to the hallowed ground of the MCG. Many Melbourne suburbs gave their names and their sporting sons to the league: Carlton, Collingwood, Essendon, Footscray (now called the Western Bulldogs), Richmond and North Melbourne (now the Kangaroos) are some of the teams comprising the now-national **Australian Football League** (AFL; www.afl.com.au). When other states joined the once exclusively Victorian league in 1982, the focus of the game shifted from a rough-and-ready neighbourhood competition to an increasingly corporate, slick and controlled national league.

Melbourne's summer love, cricket, is less of a spectacle and more of an investment. The Boxing Day Test in Melbourne attracts record crowds, but the game moves at a slow pace. Being about accumulation, there are definite down times provoking the occasional seagull

More Than a Game *John Ryan & David McClymont*

It's virtually impossible to say a bad word about the AFL grand final, the highlight of Melbourne's sporting calendar. Trying to tell a Melburnian you're not interested in the footy is like trying to tell a lemming not to throw itself off a cliff. If you find yourself in the city on this most important day of the year (usually the last Saturday in September), just give in to the mayhem. Pick a team, buy a scarf, wave a flag, have a beer, watch the match on TV, celebrate with the winners and commiserate with the losers. Come Sunday, the madness will be over for another year.

To the novice, the term 'rules' might seem to be stretching the truth. One could easily be excused for thinking that the sight of 36 men hurling themselves after the oval-shaped ball is an unsophisticated free-for-all. But to the initiated, every move, play and umpiring decision carries enormous weight and even ritual: Aussie Rules isn't described as Melbourne's main religion for nothing.

The rules are a mishmash of rugby, Gaelic football and total insanity. Players can kick or punch the ball (handpass), but not throw it. They can run with the ball, as long as they bounce it every 10 metres. They can tackle, bump and 'shirtfront' (an especially popular manoeuvre involving the near-removal of an opponent's head), but they mustn't push someone in the back. If they catch the ball after it's been kicked (a 'mark'), play can stop with the ball then played from the point where the mark occurred. A tackled player must attempt to get rid of the ball (if someone gets tackled, just scream 'baaaallll' – don't worry why).

All of these – and a hundred other little regulations – combine to create one of the most athletic, fast and physical sports in existence. If you're lucky enough to catch a blockbuster at the 'G, you'll be a convert quicker than you can scream 'You white %@* maggot!'

count. The more modern invention of the limited-overs, one-day game has a bit more sparkle, if only shimmering off the boys' colourful rayon costumes.

Australian soccer (www.socceraustralia.com.au) is still struggling to find its feet after almost qualifying for the 1998 World Cup. The Socceroos have qualified only once, in 1974. Although it doesn't attract much attention on a national level, soccer in Melbourne is hugely popular and is the city's highest participatory sport. The Greek, Italian and Croatian communities in Melbourne are probably the most ardent supporters of the game, and are responsible for popularising the sport more widely.

Rugby league (www.nrl.com.au) has recruited a small but loyal following in this town, following the success of the fledgling Melbourne Storm team in the national competition. Melbourne teams are represented in rugby union, though its popularity is nowhere near that in other Australian states.

The **Australian Open** (www.ausopen.com.au) tennis Grand Slam event is played in January at Melbourne Park. It's invariably a sell-out with over 500,000 people in attendance for day and night ladies' and men's matches. At some point during the competition, someone usually fries an egg on the heat of centre court, just because you can.

The first Tuesday in November marks the running of the **Melbourne Cup** (www.racing victoria.net.au). Over 100,000 punters strut through the gates at Flemington, where the focus is as much on fashion and champagne as on the race. Thanks to this 3.2km horse race, the state enjoys a public holiday, while the rest of the nation huddles around a TV or radio at 3.20pm. The Cup is the feather in the Spring Racing Carnival's hat (although feathers are *so* last-year), which runs from October to November.

Then there's the **Australian Formula One Grand Prix** (www.grandprix.com.au) in March, when thousands cram the stands around Albert Park Lake to glimpse the whining cars speed past. The **Bells Beach Surf Classic** (www.ripcurl.com.au) sees competitors brave the waves on the west coast.

There's some spectacle in the city's sporting calendar whatever month or week you're in Melbourne. Refer to the Sports, Health & Fitness chapter (p138) for more details, as well as suggested activities for those who want to exercise more than their eyeballs.

MEDIA

Australia's capital cities are hubs in the information exchange that occurs both globally and locally. Melbourne's denizens are blessed with a remarkably diverse number of media sources to both consume and contribute to. The city's print houses, digital producers and radio and TV broadcasters provide for an assortment of opinions and perspectives.

Melbourne Online *Meredith Badger*

- If you're curious to know how Melburnians think, visit **Melbourne Blogs** (www.melbourneblogs.net) for a comprehensive list of blogs written by local residents. Blogs are Web diaries, often updated daily, with content ranging from the journalistic to the personal.
- One popular Melbourne blog is Claire Robertson's **Looby Lu** (www.loobylu.com). Claire is a local illustrator and the stories she tells of life in Melbourne are interspersed with gorgeous illustrations of her family and her art projects.
- There's an online version of the local broadsheet, the **Age** (www.theage.com.au), which has breaking news appearing throughout the day. Sport, technology, food and entertainment are also covered and there's a My Melbourne section where readers can send in their photos of the city.
- For an alternative view try **Crikey** (www.crikey.com.au), where the team of writers keeps an eye out for corruption and dangerously inflated egos within the ranks of local politics, media and business.
- When looking for movie session times or gig guides head to **City Search** (www.melbourne.citysearch.com.au). Restaurants, clubs, shopping and accommodation are also covered. The information is updated regularly and contains both positive and negative press of the places it lists.
- **Sleepy Brain** (www.sleepybrain.net) is an online journal. While not strictly Melbourne in focus, it often covers local art or music events and interviews local talent, such as the recent Oscar winner, animator Adam Elliot.

Meredith is the author of Melbourne blog http://invisibleshoebox.blogspot.com.

Cross-media ownership laws in Australia prevent a company from owning two forms of media in the one city: it's illegal for one company to own a TV station and a newspaper, for example, in Melbourne. That said, two companies control the nation's media: Kerry Packer's Publishing & Broadcasting Ltd and Rupert Murdoch's News Corporation. The nation's sole independent broadcaster, the **Australian Broadcasting Corporation** (ABC; www.abc.net.au) includes radio, TV and online services. It's dependent on government funding, which is increasingly under threat of being reduced. Justification for funding cuts is generally underpinned with whispers that the federal Liberal government disapproves of the broadcaster's perceived left leaning. The **Special Broadcasting Service** (SBS; www.sbs.com.au) is a national broadcaster with a special mandate to refect the multiethnic and indigenous nature of Australian society.

Melbourne's commercial media is mainstream, and typically conservative and colloquial. Commercial TV and radio generally present an assenting popular-culture perspective, with newspapers being the main platform for hard news and analysis. The national broadcasters often provide for dissenting opinion, and locally produced independent media is well represented, including street press, sponsorship-based radio broadcasters and Web producers.

As is true in most Western cities, advertising is a major component of the media. Melbourne advertisers are all too aware of their market's ability to see through puerile pleas to consume. The challenge for advertisers is to strike a balance between mannered invisibility and offensive exhibitionism. Lifestyle is the biggest commodity, and advertisers perpetually find ways to creatively package their products in a sexy promise of a better quality of living.

Check the Directory for a run-down of Melbourne's newspapers and other press (p186) and radio stations (p187). The Arts chapter (p32) covers TV.

LANGUAGE

Over 250 languages other than English have been recorded as spoken in Australian communities, which have a high number of immigrants, both first and second generation. Aboriginal dialects also contribute to this number. English is the official and dominant language.

As an integral part of cultural expression, there's a firm focus in Australia to preserve language, particularly Aboriginal languages, which have been severely depleted since European settlement. In the Melbourne region, the Kulin Nation is made up of language clans that include the Woiworung and Boonwurrung.

Many Melburnians have close contact with other languages through family connections. As a result, many people have at least a basic ability to comprehend and speak a language other than English. Foreign languages are taught in schools, and an increasing number of travellers heading overseas are making the effort to study another language. Spanish is the most popular language studied at Melbourne's CAE (Centre for Adult Education).

The *Macquarie Dictionary* is generally accepted as the definitive source in Australian-English vocabulary and pronunciation. It includes etymological information and encyclopaedic entries, and aims to describe – rather than prescribe – language use, hence includes both US and British usage. US practices are becoming more common in Australian English. It's no surprise, really, considering the massive exposure American TV and cinema receive here. The current federal government's allegiance to the US administration may lead to even more US content in Australia (see p30).

Australia doesn't stand on formality, and there's a plethora of colloquialisms colouring local expression – especially in a social context. Just when you're feeling cocky (arrogantly smart) with your command of English, there'll be some obscure term to make it seem a bit warby (unkempt; decrepit). Each generation tends to have its own set of colloquialisms, such that the wrinklies don't understand the whippersnappers, and vice versa.

Many professions have their own slang, more commonly called jargon. Terms specific to a particular industry increasingly leak into the general parlance. While a few legal and scientific terms have been adopted, increasingly the most prevalent area is in corporate speech – used in the English of politics, business, bureaucracy, education and the arts. It is by nature noncommittal, self-serving and meaningless. Terms such as 'moving forward', 'strategic initiative' and 'outcome-focused' are empty expressions commonly used in public speech. Melbourne author Don Watson, in his book *Death Sentence,* argues that 'managerial language' spells the 'death of clarity and irony and funny old things called verbs'.

And then, of course, there is the influence on language from emailing and text messaging. The lack of punctuation and clipped language inherent in these forms has undoubtedly contributed to the depleted use of punctuation generally. There are dual possible effects in terms of its influence on language and expression. Does the increased use of 'bullet-point' expression influence thought patterns and limit the potential for experience? Or is it enriching language by adding new terms?

New words are constantly added to our lexicon as language grows and develops with society. Dictionaries garner new terms from literary and journalistic sources. New additions to the *Macquarie*'s last edition included 'channel-surf', 'attention deficit disorder' and 'virtual pet'. High on the list for next edition would have to be 'text messaging' and 'SMS'.

ECONOMY & COSTS

In the past five years Victoria has been Australia's pin-up economy, experiencing growth exceeding all other Australian states in building activity, retail, jobs and business investment. Development in Melbourne's infrastructure, offices and leisure facilities constitutes the largest area of growth, with one in five employees working in the property and business-services industry. The recent economic slump, which has seen the state perform below the national average, has economy-watchers baffled. The government explains the loss as a speed hump in the state's economy, attributing the decline to external factors such as drought and a subdued global economy.

One explanation for the decline in the retail sector is Victoria's ready adoption, more than any other Australian state, of e-commerce. The inevitable result of an increase in providing goods and services online is a decrease in retail jobs. Greater product demand and the resultant increase in manufacture is the projected offset to the loss in jobs.

Melbourne has a relatively low cost of living compared to other major cities, being 80% of New York, and slightly lower than Sydney. This is a defining factor in its status

Forever Young

In the last 51 years Queen Elizabeth II has aged only five times. If you compare the obverse (heads) side of coins in your wallet, you'll find an ageing Queen. Since the Queen's coronation in 1953, five portraits have been rendered of Queen Elizabeth. The latest design is from 1998, with previous designs from 1985, 1966 and 1953.

as 'the world's most livable city'. Rents in Melbourne are two-thirds that in Sydney and one-third of Singapore.

Melbourne has one of Australia's largest concentrations of tertiary education institutions. Over 25% of the city's resident population is made up of students, who contribute enormously to the city's economy. A high proportion of students are from east Asia, evident in the availability of Asian groceries and food outlets around the city's universities.

Tourism generates $9 billion a year for Victoria's economy and employs 150,000 people. It remains an area of steady economic growth, as a result of improved services and amenities and successful marketing.

This is all good news for the traveller, despite the current strength of the Australian dollar. Not only is there an increased number of facilities, they're available at an extremely reasonable cost when compared with other Western cities. You should allow at least $60 per day if staying at a backpackers hostel and self-catering. If you want your own room, to dine at the city's renowned restaurants and attend a show, count on upwards of $250. Additional to that, of course, are any must-have mementos of your visit.

Much of Melbourne's pep and style passes you by, literally, in the daily comings and goings of its denizens. Experiencing the soul of the city doesn't have to cost much or anything at all. Grab a window seat at a café or prop on the pavement and people-watch for a while. Join the throng at the Queen Victoria Market, buy some easy-to-assemble ingredients and head to a public park to dine among the giant magnolia trees. Ride a tram: there's the free City Circle tram (p52), which trundles around town with recorded commentary; or you could journey to an inner-city suburb. Walking is a great pace to explore Melbourne's nooks and crannies; don't ignore the backstreets, alleys, laneways and arcades.

Depending on the season, you could head to a suburban sports ground and watch a local footy match – what these games lack in skill, they more than make up for in spirit – or swim in the bay, run around the Tan (p142) or cycle along the Yarra River. Whatever the weather, visit the city's private contemporary art spaces (try Flinders Lane) and its public ones (NGV and ACCA). Most movie theatres have days when ticket prices are halved. Affectionately known as 'tight-arse Tuesday', they're usually on a Monday and before 4pm.

How Much?

Litre of unleaded petrol $1

Bottled water (325mL) $3

The Age newspaper $1.20

Scanlan & Theodore cardigan $400

AFL footy game $14-20

Tube of sunscreen $10

Haircut $60

Martini $13

Swim $3.50

Film processing $8

GOVERNMENT & POLITICS

A general criticism of Australia's political system is that it's over-governed. The country has three levels of government: federal, state and local. Community-focused areas, such as garbage collection and town planning, are administered by local government. Each state has its own jurisdiction in areas of education, health and emergency services. The federal government takes care of the bigger picture: immigration, trade and commerce etc.

Victoria's state government is based in Melbourne and is made up of the Legislative Council (the upper house), with 44 elected representatives, and the Legislative Assembly (the lower house), with 88 elected representatives. The government of the day must have support from a majority of members in the Legislative Assembly. Elections for the lower house are held every four years. Voting is by secret ballot and is compulsory for everyone aged 18 years and over. At the time of writing the Labor Party was in power in Victoria, with Steve Bracks as premier.

You can sit in on state parliament sessions (see p57) but don't expect a pert performance. Parliament sittings are often characterised by one voice that drones for a time, punctuated by an occasional background brouhaha that sounds a bit like a flock of seagulls just thrown a chip. It is never riveting drama. In fact, drama is a word rarely used in relation to Australia's politicians. They're generally a sedate bunch, with nary a scandalous sex-romp story in sight.

At a local level, the **Melbourne City Council** (☎ 9658 9658; www.melbourne.vic.gov.au) recognises the significant community of travellers that treads through its turf. It offers a free Greeter Service where local volunteers – who, combined, speak 20 languages – take you on a half-day tour of town; council also runs free tours of the Melbourne Town Hall (see p57). Bookings are essential; book at least two days ahead.

ENVIRONMENT

THE LAND

From a bird's-eye view, Melbourne perches at the top of Port Phillip Bay; it's about 860km south of Sydney by road. At 8806 sq km, compared to Sydney's approximate area of 4000 sq km, metropolitan Melbourne is Australia's largest city per capita and one of the largest in the world.

The city (CBD) comprises only a tiny portion (1.8 sq km). Its flat, gridlike topography defines the ordered and contained feeling of the city. The CBD is held together by a continuous green belt of parks and gardens. Inner-city suburbs thrive on the fringes of the CBD and are often included in the boundaries of the general term 'city'. The Yarra River divides Melbourne geographically and socioeconomically. Traditionally, the northern and western suburbs have been more industrial and working-class, while areas south of the Yarra and to the east have been the domain of the more affluent, and the setting for the most prestigious housing.

The sprawl of Melbourne's suburbs emanates in all directions from the city's central core. Highways and bridges duck and weave through outlying Melbourne, occasionally giving way to residential settlements. These new suburbs prop on repurposed land: cul-de-sacs, curving avenues and 'catalogue' homes have moved in where industry or parkland used to reside.

GREEN MELBOURNE

Do you want the good news or the bad news first? Victorians are the highest producers of greenhouse gas emissions per capita in the world. Melbourne's cars belch out almost half the city's greenhouse emissions. Public transport use is down to 7% of the population – the lowest in the city's history. The state's reliance on brown coal for electricity and its ever-increasing consumption of energy is another significant contributor to the state's woeful environmental record.

The good news is that the Melbourne City Council has instituted a radical policy to reduce greenhouse emissions to zero (net) by 2020. Council's strategy focuses on energy-efficient building design, which reduces the consumption and operating costs. Other council directives include implementing a marketing plan to educate city users of the need to reduce emissions, as well as making sustainable energy sources more available.

Herring Island

Theoretically, **Herring Island** (Map p212; http://home.vicnet.net.au/~herring) is open to visitors at all times. The only catch is getting to it. Unless you swim (not recommended) or have your own boat (unlikely), you're limited to the punt that ferries back and forth on weekends.

The island, perched in the Yarra River, features a native wild garden that uses naturally occurring patterns and plant species. Indigenous plants and grasses provide natural habitat for birds and animals such as parrots, possums and lizards. Designated picnic areas, with barbecues, make for a rare inner-city nature retreat just 3km from the city centre.

It's also the site of a permanent Environmental Sculpture Walk, which was installed as part of the 1997 International Arts Festival. Eminent environmental artists from Australia and abroad have works here. Made from natural materials such as stone, earth and wood, pieces are of an impressive scale – all in absolute synergy with the surrounding natural environment. The old scout hall has been architecturally redesigned into a contemporary exhibition space.

Parks Victoria (☎ 13 19 63; $2) operates the punt on weekends from Como Landing on Alexandra Ave in South Yarra. It runs between noon and 5pm from October to March.

Melbourne has great-quality drinking water; shame it wastes so much of it. Melburnians are among Australia's highest users of water per capita. The recent drought encouraged the government to implement water-use restrictions. Since the state's utilities were privatised, however, the government has limited power to control water distribution and consumption. Suppliers have also offered water-saving incentives.

Recycling is one success story, with at least 50% of solid waste recycled across the state.

URBAN PLANNING & DEVELOPMENT

Melbourne has undergone an intense stage of development of late, such that the city of five years ago is virtually unrecognisable. New precincts such as the Docklands and Federation Square have affected the rhythm of the city – containing the public in purpose-built pockets of activity. A major objective in this development process is to extend the city's appeal to a more global market – attracting business investment and visitors, as well as to create high-density housing to remedy the increased consumption of resources.

There is much debate about whether the city's developed sites look any good; debates that are informed by a personal aesthetic, as well as how an individual feels in the city's new iconic developments. Subjective preferences aside, the more subtle influences of our built environment dictate how comfortable we are interacting with it. Federation Square is Melbourne's latest icon; love it or hate it, it's an example of good architecture and planning, taking consideration of its surrounding environment and creating a topography in harmony with the landscape, while accommodating large groups of people.

Generally, greater emphasis has been placed on sustainable growth. Although the building industry's use of environmentally sustainable materials and design remains unregulated, Melbourne City Council has taken the lead in a number of city projects. Council's CH2 building, due for completion by 2005, is publicly touted as a beacon of ecologically sustainable design.

Arts

Arts

Ask any person on the street where the cultural capital of Australia is and they'll tell you Melbourne. It's a truism you'll read and hear regularly, founded in the fact that there is so much worthy art produced here. Film, theatre, music and visual arts are prolific streams of Melbourne's artistic expression.

Melbourne's landscape belongs to the arts. The Arts Centre stretches along St Kilda Rd between the National Gallery of Victoria and the concert venue, Hamer Hall, with Federation Square across the road commanding the Flinders St corner. The CBD is seemingly fertile ground, with art growing out of most surfaces: it's in the underground walkways at Flinders Street Station, sprouts out of the side of buildings in laneways across town, is stencilled on walls and thrives on city pavements. It's mostly watered with public funds and breathes stimulating life into the city.

The arts in Melbourne are highly accessible, both for sheer number of spaces and in their appeal to a broad audience. For most Melburnians, seeing a film or exhibition is part of an average week. Do some digging, though, and you'll discover there's also a keen enterprising side to Melbourne's arts scene that's less visible but no less important.

VISUAL ARTS

Melbourne has always been a city for artists – historically many of the major new artistic visions of Australia have sprung from artists, and communities of artists, based in Melbourne. A dynamic and ever-changing network of artist-run spaces, experimental events and exhibitions gives the city an exciting production-house edge, and an excellent public infrastructure of major galleries and museums offers travellers visual culture of serious polish and scale.

Melbourne's first visual arts sprang from the traditions of the Koorie (indigenous Australian) tribes who lived from and belonged to the lands we now associate with the Yarra River, Port Phillip Bay, the Dandenong Ranges, the You Yangs and the country beyond. Interestingly, the current location of many of Melbourne's key cultural institutions on the southern bank of the Yarra River is a traditional gathering and corroboree site. Both the National Gallery of Victoria, Australia (NGVA; p60) and the Melbourne Museum (p66) exhibit works of art from before and after European settlement. The art and artefacts at the Melbourne Museum's Bunjilaka Gallery provide a particularly vivid and intimate picture of Koorie culture.

> ### Top Five Galleries
>
> - National Gallery of Victoria: International (p60)
> - Ian Potter Centre: National Gallery of Victoria Australia (p62)
> - Australian Centre for Contemporary Art (p58)
> - Heide Museum of Modern Art (boxed text, p80)
> - Australian Centre for the Moving Image (p62)

The grand vistas painted by intrepid Europeans visiting the fledgling colony of Melbourne describe a very different Australian experience. These vast and encyclopaedic works offer early views of Australia as a colonial jewel. Bucolic pastures and abundant forests represent a land in the throes of colonisation and environmental upheaval, and offer intriguing catalogues of much that was on the precipice of being lost. Eugene Von Guerard's works, such as *Mount Kosciusko*, seen from the Victorian border, 1866 (NGVA) capture the wondrous difference of the Australian landscape to the European eye and reward close study with their lavish attention to detail.

In the late 19th century a generation of Australian-born artists emerged who are loved and remembered for defining a truly Australian vision of the landscape and cities of the day. The artists of the Heidelberg school took the train down the newly laid railway lines to the bush at Melbourne's fringe and camped together, sketching and working rapidly in oils to capture the bright light and dry elegance of the Australian bush. They created a heroic national iconography from the shearing of sheep and visions of a wide brown land popularly celebrated as offering a chance to all. The most widely reproduced works of Heidelberg school artists such as Tom Roberts and Arthur Streeton are majestic in scale and build grand narratives from the contemporary experience of Australians; other smaller works are surprisingly intimate and impressionistically rendered. *Lost*, 1886, by Frederick McCubbin (NGVA), portrays a young girl, almost a child, lost in the bush. The sun shines brightly on the yellowed summer grass and the repeated vertical staccato of the gum trees divides the scene creating a claustrophobic division within the infinite repetition of gum trees in the bush. While portraying an archetypal anxiety, the loss of a child to the land was a particularly poignant concern at the turn of the century as settlement of the Australian landscape continued apace. Australians love the landscape, identify with it and take pride in its complexity — harsh and mysterious, abundant and distinctive — and yet it makes us uneasy also; we feel disquiet in the very land that defines us. The disjunction of new peoples arriving in a very old land, and the experience of loss in the landscape, is an abiding anxiety explored in works of art and literature such as the iconic novel and film *Picnic at Hanging Rock*.

Visitors to Melbourne can experience some of the landscapes painted by the artists of the Heidelberg school by catching the train to Heidelberg station and walking across the Yarra River to the rambling gardens of the Heide Museum of Modern Art (see the boxed text, p80). Heide played a pivotal role in the development of Australian modernism in the early and mid-20th century. Patrons John and Sunday Reed shared their home with friends and visitors, nurturing a vibrant community of artists that included Albert Tucker, Joy Hester and Sidney Nolan. Nolan's celebrated Ned Kelly series was said to be painted at the Reed's dining-room table. The early Australian modernism forged at Heide was expressively painted and passionately connected to the emotional, social and intellectual worlds of the artists.

At the same time as the Heide artists were forging newly modern national iconographies, the lyrical watercolours of Aboriginal artist Albert Namatjira were coming to public attention. Namatjira was an innovator who painted his country in vivid jewel-like shades, a radical shift from the traditional ochres of the Arunda people of central Australia. While he was mission-raised, Namatjira regularly went walkabout, and his paintings describe the landscape he loved: white ghost gums and ochre rock outcrops with shadows of plum and mauve. Animated by myriad possibilities of light, Namatjira's works created an

Bunjilaka Gallery (left)

audience for Aboriginal art and for an Aboriginal perspective. More recently, artists such as Emily Kame Kngwarray and Clifford Possum Tjapaltjarri have created extraordinary bodies of work that establish a bridge between their traditional obligations to culture and country and the development of their own artistic language as individuals. Likewise, artists of European heritage such as Fred Williams and John Olsen have drawn upon the Australian landscape to create poetic works that newly imagine both representational space and our sense of place.

Contemporary Australian artists are strongly concerned with an Australian sense of place, as well as being actively engaged in the more universal concerns of our contemporary, globalised world. The Melbourne art scene is distinctively energised by a flourishing community of artists, experimental exhibition spaces and events. A good place to tap into this energy is Gertrude Contemporary Art Spaces (p66), where you can see exhibitions by emerging artists and get the lowdown on the newest experimental spaces. The Australian Centre for Contemporary Art (p58) generates cutting-edge programmes of exhibitions as well as developing large-scale projects with Australian and international artists. The Australian Centre for the Moving Image (p62) exhibits film and multimedia works by contemporary artists in thematic exhibitions that draw upon a rich diversity of moving-image formats.

Melbourne takes pride in being a city for ideas, a city for contemporary art. Only a small slice of the mass of work being produced will be evident at any one time, but between the commercial, public and artist-run galleries there is much to discover. The city's strength as a centre for architecture and spatial investigation is reflected in the work of contemporary artists such as Stephen Bram, Callum Morton and Natasha Johns-Messenger. The practice of the making of art and the reflective ricochet between the real and the represented are explored by Melbourne artists Ricky Swallow, Nick Mangan, Christian Capurro, Nadine Christensen and Chris Bond. The impact of technology upon our lives is a subject of much interest to artists such as Stephen Honegger, Anthony Hunt and Patricia Piccinini, artists who are empowered by the digital world as well as being thoughtfully engaged with the ethical dilemmas it generates. The politics of memory and the borders of empathy are explored by artists such as Susan Norrie, Gordon Bennett, Tom Nicholson and Louisa Bufarduci. Melbourne is a centre for cross-cultural investigation, with artists such as Kate Beynon, Sangeeta Sandrasegar, Rafat Ishak and Constanz Zikos drawing upon a diversity of cultural perspectives to find their own expressive language.

For a comprehensive guide to the city's galleries get a copy of *Art Almanac* from bookshops and newsagents.

MUSIC

With a willing audience and a swathe of music venues, there's a widely held admission that if you can't get a gig in this town, you must be lousy. That's not to say that Melbourne's musical taste is indiscriminate. Melbourne has produced some wildly successful acts and nurtures the spectrum of genres from classical to rock.

Melbourne's enviable live-music scene seems to have existed forever, played out in the city's pubs and dedicated band venues. A few years back it seemed threatened by a shifting demographic that saw DJs and decks replace drums and guitars. Pubs plugged in pokie machines in place of amps, so that music gave way to the jingle of coins and a cacophony of blips. More recently, noise complaints from residents placed additional pressure on venues that

Unbeatable Melbourne Beats

- **Augie March** *Strange Bird* – melodic, stylish experimentation
- **Cat Empire** *Cat Empire* – a music jamboree
- **Dirty 3** *Horse Stories* – electric violin, bass and drum trio: discordant and freeform
- **Nick Cave & the Bad Seeds** *Good Son* – romantically sinister, with a gothic lilt
- **Paul Kelly** *Ways & Means* – gentle and honest rock and roll

had been staging live music long before their neighbouring buildings were redeveloped into apartment blocks. Despite attacks from all sides, the Melbourne music scene is burgeoning. Where one venue closed, another opened, and strong resistance from music lovers and industry players kept many of the city's stalwart venues from closing.

While a large proportion of Melburnians avidly support the local music scene, the population itself is not large enough to retain some of the city's most successful acts. Transferring the same population percentage from, say, Melbourne to London more than doubles the audience for any given act. So, while she'll always be 'our Kylie', Ms Minogue no longer resides here. Nick Cave and the Dirty Three use their rock-star passports to live in a host of other cities, including Berlin and Sao Paolo.

For a list of live-music venues see p126. Admission prices are scandalously inexpensive: good for patrons, not so good for performers. You can head out on any night and be guaranteed to find someone, somewhere, fronting the stage bathed in blue and red spotlights. Mostly, you'll be rewarded with a polished ensemble, confidently delivering its own compositions. Keep an ear out for outstanding local performers. Of note are long-standing names such as Paul Kelly for his whimsical lyrics and guitar, Stephen Cummings for some classy lulling, Tex Perkins for some bad-arse spunk, the Dave Graney Show – self-confessed King of Pop – Kim Salmon for respectable rock and Lisa Miller for downright lovely folksy tunes. Melbourne's answer to the Strokes, Jet, are enjoying the 'new rock' revival, and energetic young standouts include Architecture in Helsinki for some cutesy brass-infused pop and Cat Empire for an upbeat fusion of styles. Mainstream mainstays include Kate Ceberano and David Bridie.

Melbourne's jazz scene is thriving (below)

Modern indigenous musicians have managed to create unique styles by incorporating traditional instruments into modern rock and pop formats. Hybrid Aboriginal music has enjoyed some popular success in Australia, with Aboriginal group Yothu Yindi and Torres Strait Islander singer Christine Anu well known around the country. Hip-hop has also proven enormously popular as a means of expression for many indigenous and Islander youth: the CD *All You Mob* is an excellent compilation of indigenous artists. Archie Roach and Ruby Hunter are two well-known and widely respected indigenous musicians currently based in Melbourne.

Every second person you speak to here has a record collection and a DJ name and moonlights at some bar or other. Melbourne's bars glide on a velvety-lounge vibe, with a section of most bar-tops in town reserved for a set of decks. Dance music has a number of subscenes. There's the big-room progressive hard-house dance parties, with big-name international and local acts. Melbourne boys Mark James, Jason Midro and Sean Quinn keep a sea of bodies pulsing. Clubs such as Honky Tonks and Revolver favour house, hip-hop and electro, or derivations thereof. House proponents include Angela Maison, Ant J Steep, Agent 86 and Boogs. Hip-hop DJs with a firm Melbourne following include Ransom and J Red.

Considering the relatively small population, Melbourne has a large number of dedicated jazz venues. The jazz scene has come a long way from the dim smoky clubs of old where a high proportion of patrons wore berets. The majority of establishments are smoke-free and take the presentation of a broad range of styles seriously. Melbourne jazz displays considerable improvisatory flair with a number of world influences, from American to Nordic and

Brazilian. Some well-respected Melbourne names include Paul Grabowsky, Vince Jones, Paul Williamson, Doug de Vries, Tony Gould, Sam Keevers, Andrea Keller, Fiona Burnett and Nichaud and Mark Fitzgibbon. The Adam Simmons Toy Band is always a hoot, proving that you can also improvise on the likes of Prince, given some excellent musicianship and a rubber chicken.

In the classical sphere, Melbourne is known for being home to the great idiosyncratic composer Percy Grainger and singer Nellie Melba. The Melbourne Symphony Orchestra performs regularly in Hamer Hall, and is well known for its spirited recitals. Chamber, choral, light opera, new music and opera performances are a feature at the Victorian Arts Centre.

Each musical genre has at least one annual festival in Melbourne, and there are festivals that bring together a wide range of styles. Music festivals profile headline international and local acts, and often run at a number of venues for a week or more. The EG section in Friday's *Age* newspaper lists what's on. Street papers such as *Beat* and *Inpress* also provide a rundown.

THEATRE

There's always a drama being acted out in Melbourne's vibrant theatre scene, from blockbuster musicals to intimate experimental fringe productions.

Melbourne's main professional theatre company, the **Melbourne Theatre Company** (MTC; www.mtc.com.au) is also Australia's oldest professional company. It stages around a dozen

Liz Jones: La Mama

Founded in 1967 as a theatre for new and experimental plays, **La Mama** (☎ 9347 6948; 205 Faraday St, Carlton) is literally the mother of independent theatre in Melbourne. If the theatre is the metaphoric matriarch, then Liz Jones – artistic director for nigh on 30 years – is the actual one. La Mama and Liz nurture Australian playwrights and artists by providing the facilities and community necessary to get shows off the ground.

In 2003, the tiny 40-seater La Mama theatre and its second venue, the Courthouse, staged 66 performances. 'We had five going at a time,' says Liz, who reads 250 scripts a year. 'I'm also considering people who just come up with an idea, a scenario or a group collaboration. Especially for the Exploration season, which is dedicated to nonscript-based works. It includes a lot of dance and multiple art forms, where people want to really try out new ideas.'

La Mama acts as a production company, of sorts. When it takes on a performance, it provides the theatre space and pays the writer and the director. Actors and others involved in a production split the door takings. Liz spends a lot of time matching writers with directors. 'You might have three or four goes at it before you get a marriage.' La Mama has an illustrious index book of actors, stage directors, set, costume and lighting designers to assist in seeing a script or idea come to fruition.

'If I want to be proactive in this 21st century, I would like to continue to encourage indigenous theatre and ensembles – groups who want to work together,' says Liz. 'When I was travelling through Europe I was really aware how conservative theatrical forms tended to be in the English-speaking countries, and how radical they were particularly in Germany, Spain, Italy and Eastern European countries. I was so much more excited by the theatre I saw in Berlin than the theatre I saw in London. I came home thinking that I did want to try and encourage that. Now, I think the key to that is the ensemble and people working together in a large group trusting each other.'

From an audience perspective, La Mama is intimate and generous. You are invited to chat to those involved in a production after a performance, and you get to participate in the raffle. 'There's such a good chance of winning, which people don't normally have in a raffle,' says Liz. The raffle tradition began in about 1990. 'I edited a book called *La Mama – the Story of a Theatre* with Betty Burstall (founder of La Mama) and Helen Garner (author). The publisher printed 3500 copies, which were not selling like hot cakes, so Betty said, "Why don't we raffle one at the beginning of each show?" We raffled the entire stock. Then I edited a book of plays, and we raffled the entire stock of that. So, now we just find a worthy book.' Your entry ticket is also your raffle ticket, which is still drawn at the start of each performance.

Seeing a La Mama performance is a little like a raffle itself. There's a similar anticipation inherent in innovative theatre. And like the raffle, you have such a good chance of being rewarded.

performances year-round at the Victorian Arts Centre. Productions are firmly focused on satisfying the company's middle-market subscriber base. It features works by well-known Australian playwrights such as David Williamson, Hannie Rayson and Joanna Murray-Smith, as well as international works. The MTC also runs a readings programme to promote and develop the works of emerging playwrights.

Playbox (www.playbox.com.au) was established in 1976 and is dedicated to the performance of Australian works. Housed in the distinctive CUB Malthouse, its programme is riskier than that of the MTC. Playbox nurtures emerging writers and actively promotes its productions in Asia.

Melbourne's numerous progressive fringe theatre companies are the essence of the city's theatre scene. The more enduring companies are responsible for premiering stellar international plays in Australia, as well as invigorating theatre's middle ground with creativity and flair. Independent theatre companies to seek out include **Red Stitch** (www.redstitch.net), the **Store Room** (www.thestoreroom.com.au), Hoist, and Ranters Theatre Ensemble.

There's a cross-pollination between theatre and TV, with writers, directors and actors working in both mediums. The glut of reality TV, which is mostly unscripted and stars nonactors, has doubled the number of professionals focusing on theatre. Fringe theatre is responsible, vibrant and stylish, with exceptionally high-calibre participants.

Melbourne's theatrical heritage is evident in the city's Victorian-era theatres – the Princess and Athenaeum. The diminutive La Mama, in Carlton (see the boxed text, p28), is an institution whose humble size and aspect is far outweighed by its place in the heart of Melbourne's theatre scene.

Established Melbourne playwrights whose works have been widely applauded include Daniel Keane, Raimondo Cortese, Matt Cameron, Louis Nowra, Michael Gow and Tobsha Learner. Emerging talents to look out for include Ben Ellis, Elise McCredie and Trudy Hellier.

The Green Room Awards are the most prestigious recognition for performing artists. Voted by their peers, the awards are held annually and acknowledge a variety of streams, including theatre, fringe theatre and cabaret.

For listings of Melbourne's theatre venues see p134.

DANCE

The body in all its beauty and skill is put on show in Melbourne's exuberant dance scene. Traditional practitioners express grace and precision in their pursuit of formal excellence. Contemporary companies are typified by innovative choreography and physicality in the extreme. **Australia Dancing** (www.australiadancing.org) is a general Web resource publishing current and historical information about dance in Australia.

Victoria's main contemporary dance company, **Chunky Move** (www.chunkymove.com), has been pushing the boundaries defining contemporary dance since 1998. Founder and artistic director Gideon Obarzanek studied with the Australian Ballet and choreographs many of the company's shows. Chunky Move is a tidy package of vital choreography, clever concepts referencing pop culture, extraordinary dancers, sleek design and smart marketing. Many Victorians have experienced at least one performance of Chunky Move's contemporary dance without realising which genre it represents. Recent works include *Tense Dave*, where an overwrought perspective, fuelled by fear and paranoia, distorted the recognisable world, and *Closer,* a screen-based interactive installation where audience members manipulated on-screen dancers with sensor pads fixed to the floor.

Danceworks (www.danceworks.com.au) is another local contemporary dance company that performs in site-specific locations and incorporates a number of art forms. A performance by **Kage Physical Theatre** (www.kagephysicaltheatre.com) is worth catching if you can.

Bangarra Dance Theatre (www.bangarra.com.au), though Sydney-based, tours with some frequency. The company presents traditional Aboriginal and Torres Strait Islander dance in a contemporary setting. Stories and characters of the Dreaming are retold through dance. As Bangarra itself puts it, the company is 'one of the youngest and oldest of Australia's dance companies'.

Chunky Move dancers (p29)

The **Australian Ballet** (www.australianballet.com.au) is the national ballet company and is considered one of the finest in the world. It performs regularly at Melbourne's Victorian Arts Centre, with a programme of classical and modern ballets. Established by artistic director Dame Peggy van Praagh in 1962, the Australian Ballet flourished under the direction of Maina Gielgud, whose creativity and vision saw the company's repertoire and reputation expand. Following a difficult period in the late 1990s, the company is once again stable, and currently under the artistic direction of the company's former principal dancer David McAllister.

A recent review of the subsidised dance sector conducted by the Australia Council's Dance Board implied that professional dance in this country is anorexic, suffering from serious underfunding. Despite the difficulties, dancers continue to contribute to the arts with exemplary élan, garnering success internationally. Independent artists and organisations are most affected by funding, generally falling through the cracks of long-term support, leaving them unable to develop substantial works that will have mass appeal. A Melbourne organisation, **Dancehouse** (www.dancehouse.com.au) is a studio setup that supports and nurtures independents. It features a programme of lectures and forums, dance classes and workshops, offers rehearsal space, and coordinates regular performances. Supported by the Australia Council, it's a terrific prop for independents to increase their skills and capacity to expand their audience reach. It's an enviable model that represents an antidote to difficulties generally experienced by individual dancers who operate outside established companies.

For a list of dance venues see p134.

CINEMA

Highly successful Australian movies aren't that representative of the population: we have our fair share of bushwhackers, that's true, but the majority of Australians would rather sit in a movie theatre than wrestle a reptile. The Hollywood influence on Australian cinema is palpable, though the story of Australian cinema is a coming-of-age tale that has audiences enamoured.

Many Australian features have screened internationally and received the red-carpet treatment, raising the country's cinematic profile and reinforcing Australia's cultural identity. A high proportion of important films were made in Victoria (see the boxed text, p31).

Excellent postproduction facilities and a number of world-class studios keep Australia neighbourly with Hollywood, which has whipped up several of its big-budget movies here, including the *Matrix* and *Star Wars* prequels. Melbourne joins Sydney and Brisbane on the list of cities boasting world-class film studios, with the recent addition at Docklands. The marked increase in the value of the Australian dollar and the high cost involved in relocating a film crew to far-flung Australia is proving to be a deterrent for Hollywood producers to use Australian facilities.

Only two film industries in the world exist without government support; they're also the two biggest: Hollywood and Bollywood. The Australian film industry, like many, is dependent on government funding. The long-term repercussions of the Free Trade Agreement signed with the US in 2004 are yet to play themselves out. The Australian 'culture' industry was vociferous in its opposition, fearing that government support for Australian-made content would be diluted, and with it, an Australian voice in film and TV.

Hollywood has traditionally set the standard for film making in Australia. For the most part, Australian films emulate the Hollywood three-act structure and seek to woo the US market by producing some quirky Australiana content in a recognisably accessible formula. Increasingly, however, Australian film-makers are shifting from the Hollywood benchmark and recognising European models of storytelling, broadening their film repertoire, along with their audience's.

Film culture is nurtured in Victoria through local funding projects, education and exhibition. Film making, screenwriting, drama and animation are taught in Melbourne's major universities. Funding for features, documentaries, shorts, digital media and game content is provided by **Film Victoria** (www.film.vic.gov.au), which also provides mentoring schemes. Federation Square has consolidated much of Melbourne's screen culture, housing the Australian Centre for the Moving Image (p62) and SBS.

Recent films made in Victoria include *One Perfect Day* (2003), which traces a classically trained musician's rise in the rave music scene; *Crackerjack* (2002), which is a comedy set around lawn bowls; and *Chopper* (2000), about the eponymous ex-crim. The quirky-comedy genre is well covered by the Melbourne-based Working Dog production company: the *Dish* (1999) and the *Castle* (1997) are supreme examples, poking fun at Australian stereotypes, with respect for their subjects.

Other films to look out for include *Proof* (1991), a poignant film about a blind photographer set in St Kilda. Uncompromising local director Geoffrey Wright's films include the savage *Romper Stomper* (1992), an early Russell Crowe show stopper about a neo-Nazi skinhead gang based in the Melbourne inner suburb of Footscray (the gang's HQ is just down the road from the Lonely Planet office!), and *Head On* (1998), the coming-of-age tale of gay sex, drugs and futility, starring small-screen star Alex Dimitriades.

Benchmark Australian films from the 1970s, which were known as the New Wave, include *Picnic at Hanging Rock, Devil's Playground* and *Mad Max*.

Famously, in 1959, the postnuclear film *On the Beach* was shot in Melbourne, depicting the city as the last place of civilisation in the world. The film's leading lady, Ava Gardner, allegedly described Melbourne as 'the perfect place to make a film about the end of the world', commenting on the city's then conservatism and staid nature. Only recently was it discovered that journalist Neil Jillett invented the quote.

Favourite Feature Films

- *Picnic at Hanging Rock* (1975; dir Peter Weir) Three schoolgirls disappear; eerie, other-dimension references.
- *The Castle* (1997; dir Rob Sitch) The Kerrigan family defend their home when it's compulsorily acquired by the government. A cracker.
- *Mad Max* (1979; dir George Miller) Before Mel Gibson found Jesus, he was a gun-toting road warrior. Cult classic.
- *Proof* (1991; dir Jocelyn Moorhouse) A blind photographer learns about trust. Intelligent and emotive.
- *Chopper* (2000; dir Andrew Dominik) The criminal world has its own etiquette and rules. Stylish and unnerving.

The prominence of film in Melbourne is evident in the number of film festivals the city hosts. Apart from the main **Melbourne International Film Festival** (www.melbournefilmfestival .com.au), there's everything from the **Melbourne Underground Film Festival** (www.muff.com.au) to Sydney-import **Tropfest** (www.tropfest.com.au), which is a free outdoor screening of short films held at the Sidney Myer Music Bowl. Other film-festival genres include foreign-made, seniors, hip-hop, queer, shorts and documentary.

Film-focused publications include *Inside Film*, devoted to the creation of screen content, available at newsagents; and *Real Time*, available free from cafés and cinemas.

For movie-theatre listings see p132.

TELEVISION

Over 99% of homes in Melbourne have one TV set, and 61% have two or more. Melburnians spend an average of 3.3 hours of each day watching the box, which is seemingly screening a constant flow of reality TV and lifestyle programmes. Free-to-air content is so laden with the stuff, you wonder whether viewers have time enough to stencil their own bathrooms, revitalise the backyard or have their own household drama, happy instead to do it vicariously through the telly.

Melburnians wake up to variety shows comprising some music, advertorials, interviews and light news. The variety-hour ratings war relies heavily on each programme's charismatic hosts: Bert Newton (affectionately known as Moonface) and Kerri-Anne Kennelly (not known so affectionately).

There's an enduring preference for the police drama in Australia. Two locally made shows with a loyal following include *Blue Heelers*, about outback cops, and *Stingers*, about undercover cops.

Locally produced lasting comedy includes *Kath & Kim*, a piss-take of suburban Melbourne, and the *Panel*, a panel discussion lampooning current issues and events.

Eat Carpet screens innovative, experimental short films from Australia and around the world. The ABC and SBS are generally good sources for nonfiction programmes. And, of course, there's the light-froth soap opera of *Neighbours* (see the boxed text, p32).

The Logies are Australia's answer to the Emmy Awards, where 2.4 million viewers tune in to watch a lot of people those from outside Australia are unlikely to have ever heard of.

LITERATURE

Australian literature examines many themes that relate to what it is to be Australian. It interprets the experience of having overseas origins, evokes a sense of place and a person's relationship in it, and re-examines history. But it also produces some excellent entertainment in the genres of crime and humour, informed by all of the above.

Neighbours

In its 18th year in 2004, **Neighbours** (www.neighbours.com) is one of Australia's most successful TV series. This weekday soap is centred on the relationships of residents in the mythical middle-class suburb of Erinsborough. Unlike American soaps, no evil characters sleep with their daughter's husband, or fake their death and re-emerge after extensive plastic surgery pregnant to their son-in-law. The most shocking raunch in *Neighbours* of late is poor old Harold (who is one of the series' most enduring characters) finding himself uncharacteristically ogling women after suffering a stroke.

The day-to-day dramas of Ramsay St beam into lounge rooms in 57 countries, with an estimated audience of 120 million. The series has launched the careers – albeit music careers – of a few Aussie notables, including Kylie Minogue, Delta Goodrem and Natalie Imbruglia, as well as the acting careers of Guy Pearce and Jason Donovan. The Melbourne Museum (p66) displays the set of the kitchen from No 26 Ramsay St, and official **tours** (☎ 9534 4755) run out to the real-life street where *Neighbours* is filmed: Pinoak Ct in Nunawading.

The Great Australian Read

- *Cloudstreet* by Tim Winton (1991) – arguably Tim Winton's best novel, the author has a gift for writing stories that are miraculous in their everydayness. *Cloudstreet* is the gorgeous story of two families and the house they share.
- *Dark Palace* by Frank Moorhouse (2000) – sequel to *Grand Days*, and set in Europe in the 1930s, *Dark Palace* records the loss of faith in the League of Nations, as Nazism takes hold. Winner of the Miles Franklin Award (2001).
- *Deadly Unna?* by Phillip Gwynne (1998) – for young adults, this fine little novel combines humour, football, race relations and politics.
- *The Hamilton Case* by Michelle de Kretser (2002) – set in Ceylon in the 1930s, this tale of intrigue and loss is sensually rendered, winning the Melbourne author a spot on the Premier's Award shortlist, as well as the Commonwealth Writers best-book award.
- *My Place* by Sally Morgan (1988) – the simple prose warms the reader to this moving autobiographical journey of the author's discovery of her Aboriginal heritage. The exploration of the Stolen Generation is good background in a heartfelt package.
- *Of A Boy* by Sonya Hartnett (2002) – the disappearance of the three Mitford children is just one of the shadows in young Adrian's life. This haunting invocation of troubled childhood won Melbourne author Hartnett the *Age* Book of the Year Award (2003) and was shortlisted for the Premier's Award (2003).
- *Shanghai Dancing* by Brian Castro (2003) – fictional biography of an Australian family's perspective on their lives before coming to Australia, set in Shanghai, Hong Kong and Macau. This challenging and intelligent work won the Premier's Award (2003).
- *The True History of the Kelly Gang* by Peter Carey (2000) – this Booker Prize–winning interpretation of Ned Kelly's trials brings him to life in language and spirit, with Carey's take depicting him as a victim of an unjust system.
- *Voss* by Patrick White (1957) – this Australian classic is no light read. A richly metaphoric, superbly written novel exploring the megalomania-fuelled era of exploration, which is contrasted with the starchy English-styled urban life.
- *The Well* by Elizabeth Jolley (1986) – eccentric Miss Hester Harper draws vital young Katherine into her lonely world on an isolated country property. Things go horribly wrong when they throw the man they accidentally killed down the well.

Australia's literary scene was long dominated by writers of British and Irish descent. It has evolved over the past few decades to better reflect the country's multicultural constitution, tackling issues of identity and diversity.

Contemporary authors such as Peter Carey and David Malouf often focus on fictitious re-interpretations of Australian history as a means of exploring personal and national identity. Thea Astley and Tim Winton, winners of Australia's most prestigious literary award, the Miles Franklin, deal with human relations while evoking a strong sense of place in the Australian landscape.

Australia turns out a respectable amount of children's fiction. Picture-book authors to look for include Mem Fox and Libby Gleeson. For older readers, the prolific John Marsden fosters a more serious aesthetic in his readers compared with contemporaries such as Morris Gleitzman and Andy Griffths.

Poetry has traditionally interpreted and re-interpreted the landscape, lifestyle and typical characters, as well as the impact of early European society on Australia's indigenous peoples. What began in sing-song bush ballads, with the likes of CJ Dennis, has evolved to contemporary musings. Well known poets include Dorothy Porter, Chris Wallace-Crabbe, Les Murray and John Tranter.

Victoria has produced plenty of outstanding writers. Some of the classic works of Victorian literature are *For the Term of His Natural Life* by Marcus Clarke, *The Getting of Wisdom* by Henry Handel Richardson, *Picnic at Hanging Rock* by Joan Lindsay and *My Brother Jack* by George Johnston. Also, look for the work of Charmian Clift, Hal Porter, Alan Marshall and Frank Hardy.

Among Victoria's contemporary writers, the best known is probably Peter Carey (now living in New York), who won the Booker Prize in 1988 for his novel *Oscar & Lucinda* and in 2002 for his novel based on the letters of Ned Kelly, *The True History of the Kelly Gang*. Helen Garner's works are mostly set in Melbourne and include *The Children's Bach*, *Postcards From Surfers*, *Cosmo Cosmolino* and *Monkey Grip*. Other contemporary

Melbourne Between the Lines

- *Loaded* by Christos Tsiolkas (1995) – the gritty story of a migrant child and his emerging sexuality, *Loaded* was made into the successful film *Head On* (1998).
- *Monkey Grip* by Helen Garner (1977) – the first novel for Garner, winning the National Book Council Award in 1978. The story of two young lovers addicted to love and heroin was made into a feature film of the same name in 1982. Garner also writes nonfiction, winning the Walkley Award for journalism in 1993.
- *Normal Service Will Resume*, published by Cardigan Press (2003) – the second collection of short fiction written by Melbourne's emerging writers; a third collection is due out late 2004.
- *Something Fishy* by Shane Maloney (2003) – the fifth comic thriller in the series linked by hapless ALP minder Murray Whelan, who somehow keeps getting involved in murder cases. Telemovies of the series were in production in 2004.
- *Three Dollars* by Elliot Perlman (1998) – multiaward-winning book that ambitiously chronicles middle-class angst in a climate of downsizing and globalisation. Perlman's latest novel, *Seven Types of Ambiguity*, was published in 2003.

Melbourne writers to look out for include Kerry Greenwood, Morris Lurie, Carmel Bird, Barry Dickins, Gerald Murnane, Robert Dessaix, Rod Jones, Andrea Goldsmith, Christos Tsiolkas, Sonya Hartnett, Clare Mendes, Fiona Capp, Michelle de Kretser and Andrew Masterson.

ARCHITECTURE

The redesign of Melbourne's major institutions reflects the city's increasingly outward-looking nature. The prim Victorian architecture for which the city has been known has shuffled aside to make way for intrepid angular newcomers. The current minimal aesthetic is complicated with exposed concrete, geometric shapes, metallic cladding and curtain-walled glass. Recent examples include Federation Square, the Australian Centre for Contemporary Art and the Southern Cross Station in Spencer St. New developments

Angling for a Future City

Approaching the city from Melbourne Airport, you'll drive beneath the Melbourne Gateway. The rake of 30m-high red beams and the single 70m yellow beam are angled so as to reach across the eight-lane Tullamarine Fwy. It's one of a string of designs by architectural doyens Denton Corker Marshall (DCM) intended to mark Melbourne as a dynamic, technologically advanced city from the future.

The DCM-designed Melbourne Museum (p66) comprises glass walls, geometric shapes and soaring angles that point away from the stately Victorian Royal Exhibition Building metres away, and to a new direction for the city's architecture. The two very different, but neighbouring, architectural styles serve almost as a 'before' and 'after' photo for a city. On a similarly imposing scale, the Melbourne Exhibition Centre (p59), also by DCM, is further evidence of the architects' preference for vast sloping surfaces and jarring angles. There's a 1950s renaissance evident in both the Melbourne Museum and the Melbourne Exhibition Centre that's both minimal and playful. Both buildings carry a sleek nostalgia that ushered them past the detractors' queue and straight through to the city's architectural fabric.

The Docklands development (p64) is often spoken about in '21st-century city' terms. For decades, this waterfront location served as the factory floor for the import/export industry of the docks. Towers of shipping containers have given way to towers of apartments designed by Fender Katsilidis and Wood Marsh. The workers of today's Docklands will be confined to an office, as opposed to a crane. And the lunchroom has multiplied into a succession of restaurants and cafés offering a world of cuisines.

The docks of yesterday were strictly reserved for work. Today's Docklands are screaming for visitors, with waterfront promenades, public spaces, restaurants and public-art projects.

And what should fittingly oversee the design-driven Docklands development, connecting Melbourne to the future? Bridges designed by DCM of course: the Bolte for those who want to get there by car, and the Webb for pedestrians and cyclists.

Building 8, RMIT University (see boxed text, p36)

have both their critics and their converts. Detractors dismiss the pervading international ambience as an empty vernacular, devoid of individual expression. Others praise recent developments for upgrading the city's facilities without compromising the surrounding environment.

Residential development has also changed the face of the city. In an effort to reduce the urban sprawl and subsequent drain on resources, high-density apartment towers dominate the skyline. Despite the increased population, many of these new apartments remain vacant. While a significant number of Melburnians are following the global downsizing trend, moving from a suburban block to a compact city apartment, it remains to be seen whether the population is large enough to fill the available space in the huge number of new developments.

Appropriately, the most prominent architectural style in the state is Victorian (1840–90), which was an expression of the era's confidence, progress and prosperity. It drew upon various sources including classical, romantic and Gothic, and as the era progressed designs became more elaborate, flamboyant and ornamental. Melbourne is widely acknowledged as one of the world's great Victorian-era cities, which accounts for the more recent *Zeitgeist* of the city concealing its vibrant treasures behind a prudish, grey exterior.

With the collapse of Melbourne's land boom in the early 1890s and the subsequent severe economic depression, a new style of architecture evolved, which came to be known as Federation. Federation style was in many ways a watered-down version of Victorian architecture, featuring simplicity of design and less ornamentation. Its evolution was mainly driven by economic necessity, but also influenced by the pending Federation of Australia (in 1901) and the desire to create a more distinctive and suitably 'Australian' style of design.

From around 1910, the most prominent style of residential architecture was a hybrid of Federation and Californian Bungalow. Art Deco also featured from the 1920s, but following the Great Depression architecture became increasingly functionalist and devoid of decoration.

Melbourne Icons

- **Federation Square** (cnr Flinders & Swanston Sts) Built in minimalist style in 2000–01. Sloping surfaces and angular metal and sandstone motifs that are loosely based on the chaos theory. A combination of both brutalism and beauty (see p62).
- **Forum Theatre** (150-152 Flinders St) Built in neogothic style in 1928, and one of the city's most atmospheric film and theatre venues, this exaggerated, Arab-inspired gem has an equally lush interior, with the southern sky rendered on the domed ceiling.
- **Manchester Unity Building** (220 Collins St) Built in Art Deco style in 1932, and the tallest building of its time, the Manchester Unity now houses dozens of lucky businesses and offices in its warrenlike interior.
- **Rialto Towers** (525 Collins St) This enormous totem to office life, built in modern style in 1985–86, is notable for its reflective exterior, which changes colour throughout the day, and for being the tallest building in the southern hemisphere. See just how tall by visiting the observation deck (p65).
- **Building 8, RMIT University** (368 Swanston St) Don't worry, you will see this colourful postmodern building constructed in 1993. This outstanding structure is a bold collage of design and ideas that smashes the solid conservative wall-to-wall aesthetic at this end of town.

In recent years, appreciation of these older styles has increased to the extent that local councils have actively encouraged residents to restore houses and buildings in sympathy with the period in which they were built. However, with the boom in medium-density housing, many of Melbourne's beautiful 19th- and early-20th-century houses and gardens have been replaced with a glut of graceless townhouses.

Visit www.walkingmelbourne.com for a comprehensive architectural database of Melbourne's historic buildings. You can also take the City Stroll walking tour (p94) for a rundown on the city's built environment.

Food

Food

Melbourne's palate is adventurous and discerning; the city's population is well versed in the art of eating. Food is an experience that surpasses its primary role as fuel – dining out is a lifestyle here. Try the Epicure lift-out in Tuesday's *Age* for regular food-focused features and reviews. The range of fresh produce available here is one of the best and broadest in the world, and Melbourne chefs are renowned for their ability to deftly and imaginatively combine and prepare them.

Fine food factors into every facet of Melbourne life, from purchasing, to preparation and consumption. Chefs and restaurateurs command positions in the media, taking on celebrity status. Some, such as Iain Hewitson from St Kilda's Tolarno (p113), appear on TV cooking programmes; others publish a variety of books, from pictorials to recipe compendiums. Melburnians are just as happy to consume professionals' advice, as they are their meals. There's a great respect for those who do food well, and home chefs are hungry to apply professional secrets and methods to their daily diet.

The culture of food in Melbourne is one of the richest in the world. Its influences, idiosyncrasies and importance generally are musts for the visitor to experience. See the Eating chapter (p100) for some of the city's staggering array of excellent dining choices.

HISTORY

Melbourne's culinary history has been profoundly influenced by the different waves of settlers and immigrants, not to mention worldwide trends. The past 50 years have seen a swing away from classic English fare, to a variety of international cuisines. WWII saw the city resorting to affordable and functional food, including the staple Spam and eggs. In the 1950s affluent British influences pervaded the menu, and dishes such as Steak Dianne appeared. In the following decade an influx of migrants began to broaden tastes, as exhibited in the preference for 'foreign' flavours such as chicken Kiev and curries. During the 1970s, ideas about societal wellbeing were shared around the fondue or a plate of cheese-cubes and cabana, and the '80s were typified by high-fat foods and cocktails: cordon bleu, avocado and creamy seafood. The 1990s saw a reaction against the excesses of the previous decade: simple, cleaner foods such as stir-fries, and roast-pepper-and-eggplant stacks with sun-dried tomatoes, goats cheese and roquette became prominent. To date, meals using organic, free-range and chemical-free produce typify the current decade.

CULTURE

Melbourne's multiethnic make-up is reflected in the variety of world flavours that is brought to the table. In an attempt to define the indefinable, Modern Australian (Mod Oz) is a term often bandied about to describe the mix of influences. It's a creative fusion of European, Mediterranean and Asian flavours prepared with Grade A

Melbourne's food is a fusion of influences

Melbourne Food & Wine Festival

Melbourne is synonymous with good food and wine, and one of the best ways to discover the city's culinary heart is to visit during the annual food and wine festival. The Melbourne Food & Wine Festival (www.melbournefoodand wine.com.au) turned 12 in 2004, serving up a feast of special events and reinforcing the city's role as Australia's culinary capital.

The two-week festival is held in March, turning the flame-burner on Melbourne's finest restaurants, most celebrated chefs and best produce. Regular events include the World's Longest Lunch (held simultaneously in the city and at two dozen regional centres across the state), superstar chef master classes, coffee workshops, a Southgate progressive dinner, and dozens of theme dinners held by Melbourne's top nosheries. The focus is on such treats as local wines, world cuisines and fresh regional farm produce.

ingredients. Don't be shy asking your waiter what *waghu* or *sumac* is if you find it on a menu: staff will proudly expound on a particular ingredient's origin and sensation.

These international influences also inspire the way diners eat in Melbourne: you can enjoy the traditional style of entrée, main course and dessert, or go for a number of plates designed to share. The shared dining experience is most evident in Asian-style ordering where several dishes are placed in the centre of the table for all to sample. Increasingly, Spanish tapas-style plates are available, intended to provide some solid sustenance while drinking with friends.

As well as the Mod Oz fusion, authentic Italian, Vietnamese, Chinese and other cuisines are prominent in enclaves about town. Uncompromising dishes such as chicken's feet are available in Little Bourke St's Chinatown, and you'll find the best bowl of *pho* (beef and rice noodle soup) this side of Saigon in Victoria St, Richmond. Authentic Italian is available in most parts of Melbourne, but is most prevalent in Carlton and Fitzroy. For tapas head to Johnston St, Fitzroy.

Food also plays an important part in many of Melbourne's social rituals. No cinema experience is complete without a choc-top (see the boxed text, p133), fish and chips are almost always consumed seaside, pies and footy are synonymous and you'll find fairyfloss (candyfloss) at the fete. These unspoken rules of where to eat what are ingrained in the social fabric and taken very seriously. Take care not to mix them up, as fish and chips at the movies will result in expulsion from the cinema and fairyfloss at the footy, well…we dare you.

Another important social ritual is the barbecue. Traditionally a man's domain, the outdoor barbecue allows males to indulge their primeval urge to play with fire. The barbecue has always been about socialising, which has meant that what was actually on the barbecue was of secondary importance. Everyone had a great time despite the shrivelled sausages and charred chops that resulted from all that hard labour. That's changing, however, with the culinary part of the equation slowly catching up – chargrilled seafood, prime cuts of meat, and vegetables all now have a place on the barbie. Barbecues for public use can be found in many of the city's parks and gardens. And technology is keeping pace with changing urban demands – tiny barbecues are now available for apartment balconies.

WHERE TO EAT

As well as restaurant, café and pub dining options described following, Melbourne has a profusion of takeaways that offer hand-held parcels to eat on the run.

CAFÉS

The European (especially Italian) influence in Melbourne remains as strong as ever – it is most evident in the vibrant café scene that dominates the city and inner suburbs. Coffee in Melbourne is the best in the world, lovingly prepared with both Italian roasts and supreme local roasts. See the Drinking chapter (p119) for more information on coffee culture in Melbourne. Café dining is generally informal and available for breakfast through to dinner; it's coffee-centric during the day and bar-focused at night. Melbourne's footpaths and laneways sport clusters of outdoor tables and chairs to cater to the city's love of alfresco dining. A ban on smoking inside all establishments where food is the main component has also contributed to the provision of outdoor dining year round. The city's notoriously changeable weather and some inglorious outlooks of parked cars and gutters are no hindrance to the café set, although many places provide pavement heating on cool days to ward off chilly breezes.

PUBS

Melbourne's pubs also offer good honest fare (see the boxed text, p121). More modern dishes, such as seafood and stir-fries, have joined the characteristic meat-and-three-veg counter-meal on pub menus. Order at the kitchen or bar, take your number and a set of cutlery and find a table. Your meal will find you. Many inner-city pubs retain their local appeal, with a relaxed retro ambience despite recent makeovers. The nicotine-

Restaurateur Profile: Paul Mathis

The chance that you'll find yourself at one of Paul Mathis' restaurants is pretty high. He's the man behind many of Melbourne's prominent eating establishments, all of which reflect the maturing of the man, as well as the city.

More than 20 years' experience culminates in Paul's biggest venture, Transport (p120) opened in 2004 – a multilevel pub whose industrialised fit-out embodies the futuristic image projected by the Federation Square precinct. 'There's a necessity to be modern', Paul says. 'The past has been done and in order to be considerably different, you need to keep reinventing yourself.' Paul's transport theme follows the tradition of naming pubs according to symbols recognisable to the community. 'In the western suburbs where I lived, all the pubs had a word that implied working-class origins: something strong and long-lasting, like the Builders Arms. Transport fits into that model, reflecting core notions of getting from here to there, wherever that place might be...and back.'

Paul's first restaurant, in Lygon St, Carlton – known for enormous serves of pasta – brought his Italian heritage to the table. In the late '80s and early '90s he opened a string of ridiculously successful cafés. 'When Blue Train (p105) and Joe's Garage first appeared, Melbourne was in a recession. We offered a cheaper alternative to the stuffy, expensive options that were around at that time.' The sleek lounge-café theme with a distinctive retro flavour inspired dozens of copycat cafés that mimicked Blue Train in particular, both in name and design.

Paul's most adventurous restaurant is the vegetarian Soul Mama (p112) in the St Kilda Sea Baths development. 'That's an establishment-type precinct with expectations for [places with] broad-reaching gastronomy and presentation. The last thing people expected was a vegetarian restaurant, because in most people's views vegetarianism is limited to a small percentage of the market. I reverted to my personal beliefs.'

The holistic approach is carried over into Paul's Japanese-style restaurant, Chocolate Buddha (p104), across from Transport in Federation Square. 'It's organic, where possible.' Taxi, Transport's midlevel restaurant also uses organic and free-range ingredients. 'Every single material here is Australian: all the timbers, metals, everything has been recycled. There's so much emphasis on environmental sustainability here from the way the kitchens are run, gas is pumped into the venue, water is recycled, and the place is heated, reflecting Paul Mathis at 42 as opposed to Paul Mathis at 22.'

Transport is already a major hub of the futuristic Federation Square, which suggests that Melburnians are more than willing to move into modernity; they'd just rather go there with a beer in one hand and an organic burger in the other. As Paul matures, imposing his personal beliefs in his restaurants, so too does the dining public. While they frequent his establishments Melburnians are literally having sustainable precepts shoved done their throats, and loving it.

stained walls and well-worn carpets evoke a past only thinly disguised by the fashionable furniture and colourful chalkboard menus.

RESTAURANTS

Restaurant dining is generally formal, with tables dressed in crisp white linen. Restaurants usually open for lunch and dinner, and are licensed to serve alcohol and/or BYO (Bring Your Own). If a restaurant is both licensed and BYO, you're generally limited to bringing bottled wine. A corkage charge will be added to your bill for BYO, which is either per person or per bottle; charges range from 50 cents to a few dollars.

Many restaurants change their menus according to the season to exploit fresh seasonal delicacies, such as figs, quinces and spring lamb, and to cater to the demand for comfort food in winter and lighter meals in summer. To be sure of a place it's advisable to make a reservation at any time of the year, and especially at weekends.

A number of Melbourne restaurants include native-animal meats on their menus. Kangaroo is deservedly increasingly popular, as a lean, tasty and relatively economical alternative to more traditional prime-meat cuts. Locals are tentative about ordering possum, however, not yet able to disassociate them from the cute, fluffy critters that inhabit suburban backyards.

Most menus have a vegetarian option and there are plenty of speciality restaurants and cafés serving only meat-free dishes. An increasing number of establishments also choose to use organic or GM-free produce. Such places are heavily patronised, reflecting the city's growing demand for sustainable and responsible consumption.

Cooks' Books

For a comprehensive range of new and out-of-print titles, head to **Books for Cooks** (Map pp206-08; ☎ 8415 1415; 233 Gertrude St, Fitzroy). Following are just a few of the excellent publications by Melbourne's favourite foodies.

- *Arabesque*, Greg Malouf – North African and Middle Eastern flavours grace this popular how-to book.
- *The Cook's Companion*, Stephanie Alexander – by the owner of Richmond Hill Cafe & Larder, this is essential for any kitchen library.
- *Ezard*, Teage Ezard – with Young Chef of the Year and Best Restaurant for Ezard at Adelphi accolades, Teage Ezard was bound to produce a bound beauty.
- *Flavours of Vietnam*, Meera Freeman and Le Van Nhan – inspirational authentic Vietnamese recipes; Meera also runs cooking classes (www.meerafreeman.com.au).
- *Modern Barbecue Food*, Allan Campion and Michele Curtis – this is the latest in a series of excellent food guides and recipe books from this duo (www.campionandcurtis.com).

SELF-CATERING

Quality produce is readily available at the vast number of emporiums and markets in the inner city (see the boxed text, p42, for some of these). Market shopping is part of the food journey, with many Melburnians incorporating it into their weekend routine. The market experience brings people closer to the source of their food. Shoppers develop a preference for particular stalls and build relationships with vendors who'll impart expert advice and recommend the choicest produce. There's a sense of community at markets where the increasing number of people who live alone engage in some friendly banter, and where stallholders still round down the bill to the nearest dollar.

CELEBRATING WITH FOOD

Melbourne's many ethnicities have specific food-related tributes, from moon cakes during new-moon celebrations to abstinence from food altogether during Lent. Generally, traditional Australian celebrations could only be described as eccentric. Christmas is celebrated with a huge cooked lunch following the English tradition, even though December is high summer here; revellers sit down to a formal meal of roast turkey or pork with

Produce Stores

DIY lunches and dinners can be a sumptuous experience equal to dining out, especially if you get your goods from one of the following speciality produce stores:

- **Essential Ingredient** (Map p212; ☎ 9827 9047; Elizabeth St, South Yarra; ☯ 9am-5.30pm Mon-Fri, 8am-5pm Sat, 10am-4pm Sun) At Prahran Market, this superstore stocks a vast array of ingredients; you can learn how to combine them at the cooking school upstairs.
- **Il Fornaio** (Map p209; ☎ 9534 2922; 2 Acland St, St Kilda; ☯ 7am-10pm) Walk into this bakery-café for a coffee, walk out with an armload of take-home dinners and doughy delights.
- **King & Godfree** (Map pp206-08; ☎ 9347 1619; 293-297 Lygon St, Carlton; ☯ 9am-9pm Mon-Sat, 11am-6pm Sun) Wines, deli, sweets and other treats: this mostly Italian-goods supplier is one of the oldest and best.
- **Richmond Hill Cafe & Larder** (Map p211; ☎ 9421 2808; 48-50 Bridge Rd, Richmond; ☯ 9am-2.30pm Mon-Fri, 8.30am-2.30pm Sat & Sun) Cheese lovers unite at this temperature- and humidity-controlled larder.
- **Simon Johnson** (Map pp206-08; ☎ 9486 9456; 12-14 St David St, Fitzroy; ☯ 10.30am-5pm Mon-Fri, 9am-5pm Sat) A range of basic ingredients and speciality products of exceptional quality is on offer here.

vegetables, followed by hot plum pudding – despite the temperature being 30+ degrees. Easter usually brings chocolate eggs delivered by a rabbit, and eating cake marks birthdays. Before a woman's wedding day, the bride-to-be and her friends celebrate with a Hens' Night. The gaggle of women generally descends on one of Melbourne's many theatre restaurants. Theatre restaurants combine food with entertainment in the form of light theatre along a particular theme, which is carried through to the décor and waiters' costumes. The occult seems to be the predominant theme, with restaurants such as Draculas, Witches in Britches and Hunchbax.

History

History

THE RECENT PAST

The last state election in 2002 resoundingly returned the Labor government to office for its second term. It didn't help the Liberal opposition that many had never heard of the party's leader, Robert Doyle. By contrast, Premier Steve Bracks was recently voted one of Melbourne's sexiest people. In 2004 the *Age* newspaper reported that it was a 'combination of his boy-next-door looks, goofily earnest manner and political smarts' that earned him a place in its top 25. The government's focus on public issues, such as education and health, has contributed to the 'nice guy' label.

Bracks' Labor government first won the public's favour with its pledge to listen to the electorate and concentrate on welfare issues after the previous government alienated the populace with its iron-fisted economic focus. From 1992 to 1999 the Liberal-National party coalition led by Jeff Kennett steamrolled the state. Its policies succeeded in turning around Victoria's failing economy, with the current government still riding its wave, but compromised social welfare, health, education and community. The Kennett government initiated the redevelopment of many of Melbourne's institutions.

FROM THE BEGINNING

ABORIGINAL HISTORY

Aborigines journeyed from Southeast Asia to the Australian mainland at least 45,000 years ago. Victoria's Aboriginal people, the Koories, lived in about 38 different dialect groups and spoke 10 separate languages. The most important social group was the clan, as the group that identified with specific tracts of land. The Aborigines' complex traditional culture was largely based on their close spiritual bond with the land. Koories led a seminomadic existence, moving within their estates according to a range of determinants, including seasonal variation and the need to be in specific places for ritual and totemic purposes.

Traditional Aboriginal religious beliefs centre on the continuing existence of spirit beings that lived on the earth during creation time (the Dreaming). These beings created all the features of the natural world and were the ancestors of all living things. They took different forms and as they travelled around, they left physical evidence of their activities, such as a tree, claypan or hill. These features are sacred sites. Individuals who are spiritually bound to a particular site are required to perform rituals and sing songs to keep the natural order.

Prior to British colonisation, the Yarra Valley region was occupied by members of the Woiworung clan of the Kulin Nation, known as the Wurundjeri.

THE EUROPEANS

In January 1788 the First Fleet sailed into Botany Bay, New South Wales, and established Australia's first colony. The fleet comprised 11 ships carrying 1030 people, including 548 male and 188 female convicts, and four companies of marines. It was not until 1803 that a small party of convicts, soldiers and settlers set sail for the south. The group landed at Sorrento on the Mornington Peninsula and established Victoria's first European settlement.

TIMELINE	1803	1835	1837
	First European settlement established at Sorrento	John Batman 'buys' land from indigenous Australians for knives, blankets, tomahawks, scissors, clothes, mirrors and flour	Named 'Melbourne' after Lord Melbourne, the British prime minister of the day

Less than a year later the settlement was abandoned due to lack of a fresh water supply and the group sailed to Van Diemen's Land (Tasmania) and founded Hobart.

The arrival at Portland of Edward Henty, his family and a flock of sheep from Van Diemen's Land in 1834, marked the first permanent European settlement in Victoria. In what has been called 'the greatest land grab in British imperial history', pastoralists and settlers flooded into Victoria. Within 10 years Europeans outnumbered the region's original inhabitants.

FOUNDING OF MELBOURNE

A Melbourne dentist with a penchant for collecting old books and manuscripts recently sold a letter that debunks all popular history about who founded Melbourne. Two Tasmanian men, John Batman and John Pascoe Fawkner, are widely acknowledged as the founders of Melbourne. However, a letter from the men's surveyor, John Helder Wedge, sheds new light about the circumstances surrounding the founding of Melbourne.

Windsor Hotel, built in 1883 (p58)

History – From the Beginning

In 1835 a group of Launceston businessmen formed the Port Phillip Association with the intention of establishing a new settlement in Port Phillip Bay. The history books say that the association's representative, John Batman, rowed up the Yarra River to the site where central Melbourne now stands, and uttered the immortal phrase, 'This will be the place for a village'. If the history books included a prologue they'd acknowledge that John Helder Wedge wrote to Batman before he left Tasmania advising him that '…the freshwater river at the head of the Port will be the place', not the site that Batman had initially selected, which lacked a fresh water supply. The rest is history.

Batman 'purchased' around 202,000 hectares of land from the local Aboriginal clans, and a settlement was established on the northern side of the Yarra River. The concept of buying and selling land was completely foreign to the indigenous population, who were given an assortment of items in exchange.

John Pascoe Fawkner and a group of Tasmanian settlers left for Port Phillip Bay six months later and settled the south of the Yarra. Fawkner became a driving force behind the new settlement. The son of a convict, he was a man of vision and worked tirelessly as a publisher, publican and self-taught bush lawyer. He spent 15 years on the Legislative Council of Victoria, where he campaigned vigorously for the rights of settlers and convicts, and for the end of transportation. By the time of his death in 1869, Melbourne was flourishing and he was known as the 'Grand Old Man of Victoria'. More than 15,000 people lined the streets to bid him farewell at his funeral.

History doesn't remember John Batman as kindly, and within four years of his dodgy deal with the Aborigines, he died of syphilis.

Estimates suggest that Victoria's precontact Aboriginal population was between 60,000 and 100,000; by the late 1840s it had dropped to 15,000 and by the 1880s to just over 800.

1838	1847	1854	1857
First newspapers roll off the presses	Melbourne is proclaimed a city	Railway from Flinders St to Port Melbourne opens	Water supply turned on

History Cast

There are some fine statues throughout Melbourne and its parklands. Many of them commemorate significant figures in the history of the city and Australia.

In the forecourt of the National Mutual building, at 447 Collins St, stand statues of Melbourne's two founders, **John Pascoe Fawkner** and **John Batman**. Beside St Paul's Cathedral, on the corner of Flinders and Swanston Sts, is Charles Gilbert's statue of a young **Matthew Flinders** who, during his voyage of 1802–03, became the first person to circumnavigate Australia and chart its coastline.

A fine statue of poet and horseman **Adam Lindsay Gordon** stands in Gordon Reserve on Spring St. Gordon shot himself on Brighton beach in 1870 after reading a review of his most recent book of poetry. Near the Shrine of Remembrance on St Kilda Rd is the statue of **Simpson and his donkey**. It was erected in memory of Private John Simpson Kirkpatrick for his bravery in helping wounded soldiers from the front line during the Allied Forces' landing at Gallipoli in WWI. Kirkpatrick was killed less than a month after the landing, aged 22.

The **Queen Victoria Monument**, in the Queen Victoria Gardens on St Kilda Rd, shows the monarch accompanied by four female figures that represent her birth, marriage, reign and death.

The Royal Exhibition Building in the Carlton Gardens is flanked by particularly voluptuous **fountain statuary**. Nearby, facing Nicholson St, stands a cute rendering of two **kangaroos**, donated by one of the colony's early settlers.

The white settlers regarded the Aborigines as a hindrance to their settling and 'civilising' of the land. The original inhabitants were dispossessed of their lands, their traditional culture was disrupted and they were killed in their thousands – first by introduced diseases such as smallpox, dysentery and measles, and later by gunfire and poison. Individual Aborigines resisted the encroachment of settlers and a number of warriors were, for a time, feared by the colonists.

EARLY DAYS

The settlement at Melbourne developed with astonishing speed and became a packing-case village of tents and hovels almost overnight. While the initial treaty with the Aborigines had no legal basis, by 1836 so many settlers had moved to Port Phillip that the administrators of NSW had to declare the area open to settlement.

Some order to the pell-mell development was provided in 1837 when military surveyor Robert Hoddle drew up plans for the new city, laying out a geometric grid of straight lines along a conveniently straight stretch of river. The broad streets were named after British kings and queens, title and all. Look at a map of Melbourne and connect parallel streets to come up with King William and Queen Elizabeth.

By 1840 there were over 10,000 people settled in the Melbourne area. As the new community grew in size and confidence, its members began to agitate for separation from NSW.

SEPARATION & GOLD BOOM

In 1851 Victoria separated from NSW, and Melbourne became the capital of the newly proclaimed colony. In the same year, gold was discovered at Bathurst in NSW. Fearing the young city's workers would take off for the northern goldfields, a committee of Melbourne businessmen offered a reward to anyone who could find gold in Victoria – and soon discovered they were sitting on the country's richest source of gold.

Within months the boom began. Every find was closely followed by hordes of hopefuls chasing the likes of the Welcome Stranger – the record-breaking nugget weighing 72kg with a current value of around $4 million. The gold rush brought about 1800

1888	1889	1905	1910
Telephone exchange opens	Electric tram begins running	Flinders Street Station built	Melbourne Cup day declared a public holiday

prospectors to Melbourne each week. Most came from England, Scotland or Ireland, but other Europeans and Americans were also among the first to arrive. Later, about 40,000 Chinese came.

Melbourne became chaotic. As soon as ships arrived in the harbour, their crews would desert and follow the passengers to the goldfields. Business in Melbourne ground to a standstill as most of the labour force left to join the search. Catherine Spence, a journalist and social reformer, visited Melbourne at the height of the hysteria. Her comments reflected concerns of the time about the effect of the gold rush on social stability: 'This convulsion has unfixed everything. Religion is neglected, education despised…everyone is engrossed with the simple object of making money in a very short time.'

Relatively few individuals struck it lucky. Scratching a living for many in outlying areas proved so difficult that it gave rise to dissent. It often seemed that local police and magistrates were using the law to oppress, rather than enforce, justice. Ned Kelly (1855–80) was a famous Victorian outlaw and defiant spirit against institutionalised injustice. Kelly presented to the authorities a hot-headed passion until his capture, and then a menacing equanimity until he was hanged at the Old Melbourne Gaol (p57). Ned was the subject of the first Australian feature film, made in 1906: *The Story of the Kelly Gang*. History repeats, with Ned as the subject of a '60s film starring Mick Jagger, and an eponymous film made in 2003, starring Heath Ledger. Ned remains as one of Australia's most enduring folk heroes.

Overall, Melbourne was bolstered by the wealth of the goldfields and the city became one of the world's great Victorian-era cities. Melburnians took some pride in their settlement, and they used their new-found wealth to build a city of extravagant proportions. Among the new migrants were tradespeople from Europe who were trained in the traditions of Renaissance-style building, and the city's architects readily put them to work. Large areas were set aside and planted as public parks and gardens. By the 1880s Melbourne was referred to as the 'Paris of the Antipodes'.

This period of great prosperity lasted 40 years. The 1880s were boom times for Melbourne, but affluence soon led to recklessness. Money from the goldfields and from overseas was invested in real estate and building works, and speculation led to rocketing land prices that couldn't last. In 1880 Melbourne hosted the International Exhibition – promoting new industrial products – in the opulent Royal Exhibition Building (p67) in the Carlton Gardens. No expense was spared in the building's construction or the exhibition itself, but this flamboyant showing off to the world was to be the swan song of a marvellous era for Melbourne.

In 1889 the property market collapsed under the increasing weight of speculation. In 1890 a financial crash in Argentina led to the collapse of several financial institutions in London; overnight, investment in Australia dried up. The 1890s were a period of severe economic depression, and it was years before Melbourne recovered.

FEDERATION TO THE DEPRESSION

On 1 January 1901, Victoria became a state of the new Australian nation. Melbourne was the country's capital and the seat of government until 1927, when the Australian capital was relocated to Canberra. The federal parliament sat at Melbourne's Parliament House, and the state parliament moved to the Royal Exhibition Building.

Melbourne again flourished in the early decades of the 20th century, but construction and development came to a shuddering halt with the Great Depression, which hit Australia hard. In 1931 almost one third of breadwinners were unemployed and poverty was widespread. During the Depression the government implemented a number of major public

1923	1950	1956	1970
Bill passed enabling women to sit in state parliament	The basic wage increased to one pound, with women entitled to 75% of this amount	Melbourne hosts the Olympic Games	The half-built West Gate Bridge collapses, killing 35 workers

Top Five: Secret Book Histories

- *Birth of Melbourne* by Tim Flannery (2004) – eminent naturalist and author Tim Flannery brings together around 70 extracts of Melbourne life from 1802 to 1903. Flannery illustrates that the development of a city is not always a pretty portrait.
- *Car Wars: How the Car Won our Hearts and Conquered our Cities* by Graeme Davison (2004) – an urban history that examines Melbourne's love affair with the car and how it shaped the city's psyche and geography.
- *Radical Melbourne: A Secret History* by Jeff and Jill Sparrow (2001) – Melbourne's political past is pegged to 50 landmarks. Take an illustrated walking tour that unveils the city's first 100 years of political and social sagas. The sequel, *Radical Melbourne II* (2004), covers the years from 1940 to 2000.
- *Melbourne Dreaming: A Guide to Aboriginal Places of Melbourne* by Meyer Eidelson (1997) – a practical guide describing and mapping places of Aboriginal significance.
- *The Melbourne Book: A History of Now* by Maree Coote (2003) – this compendium of the city is loaded with photographs, stories, graphics, impressions and illustrations.

works programmes, including the Yarra Blvd, the Shrine of Remembrance, St Kilda Rd and the Great Ocean Rd. An unlikely sporting hero was popularised by the media to help divert people's attention from the hardships: Phar Lap, the champion racehorse, became a national icon. His stuffed hide is exhibited at the Melbourne Museum (p66).

WWII TO BUST

WWII marked the beginning of a profound shift in Australia's allegiances – away from Britain and towards the USA. The war also marked the beginnings of a radical shift in Australia's immigration policies. White Australia's overwhelmingly Anglo-Celtic make-up was challenged by the arrival of non-British migrants, fleeing the upheaval of WWII in Europe. The postwar Australian government hoped that the increase in population would strengthen Australia's economy and contribute to its ability to defend itself: 'Populate or Perish' became the catch phrase. Between 1947 and 1968 more than 800,000 non-British European migrants came to Australia. The majority of migrants came by ships that docked first in Melbourne, where a large percentage of the new arrivals settled. With the demise of the insidious 'White Australia' policy in the 1970s, migrants began to arrive from Southeast Asia, adding further to the multicultural mix.

Melbourne's Victorian heritage was irrevocably altered by the postwar construction boom, a period in which architectural aesthetics worldwide hit rock bottom. Melbourne hosted the Olympic Games in 1956, and hectares of historic buildings were bulldozed as the city prepared to impress the hordes of visitors with its modernity. Construction continued in the 1960s under the Liberal premier Henry Bolte, culminating in the boom years of the 1980s. Reflecting the trends of 100 years earlier, land prices rose continuously throughout the decade, and in the competitive atmosphere of the newly deregulated banking industry, banks were queuing up to lend money to speculators and developers. The city centre and surrounds were transformed as one skyscraper after another sprang up. Even the worldwide stock market crash in 1987 didn't slow things down, but in 1990 the property market collapsed, just as it had 100 years earlier. By 1991 Australia found itself in recession once again. Unemployment hit its highest rate since the early 1930s and Victoria was the state hardest hit.

1980	1995	1998	2002
Australia's first test-tube baby born at the Royal Women's Hospital	Melbourne scientists launch a bionic ear small enough for babies	A Melbourne research team carries out mice heart transplants, expected to lead to pigs' hearts being transplanted to humans	Federation Square opens in October

Neighbourhoods

Neighbourhoods

Melbourne's metropolis radiates out from the banks of the Yarra River, about 5km inland from Port Phillip Bay. Stray slightly from the city's boundaries in any direction and you'll find yourself in one of Melbourne's colourful inner suburbs. Away from the high-rise CBD, Melbourne's neighbourhoods loosen the top button and focus on the more important business of living well. We've partitioned the city and its inner suburbs geographically, bundling them into 10 manageable parcels.

The **Central Melbourne** area is the city's heart, with major arterials conveniently ordered in a grid. A secondary network of 'Little' streets, lanes and alleys traverses the city blocks. The Yarra River has attracted a number of waterfront city precincts – seemingly self-contained microcities, such as Southgate, the casino complex and Docklands. Melbourne's two first loves, the arts and sport, have their own hubs within the city's central margins, both in the River District.

Carlton and Fitzroy, just north of town, are known for graceful Victorian-era architecture, and a vivacious café lifestyle tempered by Italian and bohemian influences. This area is bordered to the west by **Parkville and North Melbourne**, where classic Victorian streetscapes meet warehouse apartments; the University of Melbourne and Royal Melbourne Zoo are imposing landmarks here. Further north is the **Inner North** area of North Fitzroy, North Carlton and Brunswick, where frenetic multiethnic street life contrasts with sedate urban dwellings.

Abbotsford and Richmond, to the east of Central

Rialto Towers (p65)

Melbourne, include a thriving Vietnamese community and bargain retail shopping. The **South Yarra, Toorak and Prahran** area to the south is characterised by designer fashion boutiques and a thumping nightlife in and around Chapel St.

St Kilda is a spectacular and old cosmopolitan bayside suburb with terrace houses and boutiques. Its northern neighbours **South Melbourne and Albert Park** provide a sea-gazing ambience.

Williamstown, southwest of the city at the mouth of the Yarra River, has a historic maritime feel, while the **Inner West** is Melbourne's traditional working-class area, set around the city's industrial docks.

See the Greater Melbourne map (pp200–01) for a visual representation of the city and inner-suburb neighbourhood divisions. In this chapter, sights in each designated neighbourhood are listed alphabetically. Each neighbourhood section includes a boxed text of transport options, with train and tram routes and tram-route numbers shown on the relevant maps; see also the Directory chapter (p180) and the tram and train network maps (pp217–18) for more help in getting around.

ITINERARIES

One Day

Get an early-bird's eye view from the city's tallest building at the **Rialto Towers observation deck** (p65). From here you can see the central hive of the city grid, around which everything buzzes, and the river and port area to the west. Once you have your bearings, it's time to get down into it.

From the Rialto, make your way eastwards through the business-end of Collins St before weaving through Centre Way, Centre Pl and Degraves St for a taste of Melbourne's warrenlike laneways, as well as its famous coffee. You'll emerge at the graceful old edifice of **Flinders Street Station**

(p59). Walk east in its shadows until you arrive at the conspicuous hub of the city, **Federation Square** (p62). You could spend all day here, but as you have only one, best you jump on a **Melbourne River Cruise** (p53).

You'll return to **Southgate** (p61) around lunch time. There is an extraordinary range of riverfront dining options here; p104 lists a few. Back at Flinders St, flag down the **City Circle Tram** (see the boxed text, p52) to trundle about town, alighting at any points of interest you fancy.

Dine at one of the city's exceptional restaurants (p100) before seeing a theatre show or hearing a music performance (see p126). The bars are still open and you simply must experience one (p118); after all, you're only here for one day, right?

Three Days

So, you've seen the city from a building, a boat and through a tram window (see the one-day itinerary above), now it's time to really experience it. With three days you have time to participate in city life. Join the throng at **Queen Victoria Market** (p65) and buy some of the fabulous produce that Melbourne is known for. Take your goodies to the **Royal Botanic Gardens** (p60) for a picnic, or poke at a chop on a traditional Aussie barbie, located along Alexandra Ave, between the banks of the Yarra River and the Royal Botanic Gardens (Maps pp214–15 and p205).

There are sports people and arts people. If you fall into the sporty camp, spend the afternoon of day two at the city's sporting precinct **Yarra Park** (p63), perhaps watching a match or taking a tour at the **Melbourne Cricket Ground** (p63). For art lovers, instead visit the exhibits at the **National Gallery of Victoria: International** (p60) and **Australian Centre for Contemporary Art** (p58). If you're hedging, go the middle ground at the city's excellent **Melbourne Museum** (p66) and/or **Immigration Museum** (p65).

Spend day three in one of Melbourne's inner-city suburbs; try **St Kilda** (p74) – there's enough shopping, sights, dining and entertainment to sustain even the most energetic of souls for a day.

One Week

After you've worked your way through the one-day and three-day itineraries (see above), day four is the perfect time to head out of town for the night. If it's summer, go west – along the magnificent **Great Ocean Road** (p171). If you prefer the country to the coast, head to Victoria's sublime winemaking region, the **Yarra Valley** (p173).

Arriving back in Melbourne in the afternoon of day five allows just enough time to do some shopping (try along Little Collins St), or to catch up on those sights you missed in the three-day itinerary.

Days six and seven give you the opportunity to experience more of Melbourne's remarkable inner neighbourhoods. Don't miss **Carlton and Fitzroy** (p65) or **South Yarra, Toorak and Prahran** (p73).

Free for All

- Getting back to nature at one of Melbourne's parks and gardens, such as the **Royal Botanic Gardens** (p60), **St Kilda Botanical Gardens** (p76) and **Birrarung Marr** (p62).
- Trundling through town on the **City Circle tram**. The wine-coloured tram, with recorded commentary, loops along Flinders, Spring, Lonsdale and Spencer Sts before heading back to Flinders St. It runs every 10 minutes or so between 10am and 6pm (to 9pm Thursday to Saturday during summer), and you can jump on and off at any of the frequent stops.
- Musing over contemporary art works at the **Australian Centre for Contemporary Art** (ACCA; p58), Australian art at the **Ian Potter Centre: National Gallery of Victoria Australia** (NGVA; p62) and permanent collection of the **National Gallery of Victoria: International** (NGVI; p60).
- Sauntering around the **Queen Victoria Market** (p65) to see what's on offer and soak up the atmosphere.
- Book browsing at the **State Library of Victoria** (p58); it's guaranteed to provoke a thought or two...don't think out loud though, it is a library after all. Gather your thoughts under the dome of the magnificent reading room.

ORGANISED TOURS

Whether you're interested in learning more about feng shui in Chinatown, or Melbourne's history, theatre or gardens, there's a willing group to guide you through the appropriate site. The free *Me!bourne Events* guide, updated monthly, is available at the visitor information centre at Federation Square; it publishes an extensive selection of tours. Advance bookings are essential for all tours.

ABORIGINAL HERITAGE WALK
Map pp214-15
☎ 9252 2300; www.rbg.vic.gov.au; departs from visitor centre, Observatory Gate, Royal Botanic Gardens; adult/child/concession $15.50/$6.60/11; 11am Thu & Fri, 10.30am alternate Sun
Walk around the **Royal Botanic Gardens** (p60), part of the ancestral lands of the Boonwurrung and Woiworung people. Learn about song lines, bush tucker, and the traditional customs and heritage of the area's original landowners. The tour takes about 1½ hours.

CAPITAL CITY TRAIL
This 29km self-guided cycling/jogging/walking trail encircles the city, linking major parks and providing access to just about everything good in inner Melbourne. The trail starts and finishes at Southbank and follows the Yarra River to Yarra Bend Park and Merri Creek in the northeast. It passes through Royal Park and Docklands before looping back to Southbank. Pick up a brochure from the visitors centre at Federation Square and follow the identifiable plaques. See p141 for bike-hire information.

CHINATOWN HERITAGE WALK
Map pp202-04
☎ 9662 2888; http://home.vicnet.net.au; Museum of Chinese Australian History, 22 Cohen Pl; adult/concession $15/12, incl lunch $28/25; 11am Mon-Sun
After a visit to the **Museum of Chinese Australian History** (see p54) you're guided through Little Bourke St and its adjoining laneways. This is the oldest continuously Chinese quarter in Australia, dating back to 1854. The tour takes about two hours, or three hours with lunch.

CITY EXPLORER Map pp202-04
☎ 1800 858 687; Gray Line; tickets from 180 Swanston St; adult/child $33/16.50
Comfy double-decker buses circle the city constantly, allowing you to board and alight at any, or all, of the 20 stops en route. Stops include the Melbourne Museum, Rialto Towers and Royal Botanic Gardens. The bus trip includes commentary, and one stops at each sight every half-hour or so. Your day pass is valid for 24 hours, so if you start early, you might just see Melbourne in a day.

HAUNTED MELBOURNE GHOST TOUR
Map pp202-04
☎ 9670 2585; www.haunted.com.au; 15 McKillop St; adult/concession $20/18; 8pm Sat
Hear the roll call of Melbourne's restless souls when you visit the buildings and sites that they allegedly haunt. The tour runs for two hours.

MARIBYRNONG RIVER CRUISES
Map pp200-01
☎ 9689 6431; www.blackbirdcruises.com.au; Wingfield St, Footscray; adult/child from $7/4

If big industry is your thing, then cruise for an hour down the Maribyrnong River to the hulking West Gate Bridge and giant's Lego-land of the working docklands. As you pass the Coode Island petrochemical plant on your left, look for Lonely Planet's head office on your right. Cruises run on Tuesday, Thursday, Saturday, Sunday and public holidays.

MELBOURNE RIVER CRUISES
Map pp202-04
☎ 9614 1215; www.melbcruises.com.au;
adult/concession $16.50/13.20
Cruise the Yarra River upstream in this sleek boat passing the Royal Botanic Gardens, **Herring Island** (see the boxed text, p21) and the

city's sporting precinct. Or you can head down river to the port and docks. Tours depart every half-hour from Princes Walk (on the north bank of the river, east of Princes Bridge) and from Berths 5 and 6 at Southgate.

MERIDIAN TOURS
☎ 9818 0701; www.meridiantours.com.au;
city tour per person $180
These independently run city tours, that pick you up and drop you back at your city accommodation, include all the big sights and take four hours. The company, which specialises in customised tours, also operates tours further afield to the state's wine-growing areas, the Great Ocean Rd and Victoria's High Country.

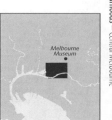

CENTRAL MELBOURNE
*Eating pp102–06; Drinking pp119–21; Shopping pp147–49;
Sleeping pp157–61*

Back in 1837, Governor Bourke insisted on messing up Robert Hoddle's neat symmetrical grid pattern for the city by adding laneways. Despite Hoddle's protests, the laneways were included to provide rear access to the main-street properties. Today, Melbourne's laneways, 'Little' streets, alleys and arcades are furtive keepers of the choicest boutiques, restaurants and bars. Turn off the well-lit pavement down the cobblestone corridor, pass the burly bouncer parked across the doorway, climb two flights of stairs and step into one of Melbourne's heaving nightspots.

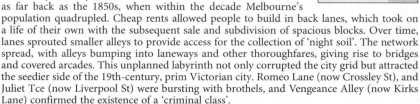

The city laneways have attracted residents and businesses from as far back as the 1850s, when within the decade Melbourne's population quadrupled. Cheap rents allowed people to build in back lanes, which took on a life of their own with the subsequent sale and subdivision of spacious blocks. Over time, lanes sprouted smaller alleys to provide access for the collection of 'night soil'. The network spread, with alleys bumping into laneways and other thoroughfares, giving rise to bridges and covered arcades. This unplanned labyrinth not only corrupted the city grid but attracted the seedier side of the 19th-century, prim Victorian city. Romeo Lane (now Crossley St), and Juliet Tce (now Liverpool St) were bursting with brothels, and Vengeance Alley (now Kirks Lane) confirmed the existence of a 'criminal class'.

Historically, certain areas attracted certain types: Flinders Lane was known for bluestone warehouses synonymous with the city's rag trade and Little Bourke St attracted the Chinese community (today's Chinatown). Areas are still known for their concentration of particular specialities: Little Collins St for superfine boutiques and Bank Pl for a conflux of cafés. Some of the city's precincts developed by chance, others by design.

Melbourne's recent developments are well-planned centres of activity. Waterfront hubs, such as Southbank and Docklands, form concentrations of residential apartments, retail shops, restaurants, cafés, promenades and public spaces. A cluster of galleries and theatres showcasing the city's arts prop together on the opposite side of the Yarra to the city's sporting arenas' hallowed turf. And the city's new public square, Federation Square, is a stylised cultural centre: the latest nucleus of recreational activity.

The flipside to the city's recreational focal points is their commercial contribution. For every cluster of visitors there's someone employed to assist them, which, added to the columns of office towers and law courts, sees tens of thousands of workers converge on the city on any given day. Add to that the thousands of transport workers, small-business employees and university students attending one of the city's institutions and you have an eclectic mix of people living, learning and labouring in a relatively small space – a space replete with carefully constructed precincts, remarkable architecture, organic laneways and resplendent gardens.

Admission to sights is free, unless stated otherwise.

Orientation

Central Melbourne continues to expand every year, stretching its geographical boundaries further in every direction. Melbourne's gridlike CBD is bordered by the Yarra River to the south, the Fitzroy Gardens to the east, Victoria St to the north and Spencer St to the west. This grid used to contain the centre of the city. New developments and enduring old-timers have loosened the boundaries a little. The city centre now generally includes the Docklands to the west, the vital area along the Yarra, and sporting precinct to the east.

We've divided Central Melbourne into three areas, moving clockwise: the East, the River Precinct (to the south), and the West. The CBD's Swanston St forms the city's East–West divide. Major attractions along the banks of the Yarra form the River Precinct.

Running through the heart of the city, Swanston St is open to vehicular traffic (other than trams) after 7pm only. A steady flow of trams plies this north–south run. So far, the street has resisted attempts to make it more upmarket – come here to buy that tram snow dome while tucking into a franchise burger.

Beside the river where Swanston St meets Flinders St is the hub of the city. It's Melbourne's main transport interchange: suburban trains depart from Flinders Street Station, and the majority of tram services pass here. It's also where you'll find Federation Square and the subterranean visitors information centre. The northern end of Swanston St is where you'll find the city's universities and student-friendly bars and cafés.

The main train station for rural and interstate services is Southern Cross Station (known as Spencer Street Station before its redevelopment) at the western end of Bourke St.

THE EAST

The East is characterised by first-class private art galleries along Flinders Lane, stupendously good bars down narrow city lanes, exclusive shopping along Collins St, top-end dining and grand hotels. It is also home to the Greek precinct, with miscellany outlets along Lonsdale St, and Chinatown. Many of the city's gorgeous gardens are also located in the East. If you're interested in seeing some of Melbourne's elegant early residential architecture and tree-lined avenues, Clarendon, Hotham and Powlett Sts are all worth a wander.

CHINATOWN Map pp202–04
Little Bourke St, btwn Spring & Swanston Sts
Red archways across either end of Little Bourke St's Chinatown are your gateways to clattering woks, glowing neons, exotic aromas and shops with floor-to-ceiling chambers of medicinal herbs and tinctures.

Melbourne's Chinatown has been thriving since the 1850s when Chinese prospectors joined the rush to find gold. The single-storey brick buildings were built in the 19th century, a time when brothels, opium dens and boarding houses were the main tenants. Today the area is chock-a-block with discount shops and authentic Chinese restaurants. It's the best place for *yum cha*, and to sate that craving for sea slug in sichuan sauce. The Eating chapter (p102) lists a few good options.

Chinatown's **Museum of Chinese Australian History** (☎ 9662 2888; 22 Cohen Pl; adult/concession $6.50/4.50; ☻ 10am-5pm) has five levels containing items of Chinese social history and significance. There's a temple in the basement, wedding gowns, artefacts from the gold-rush period and two dragons. Dai Loong dragon, whose head weighs 90kg, was retired from civic duties in 2003. The head of the Millennium Dragon, its replacement, weighs 218kg, requiring six people to hunker underneath to carry it through the streets at **Chinese New Year** (p9) and **Moomba** (p10). If you're in town during either festival and fancy being a dragon for a day, the museum is always looking for volunteers. The museum also runs the **Chinatown Heritage Walk** (p52).

Walk off your Sunday-morning *yum cha* by taking in some of the old buildings, warehouses and cobbled lanes. The building that is now **Sum Kum Lee General Store** (112-114 Little Bourke St) has been occupied by Chinese food and grocery sellers pretty much since it opened in 1888. The former **Chinese Mission Hall** (cnr Little Bourke St & Cohen Pl), built by a Chinese evangelist in 1894, is now the Po Hong Trading Company, with more Asian knick-knacks than you can poke a chopstick at.

COLLINS STREET Map pp202-04
Btwn Spring & Swanston Sts

The top end of Collins St has long been associated with that most romantic of European cities, Paris. Lined with plane trees, grand buildings and street cafés, the 'Paris end' of Collins St twinkles with grace – the trees are lit at night and exclusive boutiques, such as Hermès and Chanel, remind you that you're not mixing with the hoi polloi.

Straddling Russell St are two of Melbourne's historic churches. **Scots church** (140 Collins St) is built in the decorative Gothic style (1873); opposite is **St Michael's Uniting church** (120 Collins St), the first church in Victoria built in the Lombardic Romanesque style (1866).

The **Athenaeum Theatre** (188 Collins St), dating back to 1886, has undergone many a facelift. The Greek goddess of wisdom, Athena, sits atop the façade imbuing the theatre with temple-like qualities. During the **Comedy Festival** (p11) the venue fills with laughter and its excellent acoustics are acknowledged with many touring musicians playing here. Across the road, the opulent **Regent Theatre** (191 Collins St) was considered one of the most lavish theatres of its kind when it was built in 1929 with the advent of the talkies. Destroyed by fire and then restored in 1945, the Regent had fallen into disrepair by the 1990s. After major refurbishment it reopened in late 1996 and is now used mainly for blockbuster stage shows (p134).

For sights along the western end of Collins St, see p64.

EASTERN HILL FIRE MUSEUM Map p205
☎ 9662 2907; 48 Gisborne St; adult/child $5/2; ☼ 9am-3pm Fri, 10am-4pm Sun

Diagonally across Gisborne St from St Patrick's Cathedral is the Eastern Hill Fire Station. The old fire station building on the corner of Gisborne St & Victoria Pde, was built in 1891. Its ground floor now houses the Eastern Hill Fire Museum, which is especially great for kids, who get to clamber on a fire truck. For bigger kids there's a collection of historic fire-fighting equipment, including fire engines, helmets and uniforms, medals and photographs. Facing Albert St is the five-storey **mosaic mural** designed by Harold Freedman (1915–99), the only person to have been State Artist of Victoria, a position he held for 11 years from 1972.

FITZROY GARDENS Map p205
Btwn Wellington Pde, Clarendon, Lansdowne & Albert Sts

The city drops away suddenly just east of Spring St, giving way to Melbourne's beautiful backyard, the **Fitzroy Gardens**. The stately avenues lined with English elms, flowerbeds tucked in neatly, expansive lawns and trickling creek are a short stroll from town. At weekends, a cavalcade of wedding photographers and stretched cars deliver the princesses-for-a-day to document their white gowns and princes.

Chinatown at night (left)

The path system, which gives structure to the gardens, was first contrived as an elaborate symmetrical design that was deemed inappropriate for such a large site. It was replaced with the existing layout, which developed by happenstance with no master plan. The goal was to provide path access to the creek in the centre of the garden. The unimaginative process of working in from each corner after installing the cross-axis led to the design 'accidentally' resembling the Union Jack. There are no red, white and blue flowerbeds, so we'll have to believe the patriotic design was unplanned.

Cooks' Cottage (☎ 9419 4677; adult/concession $3.70/2.35; ☯ 9am-5pm) is actually the former Yorkshire home of the distinguished English navigator's parents. It was dismantled, shipped to Melbourne in 253 packing cases and reconstructed – stone by stone – in 1934. The cottage is furnished and decorated as it would have been around 1750, complete with handmade furniture and period fittings. There is also an exhibit on Captain James Cook's life and achievements during his great exploratory voyages of the southern hemisphere.

The **café** in the centre of the gardens has one of Melbourne's better settings. A 77-year-old hobbyist in London built the little **Tudor village** next door – Edgar Wilson's way of saying thanks for sending food to Britain during WWII. In 1932 the writer Ola Cohn carved the **Fairies' Tree** on the stump of a 300-year-old tree that had died of old age. Forty years on, the stump was treated to preserve the etched fairies, pixies, kangaroos, emus and possums. At that time a real mummified possum, about as old as the carvings, was discovered in the stump. In the northwestern corner of the gardens is the **People's Path** – a circular path paved with 10,000 individually engraved bricks.

The **Conservatory** (☯ 9am-5pm), opened in 1930, contains five different floral displays each year.

MELBOURNE CENTRAL Map pp202-04
www.melbournecentral.com.au; La Trobe St

This shopping centre complex subsumed a number of Melbourne's arcades and alleyways when it was built, as well as a lead **shot tower** dating from 1889. The old brick chimney props incongruously beneath a great glass pyramid, a staid structure in a fast-moving retail environment. In a twist of irony, the centre's redevelopment, due for completion at the end of 2004, is re-creating the alleyways and arcades it was built over. New lanes, made to look old with bluestones, create café and retail precincts. Critics believe the development continues Melbourne's trend for destroying a block with a century of character, only to replace it with a stylised copy of the original.

MELBOURNE CITY BATHS Map pp206-08
☎ 9663 5888; www.melbournecitybaths.com.au; 420 Swanston St; casual swim $4, gym $15.50; ☯ 6am-10pm Mon-Thu, 6am-8.30pm Fri, 8am-6pm Sat & Sun

Known for the swimming pool, squash courts and gymnasium, the City Baths were literally public baths when they first opened in 1860. They were intended to stop people bathing and drinking in the seriously polluted Yarra River. The baths were rebuilt on the same site in 1903 with separate entrances for men and women, as well as separate bathing areas: basement baths for the rabble and first-class baths upstairs. The squash courts and gym were added in 1983. You can still just go for a shower, too – not that you need dissuading from bathing in the Yarra.

What the…?

Why is there a giant girl peering out of a doorway at you, talking about the laneway you're standing in? She's one of Melbourne City Council's **Laneway Public Art Commissions**. The council aims to further public access to the arts by awarding a number of artists the lucrative commission each year. Artists choose from the city's many laneways where to install their contemporary, monumental piece. Preferred laneways also see a hefty amount of late-night bar traffic. You just never know when you might bump into a colossal MetCard. Laneway locations change twice annually; www .thatsmelbourne.com.au lists recent commissions.

Hosier Lane is a permanent street-gallery and the latest home of the **Citylights** project. The bluestone laneway is illuminated by 11 light boxes. Flinders Street Station is another unlikely gallery space, with **Platform** (www.platform.org .au) artists occupying the Degraves St underpass. Transport shelters, vacant shopfronts and stairwells are also subsumed by visual arts projects, often an initiative of **urbanart** (http://vicnet.net.au/~urbanart).

Melbourne's public art projects in themselves are intoxicating enough; just wait until you bump into one *after* you emerge from a city bar.

MELBOURNE TOWN HALL Map pp202-04

☎ 9658 9658; cnr Collins & Swanston Sts

The Melbourne Town Hall has been used as a civic and entertainment venue since 1870. Most famously, Queen Elizabeth II took tea there in 1954, and the Beatles waved to thousands of screaming fans from here in 1964. In 2001 the Town Hall's Grand Organ (built in 1929) was given an overhaul. You may want to take the **free tour** (11am & 1pm Mon-Fri; 1 hr) to find out exactly what having the 'biggest romantic organ in the southern hemisphere' actually means.

OLD MELBOURNE GAOL Map pp206-08

☎ 9663 7228; Russell St; adult/child $12.50/7.50; 🕑 9.30am-5pm

This sinister old prison and penal museum was built of bluestone in 1841 and used until 1929. The tiny cells display plaster casts of some of the 100 people who were hanged here. A science of the day, known as phrenology, studied the shape of the head to try to understand the criminal mind. You need only to read the museum's other displays that explain 19th-century Melbourne's dire conditions to understand that desperation may have motivated the majority of criminals.

Ned Kelly, legendary bushranger, heard the clang of the trap here in 1880. His death mask, armour and history are on display.

Night tours of the jail ham up the facts, with the ghost of a jailer talking and walking you through the space and its stories. Tours run Wednesday, Friday, Saturday and Sunday. To book, phone **Ticketek** (☎ 13 28 49; adult/child $20/13). Tours are not recommended for children under 12 years.

OLD TREASURY BUILDING Map p205

☎ 9651 2233; www.oldtreasurymuseum.org.au; Spring St; adult/concession $8.50/5; 🕑 9am-5pm Mon-Fri, 10am-4pm Sat & Sun

Built in 1862 at the height of the heady gold rush, the Old Treasury is fittingly elegant and opulent. The huge basement vaults were designed to house much of the $200 million worth of gold that came from the Victorian goldfields. Remarkably, the designer, JJ Clark, was a 19-year-old government draftsman who also designed the **City Baths** (opposite). The Old Treasury building has regularly changing exhibitions and houses the **Gold Treasury Museum**, which has three permanent exhibitions: Built on Gold, Making Melbourne and Growing Up in the Old Treasury.

Top Five Central Melbourne

- Seeing the sophisticated screen culture at the **Australian Centre for the Moving Image** (p62)
- Being brought down to size by the giant fish tanks at the **Melbourne Aquarium** (p59)
- Hearing stories from diverse cultural perspectives about settlement in Australia at the **Immigration Museum** (p65)
- Remembering that contemporary art can be accessible and inspiring at the **Australian Centre for Contemporary Art** (p58)
- Seeing the city grid, waterways and seemingly tiny buildings from the **Rialto Towers observation deck** (p65)

The adjacent **Treasury Gardens** to the south contain the **John F Kennedy Memorial**. Although Melburnians puzzle as to the significance of the late US president to their city, the setting with its attractive landscaping and water feature makes a relaxing place for a break from sightseeing.

PARLIAMENT HOUSE Map pp202-04

☎ 9651 8568; www.parliament.vic.gov.au; Spring St

Building began here in 1856 with the two main chambers – the lower house (now the Legislative Assembly) and the upper house (now the Legislative Council). The library was added in 1860 and Queen's Hall in 1879. The original plans for Parliament House included an enormous dome, which was deemed too costly. Despite being compromised, this structure is still the city's most impressive public building. Though they've never been used, gun slits are visible just below the roof, and the dungeon is now the cleaners' tearoom. Australia's first federal parliament sat here from 1901 before moving to Canberra in 1927.

You can see inside on a free half-hour tour, which takes you through both houses and the library. Tours commence at 10am, 11am, noon, 2pm, 3pm and 3.45pm each weekday when parliament is in recess. You'll need to book in advance. The tour guide points out interesting design aspects and explains the symbolism underlying much of the ornamentation. Ask about the mystery of the stolen ceremonial mace that disappeared from the lower house in 1891 – rumour has it ending up in a brothel. Another way to see the houses is to visit when parliament is sitting; phone or visit the website to find out when it's in session.

The **Parliament Gardens** to the north of Parliament House are a pleasant place to prop.

QV BUILDING Map pp202-04
www.qv.com.au; cnr Lonsdale & Russell Sts
Taking up a whole city block, this development is located on the site of the old Queen Victoria Women's Hospital. It's a medley of apartments, commercial and retail space designed by three different architects to give the impression that the block was built up over time. It's a little like a theme park of the city, with a modern architectural pastiche. The complex's retail residents comprise some of the city's finest.

ST PATRICK'S CATHEDRAL Map p205
☎ 9662 2233; www.melbourne.catholic.org.au
/cathedral; cnr Gisborne St & Cathedral Pl; 8am-6pm
One of the world's largest and finest examples of Gothic revival architecture, St Patrick's Cathedral was designed by William Wardell. Building began in 1863 and continued in stages until the spires were added in 1939. The imposing bluestone exterior and grounds are but a preview to its contents: inside are several tonnes of bells, an organ with 4500 pipes and ornate stained-glass windows.

ST PAUL'S CATHEDRAL Map pp202-04
☎ 9653 4333; www.stpaulscathedral.org.au;
cnr Flinders & Swanston Sts; Sun-Fri 8am-6pm,
Sat 8am-5pm (to 6pm in summer)
Diagonally opposite Flinders Street Station stands St Paul's Cathedral, the Anglican equivalent of St Patrick's. Built between 1880 and 1891 it is the work of distinguished ecclesiastical architect William Butterfield who designed the cathedral from England, refusing to visit Melbourne. It features ornate stained-glass windows (made between 1887 and 1890) and holds regular music programmes and services.

STATE LIBRARY OF VICTORIA
Map pp202-04
☎ 8664 7000; www.slv.vic.gov.au; 328 Swanston St;
10am-9pm Mon-Thu, 10am-6pm Fri-Sun
When the library opened in 1856, people entering were required to sign the visitors book, be over 14 years old and have clean hands. The only requirements today are that you check your bag at the door and maintain a bit of shush.

When the octagonal **La Trobe Reading Room** was completed in 1913, the reinforced-concrete dome was the largest of its kind in the world. Since 1959 the copper sheeting installed over the skylights had kept the room endearingly fusty. The sheeting was recently removed and natural light now illuminates the ornate plasterwork, oak desks and heavy chairs.

The library's collection includes hundreds-of-thousands of historical pictures, maps and manuscripts, and almost two million books, newspapers and serials. Various fascinating objects of historical interest are periodically displayed.

TASMA TERRACE Map p205
Parliament Pl, behind Parliament House
The three-storey, grey-stuccoed terraces comprising Tasma Terrace were built in 1879 and designed by Charles Webb, who also designed the famous **Windsor Hotel** (below). The restrained cast-iron decoration is one of the features of these six Victorian buildings, which are owned by, and house the office of, the **National Trust** (☎ 9656 9800; www.nattrust.com .au) – an organisation dedicated to preserving historically significant buildings across the state. The office has information on National Trust properties that are open to the public – usually stately old homestead mansions set in elegant gardens.

WINDSOR HOTEL Map pp202-04
☎ 9633 6000; www.thewindsor.com.au;
103-115 Spring St
A marvellous reminder of a more glamorous era, the Windsor is a Melbourne institution. Built in 1883 to Charles Webb's design, it was extensively restored during the 1980s and is one of Australia's grandest historic hotels. Taking tea at the Windsor (see p159) is a must for lovers of Victoriana.

RIVER DISTRICT
Melbourne's prime natural feature, the murky Yarra River, has shirked the endless jokes about its muddy character to become a grand magnet of activity. Its banks are graced with parks, promenades, bridges and some of the city's major attractions. It's a far cry from the gold-rush days when it was used for everything from a water supply to an open drain for sewage and industrial waste.

The River District is built for leisure; there's a glut of restaurants and cafés, shops and activities to suit all tastes. The city's arts and sporting precincts are clustered on opposite sides of the river.

AUSTRALIAN CENTRE FOR CONTEMPORARY ART Map pp214-15
ACCA; ☎ 9697 9999; www.accaonline.org.au;
111 Sturt St; admission free; 11am-6pm Tue-Sun

The ACCA is housed in a remarkable cathedral-like rust-coloured building, articulating the contemporary aesthetic. The interior is necessarily composed of vast spaces with the capacity to display a variety of works: from enormous installation pieces to traditional framed works. Though dedicated to showing contemporary works that generally challenge traditional artistic frameworks, ACCA isn't an alienating place: you won't be wondering if the exit sign is part of the exhibition here.

CROWN CASINO & ENTERTAINMENT COMPLEX Map pp202-04

☎ 9292 8888; www.crowncasino.com.au; Southbank
The Crown Entertainment Complex could be labelled with many an adjective, but 'subtle' most certainly wouldn't be one of them. The complex sprawls across two city blocks and includes the enormous luxury **Crown Towers Hotel** (p159) and **Crown Casino**, with over 300 tables and 2500 gaming machines open round the clock. Time is apparently irrelevant at the casino, which has no clocks and no natural light.

Thrown in for good measure are waterfalls, fireballs, a giant cinema complex, a variety of nightclubs and a 900-seat showroom. The complex also contains designer-wear and exclusive speciality shops plus a multitude of international-style bars, cafés and restaurants.

Crown is a megalopolis of fashion, food and entertainment – a highly stylised environment topped with garish glitz that's unrepresentative of any city. It answers to itself.

FLINDERS STREET STATION Map pp202-04

Cnr Flinders & Swanston Sts
Melbourne's first rail station, Flinders Street was built in 1854. Two railway workers won the design tender. This might explain why the station contained such fabulous facilities open to railway workers, now, sadly, in disrepair. In its heyday the building buzzed with a concert hall, a library, a crèche, meeting rooms, even a ballroom. Some meeting rooms were used by community groups, including the Chihuahua Club, Collingwood Cheer Squad and the Women's Action Committee. The ballroom held regular dances, including 'Saturday Dances for Lonely People'.

The station is a city landmark; beneath the clocks is a favoured meeting point. In 1999, the station and rail network was privatised, leaving little chance for the public to see beyond the station's current functional face.

Opposite the station is the city's oldest pub **Young & Jackson's**. Upstairs is the nude portrait *Chloe* painted by Jules Lefebre, which caused an outcry in the purse-lipped Melbourne of 1883. Public opposition saw the painting taken down from the National Gallery of Victoria and subsequently bought by the hotel in 1908.

GOVERNOR LA TROBE'S COTTAGE & GOVERNMENT HOUSE Map pp214-15

Kings Domain
East of the **Shrine of Remembrance** (p60), near the intersection of Birdwood Ave and Dallas Brooks Dr, is **Governor La Trobe's Cottage** (☎ 9654 4711; admission $2; ☼ 11am-4pm Mon, Wed, Sat & Sun), which is the original government house building that was sent out in prefabricated form from the mother country in 1840. Inside, you can see many of the original furnishings

The cottage provides a dramatic contrast to today's far more imposing **Government House** (☎ 9654 4711; Government House Dr; adult/child $11/5.50; guided tours Mon, Wed & Sat), where Victoria's current governor resides. It's a copy of Queen Victoria's palace on England's Isle of Wight, and was built (with no expense spared) in 1872. It's one of the most lavish and impressive examples of Italianate style in the country, and you'll need to book well in advance to take the National Trust tour. There are no tours from mid-December to the end of January.

MELBOURNE AQUARIUM Map pp202-04

☎ 9620 0999; www.melbourneaquarium.com.au; cnr Queenswharf Rd & King St; adult/child/concession $22/12/14; ☼ 9.30am-9pm Jan, 9.30am-6pm Feb-Dec
This is the best way to see sharks, with a thick glass barrier between you and them. The sub-level tunnel allows you to be surrounded by giant rays and hulking sharks, while staying pleasantly safe and dry. You can also scuba dive in the 2.2 million litre oceanarium, so occasionally you'll see a troupe of brave souls walking on the simulated ocean floor. The ground floor has the Jellies and Coral Atoll displays, while the first level has a Billabong display that rains intermittently. One of the city's most popular tourist attractions, the Melbourne Aquarium is especially good for kids.

MELBOURNE EXHIBITION CENTRE Map pp202-04

☎ 9205 6401; www.mecc.com.au; 2 Clarendon St
The Melbourne Exhibition Centre is a sleek complex designed by Denton Corker Marshall.

The trademark sharp angles, straight lines and thrusting blades are indicative of the team's architectural vision for a brave new Melbourne. The façade's highlight is the giant lettering perched on a sloping canopy against the sky. The building hosts a variety of trade exhibitions, from the Australian International Beer Awards to the Pet Expo and Mind, Body, Spirit Festival; check the website for a calendar of events.

NATIONAL GALLERY OF VICTORIA: INTERNATIONAL Map pp202-04

NGVI; ☎ 8620 2222; www.ngv.vic.gov.au; 180 St Kilda Rd; admission free; ⊗ 10am-5pm

The NGVI reopened in 2003 after extensive renovations. The original building designed by Roy Grounds was constructed from bluestone and concrete with a robust simplicity. Grounds' basic design remains. The framework of enormous walls, rough concrete columns, skylights and courtyards now contain the new gallery space.

The gallery space was designed with close consideration for the art works, regarded as Australia's best international collection. Key works, such as Rembrandt's self-portrait, feature in the open spaces, promoting a sense of discovery.

NGVI has an excellent programme of temporary exhibits, which usually attract an admission fee. There are a café, restaurant, shop and sculpture garden within the gallery behind the famous water wall.

The Australian art collection is on display at the Ian Potter Centre: NGV Australia (p62) at nearby Federation Square.

POLLY WOODSIDE MARITIME MUSEUM Map pp202-04

☎ 9699 9760; www.nattrust.com.au; Lorimer St East; adult/child/concession $10/6/8; ⊗ 10am-4pm

The Polly Woodside Maritime Museum is on the riverfront, adjacent to the Melbourne Exhibition Centre. The *Polly Woodside* is the centrepiece, perched gracefully in a dry dock. The iron-hulled, three-masted tall ship, was built in Belfast in 1885, and spent the first part of her working life carrying coal and nitrate between Europe and South America. She made the rounding of Cape Horn 16 times before ending her career as a coal hulk. Bought by the National Trust in the 1970s, she has been lovingly restored by volunteers.

Historically listed **cargo sheds** house the museum, which provides evidence of the port's importance to immigration and trade.

ROYAL BOTANIC GARDENS Map pp214-15

☎ 9252 2300; www.rbg.vic.gov.au; admission free; ⊗ 7.30am-8.30pm Nov-Mar, 7.30am-5.30pm Apr-Oct

Certainly the finest botanic gardens in Australia, and among the finest in the world, this is one of Melbourne's most glorious attractions. Sprawling beside the Yarra River, the beautifully designed gardens feature plants from Australia and around the world. Mini-ecosystems, such as the cacti and succulents area, herb garden and Australian rainforest are set amid the vast lawns. Take a book, a picnic or Frisbee; most importantly, take your time.

Along with the abundance of plant species there's a surprising amount of **wildlife**, including water fowl, ducks, swans and eels in and around the ornamental lake, and cockatoos and possums. Until recently, a large colony of flying foxes resided in the trees of the fern gully. The population escalated at an alarming rate, causing concerns for the health of the trees in which they roosted. An attempt to cull the animals met with vociferous opposition – from the public as well as the flying foxes. As a result, park staff unceremoniously banged rubbish-bin lids morning and night to prevent the animals from landing. This not-in-our-backyard approach has resulted in the colony moving to the Melbourne suburb of Ivanhoe.

The gardens are encircled by the **Tan**, a 4km-long former horse-exercising track, and now Melbourne's favourite venue for joggers. During the summer months, the gardens play host to the **Moonlight Cinema** and **theatre performances** (see the EG section of the *Age* newspaper for details).

You can pick up guide-yourself leaflets at the park entrances; these leaflets change with the seasons and tell you what to look out for at the different times of year.

The **visitors centre** (☎ 9252 2429; ⊗ 9am-5pm Mon-Fri, 9.30am-5.30pm Sat & Sun) is at the former centre for stargazers, Observatory Gate in Birdwood Ave. A guided tour of the gardens departs from the centre at 11am and 2pm daily except Saturday (adult/concession $4.50/3.50); bookings are required. Next door is the **National Herbarium**, established in 1853, which contains 1.2 million dried botanical specimens used for identification purposes.

SHRINE OF REMEMBRANCE Map pp214-15

☎ 9654 8415; ⊗ 10am-5pm

Beside St Kilda Rd stands the massive Shrine of Remembrance, built as a memorial to Victorians killed in WWI. Its distinctive design is partly based on the Temple of Halicarnassus,

Neighbourhoods – Central Melbourne

one of the seven ancient wonders of the world, and it was built between 1927 and 1934. On Anzac Day (25 April) the dawn service is attended by thousands. The Remembrance Day service at the 11th hour of the 11th day of the 11th month commemorates the time at which the Armistice of 1918 was declared. At this precise moment a shaft of light shines through an opening in the ceiling to illuminate the Stone of Remembrance. The forecourt, with its cenotaph and eternal flame, was built as a memorial to those who died in WWII, and there are several other war memorials that surround the shrine. It's worth climbing to the top as there are fine views from the balcony to the city, north along St Kilda Rd, and southwest towards the bay.

SOUTHGATE Map pp202-04
Southbank

This complex was one of the first major developments along the Southbank area, replacing billowing chimney stacks and saw-toothed factories with chichi shops and cafés. An arched footbridge crosses the Yarra River from the rear of Flinders Street Station, linking the central city to the arts precinct and to the Southgate complex itself. Promenades flank the river on both sides running all the way west to the **casino complex** (p59).

The Southgate complex houses three levels of restaurants, cafés and bars, all of which enjoy a stellar outlook over the river and city

(see p104 in the Eating chapter for some of these). There's an international food hall on the ground floor, as well as big-name boutiques, and a collection of specially commissioned sculptures and other art works.

You can take a boat cruise with **Penguin Waters Cruises** (☎ 9645 0533; adult/child $55/30; sunset) from Berth 1 to see a penguin colony. The two-hour cruise includes an on-board barbecue.

VICTORIAN ARTS CENTRE Map pp202-04
☎ 9281 8000; www.vicartscentre.com.au;
100 St Kilda Rd

The Victorian Arts Centre is easy to spot – its distinctive spire demands attention. The centre is made up of two separate buildings: the concert hall and the theatres building, linked by a series of landscaped walkways.

The Melbourne Concert Hall, renamed **Hamer Hall** in 2004 in honour of former state premier Sir Rupert Hamer, is the circular building closest to the Yarra. It's a favoured performance venue for symphonic concerts, choirs and chamber music. Most of the hall is below ground, resting in Yarra mud so corrosive that a system of electrified cables is needed to prevent its deterioration. The **Theatres Building** wears the distinctive spire, and houses the State Theatre, the Playhouse and the George Fairfax Studio. Both buildings feature works of prominent Australian artists, and in the Theatres Building

Soaking up the sunshine, Southgate (above)

the **George Adams Gallery** and **St Kilda Road Foyer Gallery** are free gallery spaces with changing exhibitions of contemporary works.

There are one-hour tours of the complex ($10) at noon and 2.30pm from Monday to Saturday. On Sunday you can visit backstage at 12.15pm ($13.50; 1½ hours). Children under 12 years are not allowed in the backstage area.

The Arts Centre undercroft shelters an **arts and crafts market** every Sunday from 10am to 5pm. Around 150 stalls peddle everything from kaleidoscopes to soaps.

The small section of park across St Kilda Rd from the Victorian Arts Centre is the **Queen Victoria Gardens**, containing a memorial statue of the good queen herself, a statue of Edward VII astride his horse, and a huge floral clock, as well as several sculptures.

Federation Square

The striking **Federation Square** (Map pp202-04; www.federationsquare.com.au) is Melbourne's public hub, imbued with a healthy cultural heart. The undulating 'square' is far from square, darting off in all directions like its fractured façade. One of the city's boldest architectural statements, Fed Square's confronting aesthetics and prominent position demanded public attention when it opened in late 2002, dividing the population into love-it and hate-it camps. The city quickly embraced Fed Square as a public space, however, gathering in the forecourt en masse for diverse events, including the huge dance-off that saw thousands taking part in the Melbourne International Festival's tap- and disco-dancing classes, peace rallies and sports broadcasts.

The public has also flocked here to be a part of the innovative celebration of screen culture at the Australian Centre for the Moving Image, and to view the NGV's Australian collection of art works. Equine buffs can visit

the **Australian Racing Museum** (☎ 1300 139 407; www.racingmuseum.com.au; admission free; tours adult/child $6/2; ☺ 10am-6pm).

A dozen or so cafés and restaurants here make for a vibrant social scene day and night. At the square's edge is the subterranean **Melbourne Visitor Information Centre** (☺ 9am-6pm), which should be a stop on any visitor's itinerary.

AUSTRALIAN CENTRE FOR THE MOVING IMAGE Map pp202-04
ACMI; ☎ 9663 2583; www.acmi.net.au;
☺ 10am-6pm

This ambitious centre is dedicated to the display, interpretation and analysis of the dominant language of the day: the moving image, in all its forms. The three-storey complex houses a screen gallery and two hi-tech cinemas. It programmes regular workshops and forums to promote education and production, and hosts film screenings and festivals. **Popcorn Taxi** (www.popcorntaxi.com.au) is a regular film event providing a forum for enthusiasts to watch films of all types and discuss the film-making process. ACMI's collection includes a comprehensive lending library with a spectacularly diverse range of films available for members.

Innovative ACMI is Melbourne's first centre devoted entirely to screen-based works. With no previous reference point and low-key marketing, the centre is slowly inching its way into the public's cultural psyche.

BIRRARUNG MARR Map pp202-04
Btwn Federation Sq & the Yarra River

Featuring grassy knolls, river promenades and indigenous plants, Birrarung Marr is a welcome recent addition to the patchwork of parks and gardens around the city. The modern sculptural **Federation Bells** that perch on the park's upper level ring out daily (8-9am, 12.30-1.30pm & 5-6pm) with specially commissioned compositions. An old railway building in the park now hosts creative workshops for five- to 12-year-olds: **ArtPlay** (☎ 9664 7900; www.artplay.com.au) runs on weekends and during school holidays. Visiting children are welcome; it's best to book to find out the times and activities on offer.

IAN POTTER CENTRE: NATIONAL GALLERY OF VICTORIA AUSTRALIA
Map pp202-04
NGVA; ☎ 8662 1553; www.ngv.vic.gov.au/ngvaustralia;
☺ 10am-5pm Mon-Thu, 10am-9pm Fri, 10am- 6pm Sat & Sun

Spongy Sidewalks

While pounding the pavement in Melbourne's CBD you may get that sinking feeling – literally – where you step on suddenly spongy ground. It looks like asphalt, but has a rubbery texture. These spongy panels laid into Melbourne's pavements are harmless to walkers, and dire for skateboarders. Designed as speed bumps for skaters, they're camouflaged to curb freewheeling momentum.

The companion gallery to **NGVI** (p60) on St Kilda Rd, the Ian Potter Centre houses more than 20,000 Australian works, including sculpture, photography and fashion.

The popular Aboriginal and Torres Strait Islander collection has its own dedicated space on the ground floor. On permanent display on the first level are works by Sir Sidney Nolan, Arthur Boyd and Albert Tucker, Australian impressionists including the Heidelberg School's Tom Roberts and Arthur Streeton, and more recent contributions from Brett Whiteley, Jenny Watson, Howard Arkley and Mike Brown.

The top floor is mainly used for temporary exhibitions.

Yarra Park

Sports fans will become pretty cosy with Yarra Park – the large expanse of parkland southeast of the city centre. This is Melbourne's sporting and entertainment precinct, attracting tens-of-thousands of adoring fans to one of its numerous world-class arenas and ovals. A footbridge over the railway line links the granddaddy of 'em all, the Melbourne Cricket Ground (MCG), with Melbourne and Olympic Parks.

This area is swarming with locals at weekends watching everything from Australian Rules football, cricket, greyhound racing, athletics, cycling to marathon dance championships. Various arenas also host weekend-long dance parties and big-name international concerts, such as James Brown and Radiohead. There's even the occasional get-rich-quick, be-the-best-you-can-be style motivational event.

MELBOURNE & OLYMPIC PARKS
Map p205

☎ 9286 1244; www.mopt.com.au; Batman Ave
These two parks have recently joined forces to become a veritable mecca for millions of sports fans. Melbourne Park comprises **Rod Laver Arena**, home to the Australian Open in January, and **Vodafone Arena**, the multipurpose venue with a retractable roof.

Olympic Park includes **Olympic Stadium** and the **Glasshouse**, home to the Collingwood Football Club and Victorian Institute of Sport.

MELBOURNE CRICKET GROUND
Map p205

MCG; ☎ 9657 8888; www.mcg.org.au; Brunton Ave
The MCG commands the sort of reverence usually reserved for holy places. MCG members are

a chosen few and worshippers in their tens of thousands come regularly, filled with hope. It's one of the world's great sporting venues, with an indefinable atmosphere comprising both tradition and the thrill of current combat.

In 1858 the first game of Aussie Rules football was played where the MCG and its car parks now stand, and in 1877 it was the venue for the first Test cricket match between Australia and England. The MCG was also the central stadium for the 1956 Melbourne Olympics, and will be centre stage for the opening and closing ceremonies of the Commonwealth Games in 2006. During 2004 extensive renovations were underway, with the mammoth construction of a new members' stand. So sacred is the members' sanctum that when the old rooms were demolished the Melbourne Cricket Club (MCC), which manages the ground, auctioned the old carpet. Incidentally, to become a member, you'll need to seek out two members to propose and second your nomination; oh, and wait approximately 20 years for the 180,000 others before you on the waiting list to be offered their places.

You don't have to be handy with the bat and ball to get the chance to stand on the hallowed turf at the 'G. **Tours** (☎ 9657 8879; adult/concession $10/6) take you through the stands and onto the ground. They run every half-hour (on nonmatch days) from 10am till 3pm and take 1¼ hours.

See p138 for details on attending an Australian Football League (AFL) footy match.

THE WEST

The West is the business end of the city. Along William St is Melbourne's legal precinct, with its imposing courts, legal eagles in horsehair wigs and billowing gowns, and the odd camera crew looking for a court-room scandal or shamed 'villain'.

The recent Docklands development has expanded the reasons for visiting the West, be it for business or pleasure.

BOURKE STREET Map pp202-04
Btwn Swanston & Spencer Sts

West of Swanston St marks the beginning of the **Bourke St Mall**. The Mall is thick with the sounds of trams clanging, Peruvian bands busking, spruikers, and general hubbub from shoppers. The expansive entrances of the city's two main department stores, Myer and David Jones, consume waves of eager shoppers, re-gurgitating them some time later with signature shopping bags.

In 2001, many Melburnians went without mail when their letters fuelled the fire that gutted the **GPO** (cnr Bourke & Elizabeth Sts). The premier corner site is being redeveloped and is due to open in 2004, with the usual array of cafés and retail outlets. On the other side of the mall, the **Royal Arcade** (www.royalarcade .com.au) built between 1869 and 1870 is Melbourne's oldest shopping mall; the upper walls retain much of the original 19th-century detail. Follow the black-and-white chequered path past souvenir, travel, food and jewellery shops to the mythological figures of giant brothers **Gog and Magog** perched (with hammers) atop the arched exit to Little Collins St. They've been striking the hour here since 1892.

If you need any outdoor or travel-related gear, head to **Little Bourke St**, west of Elizabeth St where you'll find a cluster of stores supplying all things polyfleece.

The extreme western end of Bourke St is home to some stately historical buildings, big-business office towers, power lunches and newspaper stands.

COLLINS STREET Map pp202-04
West of Swanston St

A number of Melbourne's arcades lead off from Collins St. The Block network, comprising Block Pl, Block Arcade and Block Ct, was so-named from the 19th-century pastime of 'doing the block'. Back then it referred to walking the city's fashionable area. Today, 'doing your block' means to lose your temper; obviously doing your block just isn't what it used to be.

Block Arcade, which runs between Collins and Elizabeth Sts, was built in 1891 and features etched-glass ceilings and mosaic floors. It houses some appropriately sedate retail outlets. Nestled between Block Arcade and Little

Collins St, **Block Pl** keeps hip city kids fuelled with coffee and café food, and adorns them in the latest fashion.

It's down to business along the west end of Collins St. The city's financial sector begins across Elizabeth St, but the area also has some of Melbourne's best-preserved old buildings. Bankers and stockbrokers call this area home, and it's where you'll find the **Melbourne Stock Exchange** (530 Collins St).

For sights along the eastern end of Collins St, see p55.

DOCKLANDS Map pp202-04
☎ 1300 663 008; www.docklands.vic.gov.au

Docklands' synthesised environment comprises residential apartment towers, shopping complexes, a number of dining options and public spaces. It's the latest of Melbourne's simulacrum cities within the city, designed with precincts for certain types of activity. NewQuay is the drinking and dining precinct, and Telstra Dome the venue for sports.

The 52,000-seat **Telstra Dome** (☎ 8625 7700; www.telstradome.com.au) has state-of-the-art facilities, including a sliding roof (perfect for Melbourne's changeable weather). Many AFL games take place here, as do other sporting and entertainment events. **Behind-the-scenes tours** (☎ 8625 7277; adult/child $13/5) of the venue are available.

Docklands also features new roads and Webb Bridge – symbolic of a Koorie eel trap – and substantial tracts of public space with specially commissioned art works.

The stunning waterfront location was the city's main industrial and docking area until the mid-1960s. Demand for larger berths to accommodate modern cargo vessels necessitated a move, leaving the former docklands high and (almost) dry. Several boat tours ply the area's 'Blue Park'; check the website for a full listing.

FLAGSTAFF GARDENS Map pp202-04
Btwn La Trobe, William, Dudley & King Sts

First known as Burial Hill, this is where most of the city's early settlers ended up. The hill provided one of the best views of the bay, so a signalling station was set up here; when a ship was sighted arriving from Britain, a flag was raised on the flagstaff to notify the settlers. Later, a cannon was fired when the more important ships arrived, replacing the flag raising, but the name remained.

These bustling gardens are popular with workers taking a lunch-time break to soak up some Vitamin D. The park has a children's playground, barbecues and a lawn-bowling green.

IMMIGRATION MUSEUM Map pp202-04

☎ 9927 2700; www.immigration.museum.vic.gov.au; 400 Flinders St; adult/concession $6/free; ☾ 10am-5pm

The fabulous Immigration Museum offers a moving account of immigration that uses multi-media to convey stories, both historical and modern. Housed in the Old Customs House (1858–70), the restored building alone is worth the visit; its most important space, the Long Room, is a magnificent piece of Renaissance revival architecture. The 2nd-floor galleries host a range of excellent temporary exhibitions exploring social and cultural issues, such as the various multiethnic rituals surrounding death.

QUEEN VICTORIA MARKET Map p209

☎ 9320 5822; www.qvm.com.au; 513 Elizabeth St; ☾ 6am-2pm Tue & Thu, 6am-6pm Fri, 6am-3pm Sat, 9am-4pm Sun

The Queen Victoria Market is a thriving community of over 600 traders, all bellowing special prices from behind colourful produce stalls. It's the largest open-air market in the southern hemisphere and attracts thousands of shoppers. You can buy everything the most fickle palate could desire here.

On Sunday, the produce stalls are replaced with clothing and knick-knack stalls. This is definitely the place to find those souvenir sheepskin moccasins.

The market has been on the site for more than 130 years, prior to which it was a **burial ground** (see p92).

The market is open at night in summer, on Wednesdays from 5.30pm to 10pm, when it features hawker-style food stalls. It also runs a variety of tours and cooking classes. Phone for details or visit the website.

RIALTO TOWERS OBSERVATION DECK Map pp202-04

☎ 9629 8222; www.melbournedeck.com.au; 525 Collins St; adult/concession $11.80/9; ☾ 10am-10pm

The Rialto is Melbourne's tallest structure and was once the highest building in the southern hemisphere. Its most distinctive feature is its semireflective glass exterior, which changes colour as the day advances. The observation deck is on the 55th floor; to get there you could climb the 1254 steps or decide to take the 25km/h lifts. The lookout platform provides a spectacular 360-degree view of Melbourne's surrounds – it's a great way to get your bearings. The admission fee includes a 20-minute video screening about Melbourne city.

WESTSPACE Map pp202-04

☎ 9328 8712; www.westspace.org.au; 15-19 Anthony St; admission free; ☾ noon-6pm Wed-Fri, noon-5pm Sat

One of Melbourne's oldest artist-run galleries, Westspace has a varied exhibition programme, featuring young and emerging artists working in a range of mediums from traditional forms to newer digital technologies. On the 1st floor of a 1940s light industrial building, this independent space also provides a support community to assist artists in developing their work.

CARLTON & FITZROY

Eating pp106–08; Drinking pp121–22; Shopping pp149–51; Sleeping pp161–63

These two areas have a long association with the bohemian set, sating the population's need for alternatives to the mainstream. A stop in this exceptional neighbourhood is a must for anyone interested in the city's cultural machinations.

There are two major influences in **Carlton**: the Italian community and the universities (both the University of Melbourne and RMIT University). The heady mix of intellectual activity, espresso and phenomenal food lured many to the area from the sober Anglo-Saxon city during the 1950s. European migration marked Melbourne's postwar years, with many Italians settling in and around Carlton. These days, unpretentious restaurants, and *scopa* (a card game) shops harbouring card-playing Italian men, are harder to find among the touting tourist trattorias that moved in over the past decade or so. It's far from ruined, though. You can still tuck into a plate of pasta, while Italian conversations fly over the head of the girl at the neighbouring table reading Proust.

Carlton's Lygon St has an official festival celebrating its Italian heritage (see the boxed text, p10). Unofficial celebrations effervesce along here every time Italy plays in the World Cup or Ferrari wins the Grand Prix.

In **Fitzroy** there's a lifetime of outings condensed into one suburb, with an unusually high concentration of galleries, cafés, restaurants, bars, speciality stores and pubs (the highest per capita in the state). Just one block

Transport

Tram From Swanston St, tram No 1 runs to Lygon St, Carlton. Nicholson St which links Carlton and Fitzroy, is serviced by No 96 from Bourke St. From Collins St, No 112 runs along Brunswick St, Fitzroy. From Bourke St, No 86 runs along Gertrude and Smith Sts, Fitzroy.

of the main drag, Brunswick St, contains a pub, five cafés, a perfumery, bookshop, hairdresser, bar and a clothing boutique with a busker camped out the front. The suburb's characteristic community spaces are its cafés and its gorgeous outdoor swimming pool (p143).

During the '50s, about the same time that Europeans migrated to Melbourne's inner suburbs, the government focused on providing rent-assisted housing in Fitzroy for the poor and dispossessed. The foundation for a heterogeneous community was laid. Students and artists added another layer when they moved here, attracted by the cheaper rents and varied lifestyle opportunities. Cashed-up young couples followed; they knocked down the Blu Tack–stained walls of Victorian terraces, peeled back the carpets and polished the floorboards. Then came the developers, ripping out industrial machinery from old factories and warehouses, and replacing them with upmarket appliances and flat-screen TVs.

Fitzroy contains pockets of Melbourne's highest and lowest income earners, as well as ethnic communities from around the globe. This people-mix interacts remarkably well. There's a genuine community in Fitzroy, where coffee is the social lubricant and paradoxes abound, the most pronounced of which is that the convention is unconventional.

Orientation

Lygon St is the backbone of Carlton, running all the way through to the Inner North. Rathdowne St (see p70) also runs to the Inner North and has developed its own hub of cafés and shops. Nicholson St forms Carlton's eastern border with Fitzroy.

Fitzroy's hub is busy, social Brunswick St. Gertrude St intersects the southern end of Brunswick St and has quietly accumulated the best of Fitzroy. Smith St to the east is refreshingly matter-of-fact. The western side of Smith St is Fitzroy, the eastern side is Collingwood. Johnston St to the north, between Brunswick and Nicholson Sts, is influenced by the city's Hispanic community. There's dancing, song, sangria and tapas most nights, and a festival each November (see the boxed text, p10).

CENTRE FOR CONTEMPORARY PHOTOGRAPHY Map pp206-08

CCP; ☎ 9417 1549; www.ccp.org.au; 404 George St, Fitzroy; admission by donation; ✆ 11am-5pm Wed-Sat

Experimental photo-based arts are on show here, with exhibitions changing regularly. The centre's open-entry Nikon Summer Salon attracts hundreds of local submissions and thousands of gallery patrons annually. Its biannual Leica/CCP Documentary Exhibition & Award has the best in the field vying for the lucrative prize. The not-for-profit centre also runs a lecture series and workshops in photomedia.

GERTRUDE CONTEMPORARY ART SPACES Map pp206-08

☎ 9419 3406; www.gertrude.org.au; 200 Gertrude St, Fitzroy; ✆ 11am-5.30pm Tue-Fri, 1-5.30pm Sat

Founded in 1983 as a nonprofit contemporary art complex, Gertrude Contemporary comprises

three gallery spaces and 16 studios. Through its cultural exchange and professional development initiatives it promotes emerging contemporary artists, while fostering critical debate in the community. You're guaranteed to see some quality local and international work as this is one of the city's most exciting gallery spaces.

MELBOURNE MUSEUM Map pp206-08

☎ 13 11 02; Carlton Gardens; www.melbourne. museum.vic.gov.au; adult/concession $6/free; ✆ 10am-5pm

Let go of the idea that museums are fusty old spaces with a few typed cards placed in front of fossils. The Melbourne Museum has reinvented this institution; its displays are interactive and entertaining, and all under one spiffy architecturally angled roof.

In the Australia Gallery visitors can walk through a 19th-century Melbourne street, step into a 1960's school quadrangle, duck onto a set from *Neighbours* and pay homage to the legendary racehorse Phar Lap. You can also find out what weird and wonderful things locals collect in the Community Collections display, including bow ties, Easter-egg wrappers and sneakers. The stunning Bunjilaka Gallery is the museum's Aboriginal centre, dedicated to the art, history and culture of indigenous Australians. There's also the Living Forest Gallery (a giant forest atrium), plus the Mind and Body, Science and Life, and Children's galleries. Despite its location outside central Melbourne, the museum is an unquestionably worthy detour.

The **IMAX cinemas** (p133) share the museum-complex premises.

ROYAL EXHIBITION BUILDING
Map pp206–08
☎ **9270 5000; www.museum.vic.gov.au/reb; Nicholson St, Carlton**
The stately Royal Exhibition Building, next door to the Melbourne Museum, was built for the International Exhibition of 1880. The exhibition ran for eight months and included such industrial advancements as lawn mowers and tinned foodstuffs. Still a venue for major events and exhibitions, this is the world's oldest surviving 19th-century exhibition hall. It was the site of the first Australian Parliament in 1901 and was used for the Victorian

Top Five Carlton & Fitzroy
- Topping up your energy level with a midmorning coffee and/or ice cream at **Brunetti** (p107)
- Catching a flick at **Cinema Nova** (p133)
- Browsing for the latest books and music at **Readings** (p151)
- Dining at **Mrs Jones** (p107)
- Settling in for a performance at **La Mama** (p134).

Parliament for 27 years. Beautifully restored, the building became Australia's first to win Unesco World Heritage status – in 2004. **Tours** (☎ 1300 130 152; adult/concession $4/2) operate daily at 2pm from the museum, phone for bookings.

UNIVERSITY OF MELBOURNE
Map pp206–08
☎ **8344 4000; www.unimelb.edu.au; Grattan St, Parkville**
The esteemed University of Melbourne was established in 1853. Its blend of Victorian Gothic stone buildings, functionalist brick blocks and modern showpieces sprawls from Carlton through to the neighbouring suburb of Parkville. The University is conspicuous, in its size, but also in its contributions to the community. It's behind the academic publishing house, Melbourne University Publishing Ltd

Melbourne Museum (left) frames the Royal Exhibition Building (above)

Neighbourhoods – Carlton & Fitzroy

(formerly Melbourne University Press), the literary journal *Meanjin,* and counts the Melbourne Theatre Company as one of its departments. The University houses the **Ian Potter Museum of Art** (☎ 8344 5148; www.art-museum .unimelb.edu.au; admission free), displaying the state's second-largest art collection; and the **Grainger Museum** (Map p209; ☎ 8344 5270; admission free) dedicated to the extraordinary life of Percy Grainger (1882–1961), the internationally renowned composer and pianist. Both museums are due to reopen in early 2005.

PARKVILLE & NORTH MELBOURNE

Eating pp108; Sleeping pp163

Parkville has one of the city's more unusual resident mixes: exotic animals, world-class athletes and respected students. Melbourne's largest parkland, Royal Park, houses its furry and feathered residents in Melbourne Zoo. These critters are set to be neighboured by around 6000 athletes and officials, with the establishment of the Commonwealth Games Athletes Village also in Royal Park. Also in Parkville are several buildings belonging to the University of Melbourne that sprawl over from neighbouring Carlton.

The workers' cottages and industrial warehouses of **North Melbourne** were some of the first to be transformed by inner-city gentrification. The demand for converted warehouse apartments and homes to renovate pushed property prices up and the postwar migrants who lived here out. This semi-industrial suburb near Queen Victoria Market (p65) was first populated during the gold rush of the 1850s. It was traditionally a workingmen's suburb, with the population employed in local industries. The male population formed the North Melbourne football club, one of the foundation members of the Victorian Football League (now the Australian Football League) in 1877. North Melbourne was characterised by high-density housing; the government's 'slum reclamation' project recorded some dwellings as receiving only 10 minutes of sunlight per day. By the 1960s government-assisted housing estates were established. Today, North Melbourne has a laid-back local scene lining its wide streets at the nexus of Central Melbourne and the city's west.

Orientation

Royal Pde divides Parkville from Carlton to the east. It's a broad tree-lined street, with parkland on either side. Park St forms Parkville's northern boundary with Brunswick; the major arterial, Flemington Rd, forms the boundary to the south. Elliot Ave and MacArthur Rd, bisecting the suburb, are your main access points to Melbourne Zoo.

North Melbourne is often associated

Transport

Train Upfield-line train to Royal Park Station.
Tram From Elizabeth St, tram No 19 runs along Royal Pde through Parkville. Nos 55 & 68 run from William St through North Melbourne to Parkville.

with West Melbourne (which contains the North Melbourne rail yards); Victoria St forms the boundary between the two. Errol St is North Melbourne's main shopping street; it is dominated by the town hall (built 1883), a regular venue for performing arts. Despite the area's early gentrification, Errol St is refreshingly down-to-earth and contains a number of pubs and restaurants frequented by locals and a post-theatre crowd.

ROYAL MELBOURNE ZOO Map p209

☎ 9285 9300; www.zoo.org.au; Elliott Ave; adult/child/concession $18/9/13.50; ⏱ 9am-5pm

Melbourne's zoo is one of the city's most popular attractions, and deservedly so. Established in 1861, this is the oldest zoo in Australia and the third oldest in the world. In the 1850s, when Australia was considered a foreign place full of strange plants and animals, the Acclimatisation Society was formed for 'the introduction, acclimatisation and domestication of all innoxious animals, birds, fishes, insects and vegetables'. The society merged with the Zoological Society in 1861 and together they established the zoo on its present site.

Set in spacious, attractively landscaped gardens with broad strolling paths, the zoo's enclosures aim to simulate the animals' natural habitats. Walkways pass through the enclosures; you stroll through the bird aviary, cross a bridge over the lions' park, enter a tropical hothouse full of colourful butterflies and walk around the gorillas' very own rainforest. There's also a large collection of native animals in natural bush settings, a platypus aquarium, fur seals, lions and tigers, plenty of reptiles, and a spiffy new elephant enclosure. Allow at least half a day for your visit. There's also a good selection of not-too-tacky souvenirs, as well as several snack bars and a licensed bistro.

In summer, the zoo hosts a **twilight music programme**, with performances ranging from jazz to Abba covers. The zoo also participates in the Food & Wine Festival in its Feasts with the Beasts programme. Roar 'n' Snore allows you to camp at the zoo and join the keepers on their morning rounds of the animal enclosures.

ROYAL PARK Map p209
Btwn Royal Pde & Flemington Rd
Royal Park's vast open spaces are great for a variety of activities. You'll find you quicken your jogging pace when you hear lions roaring behind you. Royal Park contains the Royal Melbourne Zoo, a number of sports ovals, netball and hockey stadiums, a public golf course and the Games Village (to be completed by 2006). The village will house athletes and officials participating in the 2006 Commonwealth Games in a mixture of permanent and temporary accommodation. In the corner closest to the University of Melbourne is a garden of Australian native plants.

INNER NORTH

Eating p108

The Inner North includes the gracious residential areas of North Fitzroy and North Carlton, as well as frenetic Brunswick – characterised by the insanely busy commercial strip of Sydney Rd.

Alexandra Pde separates the sedate old homes of **North Fitzroy** from the commercial area of Fitzroy proper. The mostly young-professional families who live here enjoy a burgeoning local scene without beckoning to the rest of the city to join them. The elegant villagelike atmosphere plays itself out in the area's quaint cafés and simmering shopping strip. Major roads skirt this area, connecting it to the rest of the city.

Like North Fitzroy, **North Carlton** has a sophisticated local scene catering to the area's residential population who live in some of the city's best-preserved 19th-century dwellings. In 1969 a group of the resident intelligentsia formed the Carlton Association who worked to preserve the Victorian edifices that lined the charming broad leafy streets.

By contrast, **Brunswick** is epitomised by the furiously paced Sydney Rd. During the gold rush, it was the main route to several goldfields, which gave rise to the throng of civic and commercial development that still exists today. The area is rich in bluestone and the many quarries here provided building materials for the fast-growing city. The incumbent population increase from the gold rush also saw an increase in crime. The Pentridge prison was established in 1850, with prisoners working in chain gangs breaking up bluestone, which was later used to build the prison's walls. Pentridge was closed as recently as 1997 and is currently being developed into housing estates – not the cheeriest of home locations.

Postwar migration saw high populations of Italians, Greeks, Turks and Lebanese settling here, which accounts for the baklava shops, Mediterranean wholesalers and Middle Eastern food outlets along Sydney Rd. Brunswick is a no-fuss neighbourhood, with a fabulously rich multiethnic

Vegemite

Open any cupboard in any Melbourne suburb – nay, any Australian suburb – and you'll find a jar of iconic black goop. Vegemite (www.vegemite.com.au) was 'discovered' in Melbourne at the Fred Walker Cheese Company in 1922. An accidental byproduct of the beer-making process, it derives from leftover brewer's yeast. This distinctive vegetable-extract spread is no longer Australian owned, but no less loved by Australians.

community. The **Brunswick Music Festival** (www.brunswickmusicfestival.com.au), held in March, 'brings a world of music to your door', with traditional, folk, contemporary, indigenous, roots and blues performers playing at a number of venues, culminating in a vibrant street party.

Orientation

The heart of North Carlton is Rathdowne St, broad and tree-lined, with a refined shopping strip to service the surrounding local neighbourhood. Drummond St, parallel to Rathdowne St, displays prime examples of the original 19th-century homes that characterise the area. After Lygon St crosses Elgin St it leaves the leisure-focused hub of Carlton proper, becoming a major thoroughfare through North Carlton to suburbs further north. Another main road, Nicholson St, forms the eastern boundary of North Carlton with Fitzroy.

Transport

Tram For North Carlton, take tram No 96 from Bourke St, which runs along Nicholson St, or No 1 from Swanston St along Lygon St. For North Fitzroy, tram No 112 from Collins St runs along Brunswick St and St Georges Rd. For Brunswick, take tram No 19 from Elizabeth St, which runs along Royal Pde to Sydney Rd.
Train Upfield-line train to Brunswick Station.

North Fitzroy is a small pocket between Nicholson St in the west and Queens Pde to the east. It is bordered to the south by Alexandra Pde and to the north by Merri Creek. The majority of activity runs along Brunswick St, which doglegs at the lush Edinburgh Gardens and feeds into St Georges Rd.

Brunswick sprawls to the west of North Fitzroy. Sydney Rd is Brunswick's spine, with the congestion starting from its intersection with Barkly St. Sydney Rd continues heading north, running all the way to Sydney.

CERES Map p210
☎ 9387 2609; www.ceres.org.au;
8 Lee St, East Brunswick

Ceres (Centre for Education and Research in Environmental Strategies) is a 20-year-old community environment project, with an objective to educate in environmental sustainability. Stroll through the Permaculture and Bushfood Nursery or the Origin EcoHouse before refuelling with an organic coffee and cake at the café. The park is popular with young families and people accessing the path to Merri Creek.

EDINBURGH GARDENS Map p210
St Georges Rd, North Fitzroy

Established European elms line the tranquil walking paths of this 140-year-old parkland. Only metres from the North Fitzroy café strip, these gardens are an ideal place to laze about on a late summer's afternoon after your caffeine fix. On weekends, wedding parties invade the rotunda while picnic blankets are spread and barbecues sizzle.

MELBOURNE GENERAL CEMETERY
Map p210
☎ 9349 3014; College Cres, North Carlton;

🕑 9am-4pm Mon & Wed-Fri, 10am-4pm Tue, 9.30am-4pm Sat, 9am-5pm Sun (office closed)

The Melbourne General Cemetery has had many homes; human bones are sometimes exhumed whenever construction takes place at the Queen Victoria Market (the cemetery's original site), but the cemetery we know today was established here in 1852. Curving paths take visitors to gravesites arranged in various denominations, displaying Melbourne's vast multicultural history. Guided moonlight tours arranged by the **National Trust of Victoria** (☎ 9656 9803; www.nattrust.com.au) are held twice a year; there are also tours every Wednesday and Sunday at 1pm for $10 per person. Bookings can be made on ☎ 0500 500 655.

PRINCES PARK Map p210
Princes Park Dr, North Carlton

Joggers, walkers and punishing boot camps make early morning pilgrimages to pound the gravel around this park, which is home to the Carlton football ground, now known as **Optus Oval** (p139). From here it's a 10-minute tram ride to Melbourne's CBD and a quick walk to the vibrant shopping strip on Sydney Rd.

ABBOTSFORD & RICHMOND

Eating pp109–10; Drinking pp122; Shopping pp151–52

This densely packed neighbourhood, sandwiched between the city and the Yarra River, contains pockets of semi-industrial streetscapes, a thriving Asian community and tracts of tranquil bushland.

Beneath the saw-toothed factory roofs, silos, chimneys and church spires of **Richmond** squat rows of workers cottages. Built in the early 1900s, the narrow streets were tightly packed with little dwellings to house the area's impoverished labourers who toiled in the tanneries, food-processing and clothing-manufacturing industries. Historically, Richmond was viewed as a poor and festering neighbourhood. The Richmond of today is a very different vision. It's a highly sought-after address associated with an industrial chic aesthetic. The factories have been remade into warehouse-style apartments and luxury offices. The homes have been renovated and refurbished several times over, and the commercial strips reflect the desires of its urban lifestylers, selling clothing and designer furniture.

Richmond's unique character comes from its working-class roots, its proximity to the city's sporting precinct and, as with all other areas, its migrant population. Richmond has a prominent population of people with connections to Southeast Asia, particularly Vietnam – most evident in Victoria St. Here you'll find an extraordinary number of Vietnamese restaurants and Asian grocers selling exotic ingredients, joss papers, woks, bamboo steamers and Buddhist iconography. There are herbalists, karaoke bars and blinking neon signs in Vietnamese characters.

North of Victoria St, the tiny residential pocket of **Abbotsford** gives way to the lush bushland verges of the Yarra River, a world away from the built-up surrounds of this city-fringe area. Here is a hidden sanctuary that belies its bustling industrial and residential location.

Orientation

Abbotsford and Richmond are bordered to the west by the ever-congested Punt Rd in Richmond and Hoddle St in Abbotsford. This is one of Melbourne's main thoroughfares and if you're driving, there's a fair chance you'll spend too much time in its gridlock. The Yarra River contains the neighbourhood to the east.

Richmond's main south–north thoroughfare is Church St. In the south, Church St proffers a burgeoning number of designer furniture and home-wares shops. Follow it north, past the old Bryant & May matchstick factory, over the railway to where it ascends to the well-to-do Richmond Hill area. The lofty rise falls away to the north before intersecting with Victoria St and the start of Abbotsford.

Victoria St, between Church and Hoddle Sts, is the place to come for the best bowl of *pho* (beef and rice noodle soup) outside Vietnam. Melburnians cram around tightly packed tables to fill up on authentic Vietnamese fare for around $10, every night of the week.

Richmond's Bridge Rd is a mecca for retail bargain shoppers. Many clothing retailers have their factory outlets and seconds stores between Punt Rd and Church St. Once Bridge Rd crosses Church St, the pace slows around the town hall to accommodate cafés, and new and used furniture stores. Swan St is a jumble of food outlets, shops and pubs. Its proximity to the MCG sees thousands trekking along here on match days seeking a postgame ale and a sympathetic ear as the day's play is dissected.

Transport

Tram Nos 48 & 75 along Flinders St will take you to Bridge Rd, Richmond. No 70, also along Flinders St, will take you along Swan St, Richmond. Swan St intersects Church St, which is serviced by tram Nos 78 & 79. Tram No 109 from Collins St heads down to Victoria St, Richmond.

Train Richmond Station is a stop on most suburban routes. For Abbotsford, take either an Epping-line train or a Hurstbridge-line train to Collingwood Station.

CARLTON BREWHOUSE Map p211
☎ 9420 6800; www.fosters.com.au; cnr Nelson & Thompson Sts, Abbotsford; ⏰ 10am & 2pm Mon-Fri; adult/concession $15/10

The Foster's beer-brewing empire runs tours of its Abbotsford operations, taking you through the brewing process from raw materials to packaging. You can sample the range of beers in the tasting room afterwards. Your brewery education will enable you to distinguish between an ale and a lager and make you a bush expert on the beer brands that come under the Foster's banner.

COLLINGWOOD CHILDREN'S FARM
Map p211
☎ 9417 5806; St Heliers St, Abbotsford; adult/concession $8/4; ⏰ 9am-5.30pm

This is a fine way to teach kids that milk and eggs don't just come from the supermarket. Paddocks with goats, cows, lambs and ponies are set in a beautiful nook by the Yarra River. Vegie gardens and an orchard promote sustainable farming practices, a theme carried through to the **Farmers' Market** (☎ 5657 2337; $2). Held every second Saturday of the month from 8am to 1pm, organic goods grown or made by the stallholders are for sale. The great food available will give you the strength to push your wheelbarrow laden with seasonal produce.

GLEADELL ST MARKET Map p211
Gleadell St, Richmond; ⏰ 7am-1pm every 2nd Sat

This little open-air market is a genuine community experience. It thrives with locals stocking up on fresh produce from spruiking stallholders. Buy a bag of nuts and shuffle between the colourful produce stalls among the shoppers' trolleys and full-to-bursting string bags.

YARRA BEND PARK Map p211
www.parkweb.vic.gov.au

Northeast of the city centre, the Yarra River is bordered by the Yarra Bend parkland, an

Top Five Abbotsford & Richmond

- Starting your day with a swim at **Richmond Recreation Centre** (p143)
- Wandering through the fabulous local market in **Gleadell St** (left)
- Lingering over brunch at **Richmond Hill Cafe & Larder** (p109)
- Walking off brunch to the tunes of bellbirds in **Yarra Bend Park** (left)
- Filling up again at one of Victoria St's fine **Vietnamese restaurants** (p109)

area much loved by runners, rowers, cyclists, picnickers and strollers.

The park has large areas of natural bushland (not to mention two golf courses and numerous sports grounds) and there are some great walks. In parts of Studley Park you could be out in the bush; with the songs of bellbirds ringing through the trees and cockatoos screeching on the banks, it's hard to believe the city's all around you. At the end of Boathouse Rd is the 1860s **Studley Park Boathouse** (☎ 9853 1972), which has a kiosk and restaurant, flocks of ducks, and boats and canoes for hire (see p140). Kanes suspension footbridge takes you across the river, from where it's about a 20-minute walk to **Dights Falls** at the confluence of the Yarra River and Merri Creek, with some great views on the way. You can also walk to the falls along the southern riverbank.

Further around the river, in Fairfield Park, is the site of the **Fairfield Amphitheatre** (Map pp200–01), a great open-air venue used for concerts and film screenings. The **Fairfield Park Boathouse & Tea Gardens** (Map pp200-01; ☎ 9486 1501; Fairfield Park Dr; ⏰ 9am-5pm Oct-Mar, Sat & Sun year-round) is a restored early-20th-century boathouse with broad verandas and an outdoor garden restaurant. You can also hire canoes and kayaks here (see p140).

Sign of the Times *Tony Macvean*

Richmond's past as a thriving industrial and manufacturing hub is graphically spelt out in its heritage signs.

Famous Richmond signs include the Nylex Plastics sign atop the silos in Punt Rd, which tells the time and temperature to thousands of commuters daily, the Skipping Girl Vinegar sign in Victoria St, the Pelaco sign in Goodwood St and the Slade Knitwear sign in Dover St. As a result of continued inner-city gentrification, land and buildings supporting these icons have been in developers' sights. To date, however, 'progress' has been resisted, with each of these signs being granted heritage protection. Heritage Victoria has prepared an inventory of Melbourne's neon heritage, so that councils are able to use planning controls to protect other signs before their switches are flicked off permanently.

Tony Macvean is a Richmond resident and avid sign spotter.

SOUTH YARRA, TOORAK & PRAHRAN

Eating pp110–11; Drinking pp122–23; Shopping pp152–53;
Sleeping pp163–64

South Yarra and Toorak are on what's commonly referred to as the 'right side' of the river – the opulent side of town. Trendy Chapel St links these elite residential suburbs to everyman Prahran, further south.

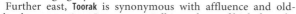

Access to **South Yarra** was by boat or punt (hence Punt Rd) before Princes Bridge was built in 1850. Its elevated aspect and large allotments enhanced the area's prestige. Demand for high-density housing led to some large blocks being subdivided in the 1920s and '30s for the construction of low-rise flats. In South Yarra's high-fashion shopping stretch designer labels outdo each other in ever-changing styles.

Further east, **Toorak** is synonymous with affluence and old-school conservatism. Luxury cars roll in and out of high-fenced properties, with mansions set behind long circular driveways. St Georges and Grange Rds are where you'll see some of Australia's biggest sprawling mansions.

Prahran is a blend of small Victorian workers' cottages, narrow, leafy streets and high-rise, government-subsidised flats for low-income earners. The name 'Prahran' is thought to have derived from the Aboriginal word *purraran*, meaning 'almost surrounded by water'. Today it would be more aptly described as 'almost surrounded by more-affluent suburbs'. People from various ethnic backgrounds, with a high proportion from Eastern Europe, live in this area. A resident student population attends the School of Design or the National Institute of Circus Arts. Prahran abounds in bars, pubs, nightclubs and recovery day clubs. Its eclectic shopping strip, aquatic centre (p143) and drinking dens keep the area thriving 24/7.

Orientation

Toorak Rd is the main artery through South Yarra and Toorak. The South Yarra end, between Punt Rd and Chapel St, is a stretch of fashion boutiques, beauty salons, specialist stores, cafés, and restaurants with fading appeal. More glamorous is the South Yarra end of Chapel St between Toorak and Commercial Rds. It's a stylish centre for designer fashion, with virtually wall-to-wall clothing boutiques (and a healthy sprinkling of bars and cafés). Fashion, is everywhere: in shop windows, sitting outside cafés and walking

> ### Transport
>
> **Train** On the Sandringham line several stations put you within easy walking distance of Chapel St: South Yarra Station in Toorak Rd, Prahran Station in Greville St, and Windsor Station at the end of Chapel St.
> **Tram** No 8 runs along St Kilda Rd to Toorak Rd, which crosses Chapel St. From here, Nos 78 & 79 run along Chapel St.

the street. The **Como Centre** (cnr Toorak Rd & Chapel St) is a sleek commercial development housing upmarket boutiques and shops, offices, cafés, cinemas and the five-star Como Hotel.

At the Toorak (east) end of Toorak Rd, between Wallace Ave and Grange Rd, is the small, exclusive group of shops and arcades known as Toorak Village. The Village is the local convenience shopping area for some of Melbourne's wealthiest citizens – don't expect any bargains. **St John's Anglican Church** (cnr Toorak & Clendon Rds) is hatch-match-and-dispatch central for any society event requiring the services of a church.

Prahran has several animated streets, the most notable being Chapel St. Prahran's section of Chapel St stretches south from Malvern Rd (the eastbound continuation of Commercial Rd) to Dandenong Rd, and is more diverse and less fashion-conscious than the South Yarra strip. Running off Chapel St by Prahran Town Hall, Greville St is the area's shopping alternative, with noteworthy retro and designer clothing shops, bookstores, gift shops and some good bars, cafés and restaurants. The Greville St arts, crafts and second-hand market (from noon Sunday) is the perfect place to recover from Saturday-night excesses. Commercial Rd is a focal point for Melbourne's gay and lesbian community, and has a diverse collection of nightclubs, bars, pubs, bookshops and cafés. Malvern Rd is another interesting shopping precinct, with a large number of antique shops and clothing boutiques.

Camberwell Market

East of Toorak is the conservative suburb of Camberwell, where twinsets and pearls are worn by many of the local women. It's also where you'll find the city's best flea market. Serious gleaners fall out of bed before dawn every Sunday to search for treasures by torchlight. It's open from 6am till noon, and six hours is hardly enough time to pick through mounds of Barbie-doll heads, old LPs, '50s clothes, cutlery, tools and photo frames. You'll find the market in the car park off Fairholm Grove, tucked in behind Burke Rd. Take a train to Camberwell Station on the Alamein, Belgrave or Lilydale lines.

COMO HOUSE Map p212

☎ 9827 2500; www.nattrust.com.au; cnr Williams Rd & Leachlade Ave, South Yarra; adult/child $11/6.50; ◷ 10am-5pm

Visit the former residence of the Armytage family who, for a century, owned this colonial mansion overlooking the Yarra. Built between 1840 and 1959, the home has been faithfully restored and contains some of the family's belongings. Set in extensive grounds, including a croquet lawn and lush flower walks, you'll appreciate what it was to be a well-known society-grazing family. Tours take around an hour: the first is at 10.30am, then half-hourly until 4pm.

PRAHRAN MARKET Map p212

www.prahranmarket.com.au; 163 Commercial Rd; ◷ dawn-5pm Tue, dawn-6pm Thu-Fri, dawn-5pm Sat, 10am-3pm Sun

The Prahran Market has been an institution for over a century. Established in 1881 it provided an outlet for the area's small farms and market gardens to peddle their wares. Back then, horses parked out the back added to rich odours of sweating carcasses and wilting produce. Car parking didn't factor into the original market design. Through the '70s and '80s a man positioned in an enclosed box, like a tennis referee, used an intercom to direct queuing cars into the next available space. He was known as 'the voice from above'. In the mid-'90s a gourmet food hall and a multilevel car park were added. Prahran's is one of the finest produce markets in the city.

It goes without saying that there are numerous stalls stocking fresh seafood, deli items, meats, fruits and vegetables. The market is also home to the **Essential Ingredient Cooking School** (☎ 9827 9047), teaching specific culture cuisines and general cooking techniques. There is **jazz** in Market Sq every Sunday from noon, and **farm animals** come to visit (Elizabeth St) each Tuesday from 10am to 1pm; just don't take the kids straight into the meat department afterwards.

Top Five South Yarra, Toorak & Prahran

- Tasting fine Italian fare at **Da Noi** (p110)
- Giving your credit card a beating in the first-rate boutiques along **Chapel St** (p152)
- Shopping for some of the city's finest produce at **Prahran Market** (left)
- Dancing all night at **Revolver** (p132)
- Sampling exquisite Polish vodka at **Borsch, Vodka & Tears** (p122)

ST KILDA

Eating pp111–14; Drinking pp123–24; Shopping pp153–54; Sleeping pp164–66

St Kilda is Melbourne's celebrity good-time suburb: its lush seaside surrounds are constantly in the limelight, home to conspicuous consumption, host to innumerable parties, replete with a reputation for a seamier side.

While the face of St Kilda has moved with the times, it remains the couthie inner-city hub established for the recreation and relaxation of the population. In Melbourne's early days, St Kilda was a sedate seaside retreat, with fashionable hotels and residences for the city's elite. The introduction of public transport brought day-trippers to the dance halls, fun park, ice-skating rink, theatres, sea baths and gardens. The mood shifted from that of a patrician village to a carnival atmosphere. St Kilda became *the* hectic centre for pleasure seekers and the wealthy folk moved on to more exclusive areas such as South Yarra and Toorak.

Melbourne Museum

The construction of flats began in the 1930s and continued for 30 years, with the area's grand old mansions either demolished or divided up. Today St Kilda has the highest number of 25- to 35-year-olds living alone in the suburb's high proportion of flats, although they're probably referred to as apartments these days. Postwar immigration brought a high Jewish population, especially from Eastern Europe. By the 1960s and '70s St Kilda had developed a reputation for seedier pleasures as a centre for drugs and prostitution. The population's homeless and unemployed unskilled labourers also gravitated to St Kilda, along with artists and students.

Top Five St Kilda

- Purchasing a luscious cake from **Monarch** (p114)
- Gorging yourself on that cake in the gorgeous **St Kilda Botanical Gardens** (p76)
- Strolling along the **foreshore** (p77) under the palm trees
- Admiring the sunset from the balcony, then settling in for some pub rock at the iconic **Esplanade Hotel** (p128)
- Catching a double-bill at the illustrious **Astor Theatre** (p132)

Since the '90s, St Kilda has returned to the forefront of Melbourne's fashionable suburbs, the place it occupied more than a century ago. It hosts the ever-popular St Kilda Festival (p10) and St Kilda Film Festival (p11), and is the venue for a variety of events each year. St Kilda's appeal is a mix of the old and the rejuvenated, the ethnic and the artistic, the stylish and the casual. It's a place of extremes – backpacker hostels and fine-dining restaurants, classy cafés and cheap takeaways, seaside strolls and Sunday traffic jams, renovated family homes, and the Sacred Heart Mission (which provides essential services for the area's disadvantaged community; rummage for a bargain at its well-stocked op shop if you're in the vicinity). St Kilda is a vibrant lifestyle-hub, far from the sanitised gloss of other urban centres.

Orientation

Fitzroy St, the wide boulevard leading down to the foreshore, still retains fragments of St Kilda's halcyon days, visible in the architecture of the George Hotel. The street has weathered a changing demographic from the glory days through the less glamorous era of amusement arcades and hamburger joints to the sophisticated restaurant strip of today that particularly comes alive at night. Fitzroy St's St Kilda Bowling Club (p141) and proximity to Albert Park Lake (p78) make it a popular spot for sneaker-clad folk on a sunny day. Some of the city's best restaurants and cafés line Fitzroy St from Lakeside Dr down to the foreshore.

Grey St, linking Fitzroy and Barkly Sts, is home to the Sacred Heart Mission.

The section of Acland St between Carlisle and Barkly Sts is famed for its continental cake shops, delicatessens, and older-style central-European cafés and restaurants, such as the long-established Scheherazade (99 Acland St). This part of Acland St became a centre for the wave of Jewish and other European refugees who settled in the area after

Transport

Tram No 16 runs down St Kilda Rd from the city to Fitzroy and Acland Sts. No 96 also goes to Fitzroy and Acland Sts but from Spencer St. No 67 runs down St Kilda Rd and will take you to St Kilda Junction or to Carlisle St a little further on.

WWII. Although fading, their influence and presence can still be experienced amid the glitzy new bars, cafés and home-ware shops that have turned this once sedate street into a bustling strip. At weekends in particular, the crowds jostle for pavement space along here.

If you follow Carlisle St across St Kilda Rd and into East St Kilda you'll find some great Jewish food shops, bakeries and European delicatessens rubbing shoulders with an influx of new cafés and bars. This precinct's distance from the spectacle of St Kilda (although short) allows for a more relaxed local atmosphere.

On the foreshore, Jacka Blvd has a few excellent waterfront restaurants, palm-lined walkways and bike paths.

Esplanade Sunday Market (below)

ESPLANADE SUNDAY MARKET Map p213
Upper Esplanade, btwn Cavell & Fitzroy Sts;
⏱ **10am-5pm Sun**
About a kilometre of trestle tables joined end-to-end carry an extraordinary array of items made by each individual stallholder. With a seaside backdrop, you can pick your way through toys, jewellery, mobiles, soaps, clothes and ornaments from over 200 stalls.

JEWISH MUSEUM OF AUSTRALIA
Map p213
☎ **9534 0083; 26 Alma Rd; adult/concession $7/4;**
⏱ **10am-4pm Tue-Thu, 11am-5pm Sun**
This dynamic and fascinating museum has interactive displays relating to Jewish history and culture since the beginning of European settlement in Australia. Permanent exhibitions celebrate the annual cycle of festivals and holy days that are integral to Jewish life, and explore the origins of Judaism. The museum also hosts regular temporary exhibitions and lectures.

LINDEN ARTS CENTRE & GALLERY
Map p213
☎ **9209 6794; www.lindenarts.org; 26 Acland St;**
⏱ **1-6pm Tue-Sun**
While the building itself dates from the 1870s, Linden Arts Centre & Gallery is a contemporary art space showing local and international work. Drop the kids in the children's sculpture garden

while you explore inside or sit in the garden. Linden also houses performance spaces and studios and holds life-drawing classes.

LUNA PARK Map p213
☎ **9525 5033; www.lunapark.com.au; Lower Esplanade; single-ride ticket adult/child $7/5.50, unlimited-ride ticket $34/24;** ⏱ **11am-6pm daily, to 11pm Fri & Sat in summer**
The famous laughing face of Luna Park has been a symbol of St Kilda since 1912. This historic amusement park was built by the same company that built the first Luna Park on Coney Island in 1903. It includes rides for all ages including the heritage-listed roller coaster (the oldest continually operating roller coaster in the world), a beautifully crafted carousel (built by the Philadelphia Toboggan Company) and the Pharaoh's Curse – the best way to see the foreshore upside down.

ST KILDA BOTANICAL GARDENS
Map p213
☎ **9209 6666; cnr Herbert & Blessington Sts**
Visit these heritage-listed gardens to see the locals relaxing; they come here to smell the roses, picnic, play bocce (Italian bowls) or just doze in the sun. At the corner of Blessington and Herbert Sts is the former caretaker's residence, now a community eco-house, with free tours on Saturday at 2.15pm.

ST KILDA FORESHORE Map p213
Jacka Blvd

St Kilda's foreshore has undergone the same rejuvenation as the rest of the suburb. The beaches have been cleaned up and topped up with sand, the foreshore parks landscaped, and bike paths built. The boats and yachts moored in the lee of the breakwater, the Canary Island palm trees planted along the foreshore and people promenading along the pier are all familiar sights. Two of St Kilda's most popular restaurants are superbly located in converted foreshore buildings: the stylish **Donovans** (p112), once a bathing pavilion, and the **Stokehouse** (p113), originally an Edwardian teahouse.

The **St Kilda Pier** and breakwater are favourite spots for strollers. In late 2003 the iconic kiosk at the pier's end burnt down, one year short of its centenary. Its reconstruction, though in accordance with heritage guidelines, will have none of the rich history of its predecessor. The kiosk was best known as Kerby's between 1938 and 1987; owner Colin Kerby became a local celebrity for rescuing over 500 people before there were police and rescue boats along the bay.

On weekends and public holidays a **ferry** (☎ 9682 9555; adult/child $6.50/3.25) runs from the pier across the bay to Williamstown, departing St Kilda hourly between 11.30am and 4.30pm, and leaving Williamstown hourly from 11am to 4pm.

On the foreshore south of the pier, the Moorish-style **St Kilda Sea Baths** (☎ 9525 3011; 10-18 Jacka Blvd) has undergone major redevelopment, with the complex containing a health club, shops and food outlets. The 25m saltwater swimming pool is the highlight.

SOUTH MELBOURNE & ALBERT PARK

Eating pp114–15; Shopping pp154; Sleeping pp166

If you're starting to feel landlocked and anxious to see the horizon, these residential suburbs bordered by the bay make for a pleasant inner-city jaunt. Each has a local shopping strip with the requisite cafés and modish designer stores.

The streets in **South Melbourne** have an introspective quality, winding among solid Victorian terrace homes before turning back on themselves. When you do make your way out into the open, it's to the sweeping waterfront broken by a number of weatherworn piers. South Melbourne's humble beginnings as a shantytown of canvas and bark huts belie its current status as the preferred suburb for moneyed professionals. The area was originally called Emerald Hill, after the grassy knoll of high ground that rose above the muddy flatlands. Its government-funded housing towers recall South Melbourne's history as an area known for providing community services, and contribute to its mix of residents from diverse backgrounds. As well its leisurely paced shopping strip, South Melbourne has a more commercial hub serving the ad agencies, market researchers and film-related businesses in the area.

West from South Melbourne, **Albert Park** is a villagelike suburb that you'll most likely pass while strolling its waterfront. Like its neighbour, many residents are young families or the upwardly mobile. The majority of its Victorian terrace houses and cottages have been faithfully restored, which is part of the area's gracious appeal.

The waterfront continues north to Port Melbourne and Station Pier – the passenger terminal for the daily ferry service between Melbourne and Tasmania, across Bass Strait. A number of housing estates have sprouted inland from the bay. These cartoon-colourful high-rises give the surreal impression that thousands of Noddy and Big Ears characters just moved into the area. This once semi-industrial end of the bay has layers of development that conceal its working-class port origins.

Top Five South Melbourne & Albert Park

- Walking or running around beautiful **Albert Park Lake** (p78)
- Dipping your chopsticks into delicate Japanese food at **Misuzu** (p114)
- Browsing through the clothing and other special things at **Husk** (p154)
- Joining the throng at **South Melbourne Market** (p79)
- Strolling along the foreshore at **Albert Park Beach** (p78)

Orientation

South Melbourne's city boundary is gradually shrinking as the City of Melbourne expands south. Emerald Hill, bordered by Clarendon, Park, Cecil and Dorcas Sts was the first area to be built upon and is now a heritage-conservation area. The main street running through the heart of South Melbourne from Spencer St in the city to Albert Park Lake is Clarendon St. In the central shopping section, many of the original Victorian shopfronts have been restored and refitted with verandas, and you'll find all sorts of shops and a few pubs (the survivors from the days when the area boasted a pub on every corner). The area around the market, on Cecil and Coventry Sts, is a secondary focus of activity created by and for market-goers. Bridport St, between Montague and Merton Sts, is a lively local shopping area. Here you'll find some stylish cafés, tempting delicatessens and a few exclusive speciality shops and boutiques. Just north of the shopping centre is the suburb's backyard, St Vincent Pl – a formal Victorian garden surrounded by beautiful terrace houses.

Pick up some takeaways along Victoria Ave in Albert Park on your way to the beach. Kerferd Rd is another main thoroughfare that'll pop you out on the waterfront at the eponymous pier. Beaconsfield Pde, from South Melbourne through Albert Park, has a constant stream of traffic – both on the road and on the promenade. In-line skaters, cyclists and pedestrians all share pavement space here.

Transport

Tram No 1 trundles along St Kilda Rd to South Melbourne and Albert Park. Alternatively, take No 112 from Collins St.

ALBERT PARK LAKE Map pp214-15
Btwn Queens Rd, Fitzroy St, Aughtie Dr & Albert Rd

Pairs of elegant black swans will give you their inimitable bottoms-up salute as you circumnavigate the 5km perimeter of this stunning lake. Water birds share the lake with dozens of small sailing, rowing and remote-controlled boats. You can hire sailing boats from the **Jolly Roger School of Sailing** (☎ 9690 5862; Aquatic Dr South). Joggers, cyclists and dogs share the path around the lake on any given day. The outdoor activity ripples out to the surrounding parkland, sports ovals and golf course. Also on the periphery is the **Melbourne Sports & Aquatic Centre** (see p143), with an Olympic-size pool for starters. Lakeside Dr was used as an international motor-racing circuit in the 1950s, and since 1996 the revamped track has been the venue for the **Australian Formula One Grand Prix** each March; see p140 for more details.

Melbourne's Aboriginal Places

Although more than 160 years have passed since Melbourne was colonised, traces of the area's Aboriginal past remain. For a different perspective on some of Melbourne's attractions, visit the following sites.

- **Burnley Park** (Map pp200–01) has a corroboree tree (now a stump) that is a site of spiritual significance for the Wurundjeri people. The tree was a marker of clan territory, a site for meetings and formal corroborees. Other corroboree places include the sites of the Supreme Court, the Melbourne Town Hall and Emerald Hill (South Melbourne).
- **Fitzroy Gardens** (Map p205) has a scarred tree that is not far from Cooks' Cottage.
- **Queen Victoria Market** (Map p209) is on the site of Melbourne's pioneer cemetery. Few visitors enjoying the market's vibrancy realise that buried beneath the produce stalls lie around 10,000 graves, which makes building renovations a tricky exercise. The section reserved for Aboriginal sites lies under sheds F to J, near Queen St.
- **St Kilda Junction** (Map p213) has a corroboree tree that is now surrounded by traffic and fumes, and is believed to be around 300 years old. The site was both a meeting area and a fringe camp used by survivors of white settlement. The area was bordered by wetlands, a great source of food. Today the wetlands form the basis of nearby Albert Park Lake.
- **Yarra Park** (Map p205) is home not only to the MCG, but also to two ancient trees whose trunks were scarred by the removal of their bark to build canoes. Incidentally, it is thought that a form of Australian Rules football was played by Aborigines, using a possum skin as a ball.

FAWKNER PARK Map pp214-15
Off Toorak & Commercial Rds

This huge expanse of open grassy fields is loved and used by the area's sports folk and small lap-dogs alike. Walkways lined with elms, oaks and Moreton Bay fig trees provide structure to the otherwise open fields. The fields, leased as recently as the 1920s for cattle grazing, are now used for all manner of sports. Barbecues and Art Deco pavilions are available for public use.

SOUTH MELBOURNE MARKET
Map pp214-15

☎ 9209 6295; cnr Coventry & Cecil Sts; ☾ 8am-2pm Wed, 8am-6pm Fri, 8am-4pm Sat & Sun

The compact South Melbourne Market has been operating on the same site since 1864. This neighbourhood institution sells everything from carpets to *bok choy*. The market's labyrinthine interior is packed to overflowing with an eccentric collection of stalls. Turn a corner and you could find organic wine, a hairdresser, a masseuse or a novelty singing trout. The produce is excellent, the pace is leisurely and the surrounding streets are conveniently dotted with good cafés. Join the queue at South Melbourne Market Dim Sims & Spring Rolls on the market's Cecil St frontage to experience the singular pleasure of Cheng's dim sims, regularly voted Melbourne's best by those in the know.

WILLIAMSTOWN
Eating pp115

Neighbourhoods – Williamstown

Wondering where to wear that white cap with the embroidered anchor? **Williamstown** is the place. This historic seafaring town is full-steam-ahead on sunny afternoons, its pavements packed with café-dwellers enjoying the view over Hobsons Bay to the city.

Back in 1837, two townships were laid out simultaneously at the top of Port Phillip Bay: Melbourne, the main settlement and Williamstown, the seaport. With the advantage of the natural harbour of Hobsons Bay, Williamstown thrived and government services such as customs and immigration were based here. Many early buildings were built from locally quarried bluestone and the township quickly took on an air of permanence.

When the Yarra River was deepened and the Port of Melbourne developed in the 1880s, Williamstown became a secondary port. Tucked away in a corner of the bay, it was by-passed and forgotten for years. Its rediscovery was inevitable, and these days (especially on weekends) crowds of day-trippers take ferry rides across the bay to enjoy the historic seaside atmosphere and to promenade along the Esplanade with the bay on one side and the Botanic Gardens on the other. 'Willy' also has a quaint little beach.

The independently operated **Williamstown Information Centre** (☎ 9397 3791; www.williamstowninfo.com.au; Commonwealth Reserve; ☾ 9am-5pm) is between Nelson Pl and the waterfront. A series of self-guided heritage-walk brochures are available covering the waterfront and seaside areas. Commonwealth Reserve is also the site of the **craft market** (☾ 10am-4pm), held on the third Sunday of every month.

Orientation

Nelson Pl is Williamstown's main waterfront street. It's lined with gracious historic buildings blessed with exceptional views of the city. Many of Nelson Pl's buildings contain restaurants, cafés and galleries that keep a constant leisurely pace. Between Nelson Pl and the bay are Commonwealth Reserve and Gem Pier – the main departure point for ferries. Past the café strip Nelson Pl changes name to Battery Rd. Battery Rd is made from bluestone extracted by convict labour; it's thought that Ned Kelly (p47) contributed to building the retaining wall in 1873. Battery Rd leads to the historic Point Gellibrand Coastal Heritage Park. This was the first disembarkation point for early Victorian settlers, and contains the Timeball

Transport
Train Williamstown-line train to Williamstown Station.
Boat See p80.

Tower – once used as a lighthouse – and old Fort Gellibrand. Battery Rd turns into the Esplanade, with the Williamstown Botanic Gardens and tiny Williamstown Beach.

When you start to tire of the historical theme-parklike ambience of the waterfront, head down Ferguson St. It's Williamstown's local shopping precinct, and well worth a wander for its cafés, restaurants and shops.

Neighbourhoods – Williamstown

CUSTOMS WHARF GALLERY Map p216
☎ 9399 9726; www.customswharfgallery.com;
126 Nelson Pl; adult/concession $2/1; ⏰ 11am-5pm
The old Customs building, built in 1876, houses changing exhibitions by local and interstate artists in its 12 rooms. Paintings, photographs, sculpture and old books adorn the gallery spaces, with stunning views over the bay from the first floor.

GEM PIER Map p216
Syme St
Gem Pier is where passenger ferries dock to drop off and collect those who visit Williamstown by boat. It's a fitting way to arrive, given the area's maritime ambience. **Williamstown Ferries** (☎ 9506 4144; www.williamstownferries .com.au) plies across Hobsons Bay, stopping at Southgate (daily) and St Kilda (weekends), visiting a number of sites along the way, including **Scienceworks** (below) and **Docklands** (p64). **Melbourne River Cruises** (☎ 9629 7233; www.melb cruises.com.au) also dock at Gem Pier travelling up the Yarra River to Southgate. Ticket prices vary according to your destination. Pick up a timetable from the visitors centre in Williamstown or at Federation Square, or contact the companies directly; bookings are advised.

Also on Gem Pier, you can board the WWII minesweeper **HMAS Castlemaine** (www.hmas castlemaine.com; adult/child $5/2.50; ⏰ noon-5pm Sat & Sun), which has been converted into a maritime museum, with nautical exhibits and memorabilia.

SCIENCEWORKS & MELBOURNE PLANETARIUM Map pp200-01
☎ 9392 4800; http://scienceworks.museum.vic.gov .au; 2 Booker St, Spotswood; adult/concession $6/free, including Planetarium show adult/child/concession $12.50/4/5; ⏰ 10am-4.30pm
Scienceworks museum and the Melbourne Planetarium are both under the same roof in Spotswood, in the shadow of the West Gate Bridge.

Scienceworks was built on the site of the Spotswood pumping station, Melbourne's first sewerage works, and incorporates the historic buildings. The museum has a huge, fascinating array of interactive displays: you can spend hours inspecting old machines, pressing buttons, pulling levers and learning all sorts of weird facts and figures. Scienceworks is *very* popular with school groups and can get crowded; the quietest times are weekday afternoons during school terms and Saturday morning. The museum is a 10-minute signposted walk from Spotswood train station.

The **Melbourne Planetarium** re-creates the night sky on a 16m-domed ceiling using a hi-tech computer and projection system. In the comfort of a reclining chair you can dip through a wormhole or ride the rings of Saturn. Several shows suitable for children of all ages also screen.

WILLIAMSTOWN RAILWAY MUSEUM
Map p216
☎ 9397 7412; Champion Rd; adult/child $5/2;
⏰ noon-5pm Sat, Sun & public holidays, noon-4pm Wed & school holidays
Train-spotters among us will appreciate the collection of old steam locomotives, wagons, carriages and old photos here. Kids will appreciate the ministeam-train rides. Operated by the Australian Railway Historical Society, it's part of the Newport Rail Workshops in North Williamstown.

Museum of Modern Art Detour

In the eastern suburb of Bulleen, the Heide **Museum of Modern Art** (☎ 9850 1500; www.heide.com.au; 7 Templestowe Rd; adult/concession $12/8; ⏰ 10am-5pm Tue-Fri, noon-5pm Sat & Sun) is on the site of the former home of the late John and Sunday Reed, under whose patronage the likes of Sir Sidney Nolan, John Perceval, Joy Hester, Albert Tucker and Arthur Boyd created a new movement in the Australian art world (see also p24).

Known as Heide, the gallery has an impressive collection of 20th-century Australian art. The sprawling grounds are an informal combination of native and European trees, with a carefully tended kitchen garden and scattered sculpture gardens running down to the banks of the Yarra River.

Heide is signposted off the Eastern Fwy; otherwise, catch a Hurstbridge-line train to Heidelberg Station, then bus No 291.

INNER WEST

Eating pp115–16

This industrial heartland is characterised by the working dock-lands. The day-and-night rhythms of this area are mesmerising. Giant machines driven by unseen operators stack enormous bricks of solid colour that come and go on immense ships. Here is Melbourne's main working-port area. The surrounding suburbs have a long association with the working class and a reputation as a genuinely inclusive community.

Located on the western verge of the city, you may pass through the light industry of **West Melbourne** on your way to Footscray. The Inner West's focus is the Maribyrnong River. Once a conduit for heavy industry and effluent, the river is now given over to leisure pursuits. Regular cruises run along here (see p52), and the rejuvenated riverside incorporates wetlands, a bike path and a promenade. The area's 'capital' is the fabulously unfussy **Footscray.** Over 40% of Footscray's resident population was born outside Australia, the majority in Vietnam, China, Italy and Greece. More recently, a significant African population has settled in Footscray. Also settling in Footscray are young home-buyers eager to own a slice of the inner-city. House prices are rocketing, but the inevitable gentrification remains curbed for the moment. The spirit of Footscray is represented by its traditionally underdog, much loved AFL team the Western Bulldogs.

Footscray's enormous wholesale markets along Footscray Rd are not open to the public, but you can join a tour with **Point Nepean** (☎ 5984 4276; adult/concession $20/17). Set your alarm clock; tours leave at 5.15am and run for three hours through the flower market, fish market, and fruit and vegetable market.

Neighbouring Footscray, **Yarraville** was recently discovered by young families as an affordable suburb close to the city. It has since developed a villagelike atmosphere in its shopping strips, while retaining its fabulous heritage, evident in the gorgeous Art Deco Sun Theatre and the local pubs, with basic pub-grub and honest charm.

Orientation

West Melbourne, between Spencer St and the new Docklands development, is separated from North Melbourne along Victoria St. The major arterials of Footscray Rd and Dynon Rd carry a huge amount of traffic, heavy with trucks moving in and out of the working docklands area. Footscray's hub is along Barkly St. Here you'll find the Foot-scray Market and an abundance of Vietnamese restaurants, grocers and Asian food marts. Near the east end of Barkly St, Footscray train station pipes classical music over loudspeakers in an attempt to discourage youth from loitering. The beautiful Edwardian gardens of Footscray Park are located on Ballarat Rd, next to the famous Flemington Racecourse – home of the Melbourne Cup.

Yarraville centres on its train station, with the main shopping area along Anderson St. It has a burgeoning local café scene and features a number of speciality stores.

> **Transport**
>
> **Train** To reach Footscray, take a Williamstown- or Werribee-line train to Footscray Station. Yarraville is on the Williamstown line.

FOOTSCRAY COMMUNITY ARTS CENTRE Map pp200-01

☎ 9362 8888; www.fcarts.org.au; 45 Moreland St; ⏰ 9.30am-7pm Mon-Thu, 9.30am-5pm Fri, noon-4pm Sat & Sun

Borrow a beach mat from the **Big Fish Café** (⏰ 9.30am-4pm) to lounge on while you eat your vegie wrap or slurp your soup beside the Maribyrnong River, then stroll through **Gabriel Gallery** (⏰ 9.30am-5pm Mon-Fri, noon-4pm Sat & Sun), which profiles art works by people who've recently arrived in Australia. Both are housed in the historic former piggery of Mr Henderson, Henderson House. The complex includes the adjoining warehouse, which is a physical training area for the Women's

Trugo

Something like a hybrid of lawn bowls and croquet, Melbourne rail workers invented Trugo in the 1920s. Not surprisingly, every aspect of the game relates to trains. Solid rubber rings used as buffers between carriages were knocked about with a sledgehammer, since replaced by a lighter wooden mallet. The pitch's length is that of a train carriage and the goals are the same width apart as an open doorway to a carriage.

A team consists of eight players. Each has six turns at hitting four rings through the goals: a 'true go' according to legend. Men prefer to take a swing backwards through the legs, while the ladies prefer the putt-style swing. **Footscray** (☎ 9687 4916; 38 Windsor St) and **Yarraville** (☎ 9314 3348; 48 Fehon St) each have a Trugo club if you want to get on board.

While the Connecticut Extreme Croquet Society showed some interest in the game, it's currently played exclusively by Melbourne's older generation.

Circus. There are also regular music and theatre programmes promoting the centre's charter of facilitating community arts in multiethnic Footscray.

FOOTSCRAY MARKET Map pp200-01
☎ 9687 1205; cnr Hopkins & Leeds St; ☿ 7am-4pm Tue & Wed, 7am-6pm Thu, 7am-8pm Fri, 7am-4pm Sat
This frenetic covered food market is laden with seductive produce: you'll find lotus flowers, pigs' ears, coriander and cassava root. There's also an excellent range of fresh seafood, some of it still swimming. From the food court, take the elevator to the top floor for a giddying view over the railway and docklands to the city and West Gate Bridge.

LIVING MUSEUM Map pp200-01
☎ 9318 3544; www.livingmuseum.org.au; Pipemakers Park, Van Ness Ave, Maribyrnong; admission free; ☿ 10am-4pm Mon-Fri, 11am-4pm Sun
This community museum promotes local participation in its programme of documenting and interpreting the area's social, industrial and environmental history. It keeps 400 oral histories on various topics, such as migration, the role of women, and the meat industry. There's also a collection of photographs, maps, plans and drawings. It's set in the grounds of Pipemakers Park, featuring a Discovery Park, wetlands area and indigenous gardens, which re-create the landscape of the basalt plains and valley as it was before white settlement.

1 Golfers, Albert Park (p141)
2 Autumn gold, Fitzroy Gardens (p55) **3** Outdoor activities, Albert Park Lake (p78) **4** In-line skater, St Kilda foreshore (p141)

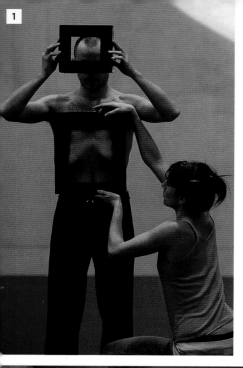

1 *Chunky Move contemporary dancers (p135)* **2** *Princess Theatre (p134)* **3** *Live music, Evelyn Hotel (p128)* **4** *Night Cat (p129)*

1 *Croft Institute (p119)* 2 *Upstairs at Revolver (p132)* 3 *Cookie (p119)* 4 *Polly (p121)*

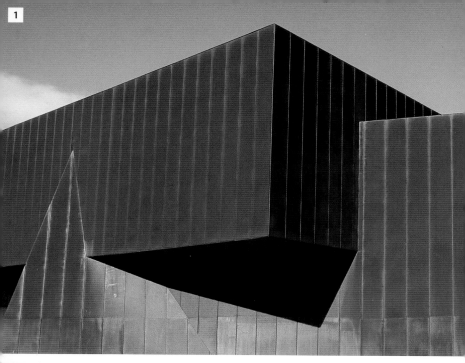

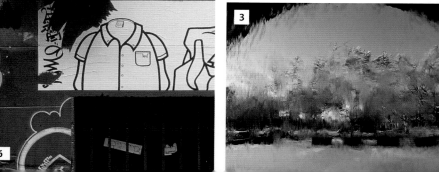

1 Australian Centre for Contemporary Art (p58) *2* Victorian Arts Centre (p61) *3* Water wall, National Gallery of Victoria: International (p60) *4* Melbourne City Council laneway commissions (boxed text, p56)

1 *Fantastic food, Federation Square (p62)* 2 *Alfresco dining, Southgate (p61)* 3 *Roast ducks, Victoria Street (p71)* 4 *A barista demonstrates his art*

1 Café culture, Block Place (p64)
2 Old Melbourne Gaol (p57) 3 City Circle Tram (boxed text, p52) 4 The clocks, Flinders Street Station (p59)

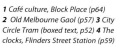

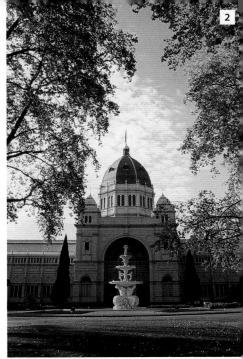

1 Como House (p74) *2* Royal Exhibition Building (p67) *3* Luna Park (p76) *4* Gem Pier (p80)

1 Owl (p153) 2 Jasper (p149)
3 Queen Victoria Market (p65)
4 Royal Arcade (p64)

Walking Tours

Walking Tours

Exploring Melbourne's alleys, laneways and arcades necessitates a bit of legwork: walking is the only way to discover these gems hidden among the city's main streets. The city's central grid of straight intersecting streets makes it easy to navigate. Melbourne is almost entirely encircled by parks and gardens, rivers and the bay. Walk a couple of kilometres in any direction and you'll hit one of these natural beauties; and if you run out of puff, there'll be a tram, train, bus or boat within metres, going your way.

RADICAL MELBOURNE

There are two sides to Melbourne. Often seen as stuffy and respectable, the city also has a long-standing radical tradition. This walk gives you a glimpse into Melbourne's unruly past.

Start at the **Flagstaff Gardens 1**. This lush park played a dual role in early Melbourne. As one of the highest points in the settlement, the flagpole on the hill served to communicate with Williamstown as ships

> **Walk Facts**
>
> **Start** Flagstaff Gardens
> **End** Trades Hall
> **Distance** 5km
> **Duration** 2½ hours
> **Fuel Stop** Trades Hall bar

arrived. The lower area provided the earliest cemetery. Among the half-dozen bodies interred here lies a settler named Charles Franks. His death in 1836 was probably at the hands of indigenous Australians and the leaders of the colony killed perhaps 10 Aboriginal people in a reprisal raid.

Walk down Peel Street to the **Queen Victoria Market 2** (p65). The area that's now Melbourne's largest open-air market was the city's biggest cemetery between 1838 and 1920. The demands of commerce saw the prime real estate ceded to local traders. Identifiable graves were disinterred but some 9000 corpses remain buried under what's now the car-park area. They include the bodies of the first people executed in the city, the Aboriginal resistance fighters Robert Smallboy and Jack Napoleon Tunerminnerwail (see p93 for more details). Most of the cemetery wall remains intact – a brown and cream arched brick wall running through the middle of the market.

Head down to 383 Latrobe St – the **headquarters of the Australian Federal Police 3**. In the late 1980s, Melbourne was the centre of a thriving computer-hacker scene. When a computer 'worm' originating from Melbourne disrupted a controversial plutonium-powered NASA (National Aeronautics and Space Administration) launch in 1989, police established one of the world's first computer crime teams in this building.

At 293 La Trobe St, you'll find the **Duke of Kent Hotel 4**. The room that is now a beer garden was in 1937 the home of the New Theatre, a left-wing drama society affiliated to the Communist Party. It established its own theatre after the government banned its antifascist plays on the grounds that they might be offensive to a friendly government – that is, Nazi Germany.

Turn right into Elizabeth St. The Aussie Disposals store at 283 Elizabeth St used to be known as **Socialist Hall 5**, the office of the Victorian Socialist Party (VSP). Founded in 1906 by the famous English agitator Tom Mann, the VSP ran political meetings, a Socialist Sunday school and a choir led by Tom's wife, Elsie. It also campaigned for free speech and against unemployment. Some of its members went on to found the Communist Party of Australia.

Turn left into Lonsdale St and left again into Swanston St. After crossing Little Lonsdale St you'll come to the recently renovated **State Library of Victoria 6** (p58). Today the forecourt is the customary gathering place for protests and demonstrations. During the 19th century, the strict enforcement of the Presbyterian Sabbath meant the library remained closed on

Sunday, the one day on which working people might have been able to use its facilities. Anarchists, socialists and sundry other agitators joined forces in a long-running campaign against Sunday closing. Rallies for the right to use the library saw a number of activists imprisoned on charges of 'insulting behaviour', 'loitering' and 'taking part in a procession'. The library eventually relented in 1904.

Continue along Swanston St and cross La Trobe St. On your right is **RMIT University 7**. Among the postmodern architecture, you'll see the columns of a much older building. Today it's called Storey Hall, and hosts various university functions. In 1916 it was known as Guild Hall, and provided the base for the Women's Political Association (WPA). The WPA was founded by Vida Goldstein, the first woman in the British Empire to stand for parliament. Her organisation campaigned for equal pay, international female suffrage and equal divorce rights. During WWI the WPA agitated against conscription and militarism, and supported the Russian revolution.

In the middle of RMIT university campus, you'll come across Bowen Street; walk north along it until you emerge in Franklin St. The **hill 8** on which you're standing was used for public executions in 1842. On 21 January, Jack Napoleon Tunermenerwail and Robert Smallboy – who had led a guerrilla campaign against settlers near Bass River – were hanged before a crowd of 6000 people. As the sentencing judge explained, the punishment was 'not one of vengeance but of terror…to deter similar transgressions'. The same year, an Aboriginal man identified only as 'Roger' was hanged for killing a white man in the Mt Rouse area, possibly in reprisal for the molestation of Aboriginal women. Three white bushrangers were also executed here.

If you keep walking along Franklin St then east along Victoria St, you'll see the **Eight Hour Day monument 9**. The three '8's on the top of the statue represent the slogans of working class agitation of the 1850s – eight hours' work, eight hours' rest and eight hours' recreation. Stonemasons working at Melbourne University led a march through the city in 1856. In that year, Victorian workers became some of the first in the world to enjoy the eight-hour day. The monument was completed in 1903, and unveiled by the veteran socialist Tom Mann.

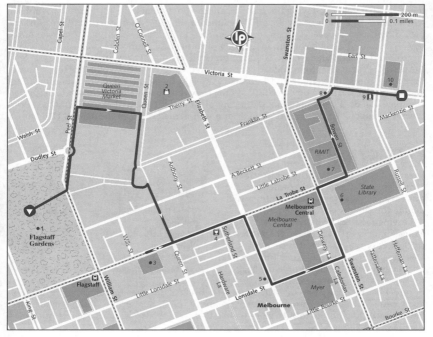

State Library of Victoria (p92)

Across the road is **Trades Hall 10**, one of the oldest purpose-built union buildings still in use. Unionists raised a substantial amount of money to construct a 'working class parliament', deliberately employing the same architect who designed the Melbourne Town Hall, Joseph Reed. In its early years, the building functioned as an educational centre for workers, providing classes on everything from mathematics to landscape painting. The tower at the top once housed a radio station, in an attempt to provide a union response to right-wing electronic media. Plaques inside commemorate the eight hour day and the unions' role in the defeat of legislation to introduce conscription during WWI. The building today houses numerous community and activist groups, as well as being the venue for union meetings and alternative theatre. You can check out the New International Bookshop, which specialises in radical books and magazines. But you might prefer to head up the stone stairs (worn down by generations of workers' boots) for a well-earned drink in the Trades Hall bar.

CITY STROLL

Weave through Melbourne's historic arcades, laneways and less crowded streets; this easy walk takes you past buildings that denote the city's architectural heritage.

Leaving **Federation Square 1** (p62) head west along Flinders St. Pass **Flinders Street Station 2** (p59) across the road, and turn right into Degraves St with its cafés and tiny shops. As you approach Centre Pl note the beautiful **Majorca Building 3**, on the corner of Centre Pl and Flinders Lane, one of Melbourne city-dwellers' most sought-after addresses. Follow Centre Way arcade through to leafy Collins St (p64); this section of the famous street has retained much of its former glory thanks to classic 1930s buildings such as **Lyric House 4** (No 248), **Kodak House 5** (No 252) and **Newspaper House 6** (No 247).

Walk Facts

Start Federation Square
End Chinatown
Distance 2.5km
Duration 2 hours
Fuel Stop Café Segovia (p105)

Cross the street and enter the Australia on Collins shopping mall, taking the escalator to the 1st floor to exit into Little Collins St. Pop into the nearby **Royal Arcade 7** (p64). Head back to Collins St by taking **Block Pl 8** a few steps to the right. This atmospheric alleyway is clustered with some of the city's most popular cafés and threads its way to the **Block Arcade 9** (p64).

Turn left into Collins St and head east to Swanston St, where you'll pass some fine boutiques, and the glorious **Manchester Unity Building 10** (p36) on the corner of Collins and Swanston Sts, a 1930s Commercial Gothic Modern marvel. The **Melbourne Town Hall 11** (p57) on the opposite corner, designed by Joseph Reed, is a classic example of gold-boom ostentation, and was the model for many a suburban town hall.

Continue east along **Collins St** (p64), known as the Paris-end of town. The gorgeous **Regent Theatre 12** (No 191) is just beyond the former city square. Opposite the Regent Theatre and hidden behind the white classical façade of the **Baptist church 13** (No 170) is an 1845 structure, making it the oldest Baptist church in Victoria. The corner of Russell and Collins Sts is watched over by **Scots 14** and **St Michael's churches 15**, textbook examples of High Victorian architecture by the prolific Joseph Reed.

At the end of Collins St, cross Spring St to Macarthur St, passing the back garden of Parliament House (diagonally to the left), and walk along to **St Patrick's Cathedral 16** (p58). Loop around Albert St into Spring St and then turn into Little Bourke St for a jaunt through **Chinatown 17** (p54).

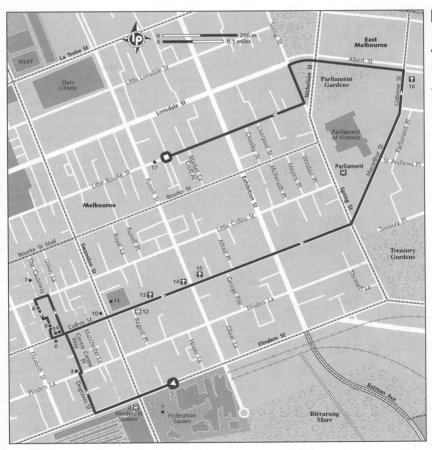

GALLERY HOP

See what Melbourne artists have to say for themselves by viewing their interpretations of contemporary culture. The following galleries are generally open from 11am to 5.30pm Tuesday to Friday and between 1pm and 5pm Saturday. See also the boxed text, p146, for a rundown on buying art.

Start at the **Australian Centre for Contemporary Art 1** (p58), then walk up Grant St (past the *Vault* sculpture, unaffectionately known as the *Yellow Peril*) to St Kilda Rd and the **National Gallery of Victoria: International 2** (p60). Cross the Yarra River at Princes Bridge – copping an eyeful down to Southgate and beyond – then cross over to Federation Square, ducking into the **Australian Centre for the Moving Image (ACMI) 3** (p62) and **Ian Potter Centre: NGV Australia 4** (p62).

Venture up Swanston St and take a right at Flinders Lane: once the hub of clothing manufacture, now the centre for commercial galleries. Don't miss the **Anna Schwartz Gallery 5** (☎ 9654 6131; www.annaschwartzgallery.com; No 185), **Gallery Gabrielle Pizzi 6** (☎ 9654 2944; www.gabrielle

pizzi.com.au; No 141) the **Flinders Lane Gallery 7** (☎ 9654 3332; www.flg.com.au; No 137), **Fortyfivedownstairs 8** (☎ 9662 9233; www.fortyfivedownstairs.com; basement, No 45) and **Span 9** (☎ 9650 0589; www.spangalleries.com .au; No 45). For excellent new design and craftworks visit **Craft Victoria 10** (☎ 9650 7775; www.craftvic.asn.au; No 31).

Turn left up Spring St, then left down Bourke St for around 200m until you reach Crossley St. Here you'll find **Gallery Funaki 11** (☎ 9662 9446; No 4) and **Crossley & Scott 12** (☎ 9639 1624; www.crossleyscott.com.au; level 2, No 26-29).

While you are processing that lot, walk right at Little Bourke St to Nicholson St. Turn right at Albert St, left at Gisborne St over Victoria Pde to Brunswick St, Fitzroy.

After a quick stop at **Alcaston 13** (☎ 9418 6444; www.alcastongallery.com.au; 11 Brunswick St), turn right into Gertrude St – marked by the fabulous carpet shop. This stretch is an artist's delight, lined with galleries and art suppliers. Start at **Dianne Tanzer Gallery 14** (☎ 416 3956; www.diannetanzergallery.net .au; No 108) showcasing emerging artists. Before you reach **Intrude 15** (☎ 9417 6033; www.intrudegallery.com.au; No 122) you'll pass its companion venue Intrude2 at 114 Gertrude St. **Seventh 16** (☎ 0407 112 482; No 155) across the road, is an artist-run space with a new show every two weeks. Cross back to the exciting **Gertrude Contemporary Art Spaces 17** (p66). **Australian Print Workshop 18** (☎ 9419 5466; www.australianprintworkshop.com; 210 Gertrude St) is the longest-running public-access print workshop in Victoria, and presents a broad collection of individually editioned prints by Australian artists.

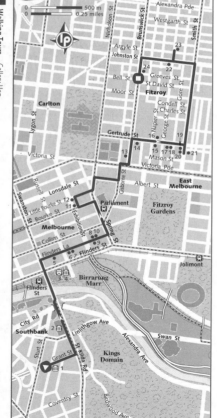

Turn right at Smith St to the artist-run **69 Smith 19** (☎ 9432 0795; www.vicnet.net .au/~smith69; No 69). Close by are **Charles Smith 20** (☎ 9419 0880; www.charlessmithgallery .com.au; No 65) and **Australian Galleries: Works on Paper 21** (☎ 9417 0800; No 50), representing established contemporary artists.

Double back down Smith St and turn left into Johnston St for a look in at the artist-run **Conical Inc 22** (☎ 9415 6958; www.conical.org.au; 3 Rochester St), and the **Centre for Contemporary Photography (CCP) 23** (p66; ☎ 9417 1549; www.ccp.org.au; 404 George St). A left into Brunswick St will take you up to **Sutton Gallery 24** (☎ 9416 0727; www.suttongallery.com.au; 254 Brunswick St) – a quality commercial space.

There are heaps of eating and drinking options around here if you need some sustenance; otherwise take tram No 96 or 112 back into the city.

ST KILDA

They say it's the ions emitted by the sea that attract us to seaside areas. If that's true, then St Kilda's air must have an oversupply, as it attracts *a lot* of people. There's an indefinable energy in St Kilda that's infectious. The area retains its original status as a seaside entertainment hub, with a fun park, some lively watering holes and, most notably, fabulous food options. Stellar cafés and restaurants accompany you all the way on this seaside circuit, so come hungry. See p111 for some suggestions.

Walk Facts

Start St Kilda Junction
Finish Corner of Fitzroy & Acland Sts
Distance 3.5km
Duration 2½ hours
Fuel Stop Monarch Cakes (p114)

From the top of Fitzroy St – near St Kilda Junction – head down towards the waterfront. Just past Lakeside Dr to your right is the palm-fringed **Albert Park Lake 1** (p78). Take a detour and jog around its 5km circumference if you're feeling frisky. Further along, before you cross Canterbury Rd, is the **St Kilda Bowling Club 2** (p141). Lawn bowls have become a popular Sunday activity for the St Kilda set; pop in if you feel like throwing your weights around on the green.

Many of the ageing buildings along Fitzroy St recall its heady past as a fashionable strip for day-trippers. The **George Hotel 3**, on the corner of Grey and Fitzroy Sts, was built in 1857. Then known as the Seaview, it has seen St Kilda's status rise and fall, and rise again. As with most of the buildings along here, the George now houses a fine restaurant, the Melbourne Wine Room (p112).

If it's a Sunday, when you reach the waterfront take the Esplanade and browse at the **Esplanade Sunday Market 4** (p76). Also on the Esplanade is the **Esplanade Hotel 5** (p128). This institution of live music, pub grub and sticky carpet has for years resisted developers' attempts to turn it into apartments.

No matter what day it is, take a stroll along **St Kilda Beach 6** (p77); on the distant headland to your right are the working docklands.

Turn up Cavell St. You'll soon come to the gracious **Palais 7** on your left. Built in

1927, it was one of the largest and best picture palaces in Australia; it seats over 3000 and is still used as a venue for live music. To your right, the scenic railway rises and dips above the fence-line of **Luna Park 8** (p76).

Turn right into the frenetic section of Acland St (p75). Then take a left at Barkly St, past its funky little boutiques, until you reach the **National Theatre 9** on the corner of Barkly and Carlisle Sts. The National houses a ballet and drama school, and stages everything from school productions to the local tap-dancing extravaganza at the end of each year.

Turn left at Carlisle, which will lead you back to Acland St. Take a right up the quiet, residential section of Acland St. Stop in at **Linden Arts Centre & Gallery 10** (p76) at No 26, set among some of St Kilda's crumbling terrace beauties, before popping back out at Fitzroy St. Tram Nos 16 and 96 run along here and into the city.

Eating

Eating

Melbourne's outstanding culinary reputation comes from the array of amazing quality produce used in innovative applications by its creative chefs. The city has a population of captive and savvy consumers who count dining out as part of their weekly entertainment. Dining options in this town are everywhere, and almost as conspicuous as footy.

Melbourne's diverse menus are all-embracing and egalitarian, and also offer a number of special-occasion options. And while food is a serious business, the city's businesses devoted to food don't take themselves too seriously. Dining is flexible to cater to the diverse desires of the city's population: order a number of small plates to share or go the whole three-course option. There's also a pervading café culture (see the boxed text, p119), with a steam-driven coffee machine at the centre of informal surrounds. And for those times when only a good honest counter meal in unfussy local surrounds will do, try pub dining (see the boxed text, p121).

The Food chapter (p38) has more on Melbourne's eating scene.

Top Five Eat Streets

- **Fitzroy St, St Kilda** (p111) International flavours, with finesse.
- **Brunswick St, Fitzroy** (p106) There's at least one of everything here.
- **Lygon St, Carlton** (p106) Honest Italian fare.
- **Chapel St, Prahran** (p110) A world of great potentials line up here.
- **Little Bourke St, Chinatown** (p102) It's all yum – from *yum cha* to *tom yum*.

The Colonial Tramcar Restaurant (boxed text, right)

Meals on Wheels

Melbourne's most popular attractions include its trams and restaurants, but it's the combination of both that has made the **Colonial Tramcar Restaurant** (☎ 9696 4000) an enduring favourite. The fleet of 1920s trams has been well and truly given the full colonial make-over with plenty of opulent touches and period detail. Stabilisers have also been fitted to ensure a steady and incident-free ride, and one-way glass windows have been installed for privacy as you tram it through the city streets in style.

There are two evening sittings daily: early dinner is from 5.45pm to 7.15pm and costs $66 a head, which includes three courses and all drinks; late dinner is from 8.35pm to 11.30pm and is $93 ($104 on Friday and Saturday), which includes five courses and all drinks. Book at least a week ahead; Friday and Saturday sittings are generally booked up two to three months in advance.

Opening Hours

Cafés and restaurants generally open seven days a week. Those restaurants that do close shut the doors on Sunday and/or Monday. Cafés open for breakfast from around 8am, with a few early openers cranking the coffee machine by 7am for nine-to-fivers. They run through lunch and dinner, closing the kitchen at around 10pm. Most restaurants are open for lunch from around noon until 3pm and for dinner from 6pm until 10ish. In this chapter we indicate whether an establishment is open for breakfast, lunch and/or dinner.

How Much?

Eating in Melbourne can be as thrifty as a $3 sushi roll, a $7 bowl of *pho* (beef and rice noodle soup) or a hearty breakfast hovering around the $10 mark. At mid-range places you can expect to pay between $15 and $25 for a main course. At the city's top restaurants you'll be looking at paying from $30 to $50.

Booking Tables

It's generally first come first served at Melbourne's informal cafés. Busier establishments have a bar or lounge area where you can have a drink until your name is reached on the waiting list. Restaurants will take bookings for lunch and dinner, so call ahead if you want to ensure a seat. We've included reservation recommendations for those restaurants that frequently fill up fast.

Tipping

Tipping is not compulsory in cafés and restaurants, but is always appreciated. The standard tip for good service is 10% and between 15% and 20% for something exceptional. If you've had lousy service, feel free to express your displeasure by not leaving a tip.

Self-Catering

The extraordinary range of quality produce in Melbourne simply has to be seen, sampled and savoured.

Markets are a great way to shop, soaking up a little local atmosphere while purchasing some of the fine seasonal produce for which the city is known. The deli section of the Queen Victoria Market (p65) will sort you out for tasty titbits that are perfect for a picnic. There's an increasing number of speciality produce stores in Melbourne (see the Food chapter, p38), with outlets limiting the lines they stock. The general philosophy is to do a little, but to do it exceptionally well, providing excellent advice and service. You can find outlets specialising in cheese, Italian produce, organic groceries, pies and chocolate.

Coles and Safeway are the two big supermarket chains; you'll find one (or both) in every neighbourhood.

CENTRAL MELBOURNE

The city is where epicurean Melbourne really shows off. Dining options are spread all over town but, like its bars, many are hidden down little streets and laneways. The majority of the city's restaurants are licensed, with each drinks list rounding out the complete dining experience.

THE EAST

BECCO Map pp202-04   *Modern Italian*
☎ 9663 3000; 11-25 Crossley St; mains $23-30;
◔ lunch & dinner Mon-Sat

Sexy in the best possible taste, Becco is a long-established favourite for an eclectic mix of diners and bar babes from the business, arts and fashion circles. Staff are invariably attentive, adding to the lively vibe. After dinner, try the upstairs bar where you can keep one eye on the comings and goings through the video camera trained on the laneway below.

BISTRO 1 Map pp202-04   *Modern European*
☎ 9654 3343; 126 Little Collins St; mains $26-32;
◔ lunch Mon-Fri, dinner Mon-Sat

Slide onto the black leather banquette and make your selection from the modern bistro menu. A suggested wine to match your meal accompanies each menu item. Offering mostly Australian wines, this licensed establishment stocks a prime selection. Classic menu items include roast pork and beer-battered whiting. Bistro 1 is popular for business lunches and postbusiness bevies at the adjoining café-bar.

CHEZ PHAT Map pp202-04   *Modern Australian*
☎ 9663 0988; level 1, 7 Waratah Pl; mains $18-25;
◔ dinner Tue-Sun

Duck down the Chinatown laneway, past the dumpsters and up a flight of stairs to Chez Phat. The capacious interior, mix-and-match furniture and earthy colours lend the Phat a modern '70s ambience. Covering the spectrum of flavours and styles, there's a playful inventiveness in the menu, which includes a number of Spanish-style dishes to share.

EUROPEAN Map pp202-04   *European*
☎ 9654 0811; 161 Spring St; mains $18-25;
◔ breakfast, lunch & dinner

It looks like it's been here forever, with recycled-wood panelling, black-and-white checked floor and, well…European ambience. Comfort dishes run through from panettone with poached fruit for breakfast, to hearty favourites such as rib eye in red wine, and osso bucco. The extensive wine list reads like a who's who of European wines.

EZARD AT ADELPHI
Map pp202-04   *Modern Australian*
☎ 9639 6811; 187 Flinders Lane; mains $29-32;
◔ lunch Mon-Fri, dinner Mon-Sat

Right up there with the best, and located in the basement of the Adelphi Hotel, celebrity chef Teage Ezard has earned his Best Young Chef accolades. Oyster shooters with *mirin* are a great start, followed by winning Asian-inspired dishes. A balmy night at the upstairs bar around the lap pool that protrudes out over the street is an added bonus.

FLOWER DRUM Map pp202-04   *Chinese*
☎ 9662 3655; 17 Market Lane; mains $35-45;
◔ lunch Mon-Sat, dinner daily

The Flower Drum continues to be Melbourne's most celebrated Chinese restaurant. The finest, freshest produce prepared with delicate professionalism keeps this Chinatown institution booked out for weeks in advance. Sumptuous, yet not exaggerated, the ostensibly simple food is delivered with the slick service you'd expect, in elegant surrounds. You may be there for only a few hours, but the experience is lasting.

GROSSI FLORENTINO Map pp202-04   *Italian*
☎ 9662 1811; 80 Bourke St; mains $38-45;
◔ lunch Mon-Fri, dinner Mon-Sat

If you're into grand dining or celebrating a special occasion, Grossi Florentino will impress. The opulence distinguishes itself in every detail, from lush murals on the walls to silverware for each table. The Cellar Bar next door is fashionably brooding, intimate and more affordable: a great place to have a special bowl of pasta ($16) and a glass of ripe Chianti.

Transport

Trams are generally the best way to get about town. The city's vast network will drop you virtually outside all of the city's eating establishments. See the boxed text, p54, for transport options around Central Melbourne, or check the Tram Network Map on p218.

IL SOLITO POSTO
Map pp202-04   *Italian*

☎ 9654 4466; basement, 113 Collins St, enter from George Pde; mains $27-35; ☯ breakfast, lunch & dinner

You will feel right at home at 'the Usual Place'. It's warm, vibrant and welcoming, just like the staff. Walk into the bar serving snacks, edgy cocktails and offering an impressive wine list. Enjoy spaghetti *vongole*, crusty bread, a beautiful glass of white at the bar, or venture downstairs for more formal dining.

KUNI'S
Map pp202-04   *Japanese*

☎ 9663 7243; 56 Little Bourke St; mains $12-27; ☯ lunch Mon-Fri, dinner Mon-Sat

Prop at the bar for fresh-made sushi and *sashimi*, or order from the breezy dining room. Kuni's does culinary classics with the same steadfast reliability as a Japanese-made car. Noodle dishes are typically uncomplicated and delicate, and the *shumai* (prawn and scallop dumplings) are as soft as clouds. Kuni's is licensed and BYO wine only.

MO MO
Map pp202-04   *Modern Middle Eastern*

☎ 9650 0660; basement, 115 Collins St, enter from George Pde; mains $26-30; ☯ lunch Mon-Fri, dinner Mon-Sat

Mo Mo is a welcome trip through the Middle East, with celebrity chef/author Greg Malouf as your guide. Malouf's deservedly excellent reputation is built on his ability to prepare authentic ingredients with deft wizardry. The adjoining rooms are reminiscent of a ducking-and-weaving market bazaar, minus the carpet sellers and apple tea.

MOVIDA
Map pp202-04   *Spanish*

☎ 9663 3038; 1 Hosier Lane; meals $15-23; ☯ lunch Mon-Fri, dinner daily

Neighbouring **Misty** (p120), one of Melbourne's original laneway bars, Movida does Spanish dining without the jugs of sangria and drunken backpackers dancing on the bar. Instead, the scene is hip city types washing down tapas and *raciones* – larger dishes to share between two – with glasses of Spanish wine.

SUPPER INN
Map pp202-04   *Chinese*

☎ 9663 4759; 15 Celestial Ave; mains $15-30; ☯ dinner

So, the word's out: bar boozers queue behind families who got there just before the group of students. Open until 2.30am, the Supper Inn is a favourite for late-night noodles, claypots or *congee*. The décor is nothing flash and the service can be blunt, but the quality dishes are excellent value. Supper Inn is licensed and BYO.

Top Five Central Melbourne Eats

- Becco (opposite)
- Mecca (p105)
- Movida (left)
- Supper Inn (left)
- Pellegrini's (p104)

VERGE
    Modern Australian

☎ 9639 9500; 1 Flinders Lane; mains $18.50-28; ☯ lunch & dinner Mon-Sat

This stylish split-level corner establishment is like an inside-out terrarium: enclosed in glass, it has a gorgeous leafy aspect out to Treasury Gardens. A back-slapping bar with a loyal following of chic city dwellers tempers the sleek, minimalist interior. The menu combines Asian and European influences, with dishes as refined and lustrous as the décor.

YU-U
Map pp202-04   *Japanese*

☎ 9639 7073; 137 Flinders Lane; mains $5.50-15; ☯ lunch & dinner Mon-Fri

There's no signage and the doorway is nondescript, so it's easy to miss, but try not to. This sparsely decorated basement restaurant does smart Japanese fare, artfully presented and assuredly delivered. Go for the set lunch menu ($15) of *bento* boxes, soup and noodles. Dinner is a progression of small dishes that substantiate your sake intake. Bookings are advised.

Cheap Eats

DON DON
Map pp202-04   *Japanese*

☎ 9670 9670; 321 Swanston St; mains $5-7; ☯ lunch Mon-Fri

Students, retailers and city kids swamp this uptown Japanese outlet. The prices are unbelievably cheap, incommensurate with the quality *bento* boxes, bowls of curry and noodles. Join the throng at this informal eatery to wolf down a lunch at an up-tempo pace.

LOUNGE
Map pp202-04   *Café*

☎ 9663 2916; level 1, 243 Swanston St; mains $10-15; ☯ lunch & dinner

Über-cool student types hang around pool tables and on the leafy balcony, picking at giant plates of nachos or hoeing into burgers and chips. At night, the lights go down and the beats are turned up when the Lounge segues into a lively, always-buzzy nightspot (see p132).

Eating – Central Melbourne

PELLEGRINI'S ESPRESSO BAR

Map pp202-O4 *Italian*

☎ 9662 1885; 66 Bourke St; mains $12-14;
🕑 lunch & dinner

This is *the* classic Melbourne coffee bar, with a reputation built over decades. It's squishy and the food's rudimentary, but we love it. Prop at the bar for an espresso any time of day, or for a plate of classic pasta at lunch or dinner time.

RIVER DISTRICT

CECCONI'S Map pp202-O4 *Italian*

☎ 9292 6887; ground level, Crown Entertainment Complex; mains $30-35; 🕑 lunch Sun-Fri, dinner daily

If the dice fell your way at the casino, then splash some cash at upmarket Cecconi's. Soaring ceilings, sandstone columns and back-lit urns are the setting for equally handsome Italian fare. The menu occasionally veers from the traditional, and there are plenty of pasta, meat and fish dishes to choose from. An extensive wine list also.

CHOCOLATE BUDDHA

Map pp202-O4 *Japanese*

☎ 9654 5688; Federation Sq; meals $14-20;
🕑 lunch & dinner

Slurping organic soup noodles, or sharing *gyoza* and the steamed soya beans *edamame* is a relaxed way to enjoy the vibe at Federation Square. Communal tables create a friendly atmosphere here. Only the complex rules for ordering here lack Zen calm. Dishes don't come out together and there's no food service at some tables; best you wait to be seated.

EQ Map pp202-O4 *Mediterranean*

☎ 9645 0644; Hamer Hall, Victorian Arts Centre; 100 St Kilda Rd; mains $20-27; 🕑 lunch & dinner Tue-Sun

Theatregoers grabbing a meal before or after a show are treated to the spectacle of city views from EQ's river-front terrace. The Mediterranean-inspired menu offers small plates to share, such as *saganaki* or dips, as well as hearty mains to keep to yourself. You'll want to guard your stuffed free-range chook from friends' prying forks.

KOKO Map pp202-O4 *Japanese*

☎ 9292 6886; level 3, Crown Entertainment Complex; mains $25-40; 🕑 lunch & dinner

A favourite spot for Melburnians dining out on someone else's expense account, this Japanese restaurant combines a sushi bar, *teppanyaki* tables and a very traditional, yet faultlessly fresh, à la carte menu. It doesn't exactly hum with atmosphere, although negotiating the edge of the decorative pond after a few sakes can be very diverting.

Owner Sisto Malaspina outside his iconic Pellegrini's Espresso Bar (above)

Eating – Central Melbourne

MECCA Map pp202-04 *Middle Eastern*
☎ 9682 2999; mid-level, Southgate; mains $25-30;
◔ lunch & dinner

Follow the spice trail to this mecca for lovers of Middle Eastern flavours. Offering Moroccan, Egyptian and Lebanese influences, the menu comprises confident combinations of prime ingredients. Sink your teeth into some *harissa*-spiced barramundi on the river-side balcony and suddenly the Yarra looks like the Nile. After demolishing the delectable nougat parfait, you'll think you're in heaven.

SCUSAMI Map pp202-04 *Italian*
☎ 9699 4111; mid-level, Southgate; mains $22-50;
◔ lunch & dinner

Feast your eyes on the city views, then feast on Scusami's outstanding dishes. This long-running restaurant has been teasing the city's culinary senses for over a decade. An excellent range of wines is offered by the glass to complement the classic and contemporary Italian fare. Expect a sprinkling of luxurious ingredients such as porcini mushrooms and truffle oil.

WALTER'S WINE BAR
Map pp202-04 *Modern Australian*
☎ 9690 9211; upper level, Southgate; mains $25-35;
◔ lunch & dinner

As the name suggests, Walter's has wine – 22 pages of it. Professional service and a tinkling piano accompaniment set the tone for this self-proclaimed fancy bistro. The menu has Italian leanings, with dishes such as tomato-and-zucchini lasagne keeping company with a generous quail *saltimbocca*. Going for dessert provides the doubly good opportunity of dipping into a soufflé and a glass of sublime dessert wine.

Cheap Eats
AUTOMATIC Map pp202-04 *Café*
☎ 9690 8500; ground level, Crown Entertainment Complex; dishes $5-20; ◔ breakfast, lunch & dinner

Another concept of Paul Mathis (see the boxed text, p40), Automatic combines a winning formula of well-priced meals in low-key surrounds. Come for bacon and eggs, wood-fired pizza, calzone or Turkish *pide*.

BLUE TRAIN Map pp202-04 *Café*
☎ 9696 0111; mid-level, Southgate; dishes $6-15;
◔ breakfast, lunch & dinner

Cavernous Blue Train keeps a frenetic pace, pumping out basic food inspired from all corners of the globe. Wood-fired pizzas, salads and dhal are turned out with factory-like efficiency. If there's a waiting list for a table, you can hang in the lounge with a drink until they're ready for you.

THE WEST
LIVEBAIT Map pp200-01 *Seafood*
☎ 9642 1500; 55b New Quay Promenade, Docklands; mains $20-35; ◔ lunch & dinner

It's as if the seafood at this unaffected eatery were from the Mediterranean Sea, picking up flavours from Spain, Greece and Italy on their journey to your otherwise bare table. Stellar views to the city are a bonus. Livebait is great for the little snappers, too, with a special kids' menu featuring that perennial favourite, fish fingers.

SUD Map pp202-04 *Italian*
☎ 9670 8451; 219 King St; mains $22-26;
◔ breakfast Mon-Fri, lunch & dinner Mon-Sat

Sud brings real style to the business end of town, and throngs of suits file in here every lunch time to sample spectacular southern Italian cooking. The menu, writ large on the walls, changes daily. This is one of the few places in the city where you can escape the tastes of Tuscany and relish the joys of the south.

SYRACUSE Map pp202-04 *Mediterranean*
☎ 9670 1777; 23 Bank Pl; mains $20-25;
◔ breakfast, lunch & dinner

Syracuse's lush interior of marble-topped tables and columned archways is set in a grand old Victorian building tucked away in a cobbled laneway. This is *the* place in the city for delicious tapas in the evening, hearty meals at lunch time, and excellent wines and a shabby-chic European ambience any time.

Cheap Eats
CAFE SEGOVIA Map pp202-04 *Café*
☎ 9650 2373; 33 Block Pl; dishes $8-15;
◔ breakfast & lunch daily, dinner Mon-Sat

Segovia was here long before a hole in the wall could constitute a café. Popular from sunrise to sunset, people spill out into the laneway, merging with patrons from surrounding cafés. Tuck your shopping bags under the table and stop in for a focaccia or light pasta meal.

DEGRAVES ESPRESSO BAR

Map pp202-04   *Café*

☎ 9654 1245; 23 Degraves St; light meals $7-13;
☺ breakfast & lunch

The rickety cinema seating and fashionable gloom make Degraves a quintessential Melbourne laneway experience. If you've overindulged in that other Melbourne laneway experience, the hip little bar with no signage, beat your hangover with poached eggs or French toast with maple syrup from the all-day breakfast menu.

CARLTON & FITZROY

Between these two suburbs, you could eat at a different restaurant each day for around a year and still not have been to them all. Carlton's Lygon St is still heavily influenced by its Italian heritage. After crossing Grattan St (coming from the city) the staged smiles and antics from the spruikers outside the many tourist restaurants give way to a more local setting, marked by unfussy bistros.

Most of Fitzroy's action is on Brunswick St around Johnston St, though Gertrude St shouldn't be overlooked. There are more options than you thought possible along Brunswick St. It's where Mongolian meets Malaysian, Russian cafeteria meets Italian café, and Spanish tapas bar meets vegetarian barn.

See the boxed text, p66, for transport options to these areas from the city.

ABLA'S Map pp206-08   *Lebanese*

☎ 9347 0006; 109 Elgin St, Carlton; mains $12-16;
☺ lunch Thu-Fri, dinner Mon-Sat

Grab a bottle of your favourite plonk and settle in at homely Abla's. If you're here for the compulsory banquet on Friday and Saturday night, bring a couple of bottles to see you through the 13 courses. Steered by chef and proprietor Abla Amad, the kitchen produces a steady flow of Lebanese flavours, from *baba ghanoush* to *majadra* – lentils and rice with yogurt. Leave room for a stiff coffee and baklava.

BLUE CHILLIES Map pp206-08   *Malaysian*

☎ 9417 0071; 182 Brunswick St, Fitzroy;
mains $10-20; ☺ lunch & dinner

The dark-wood shelving artfully stacked with Asian produce makes for ambient casual dining at Blue Chillies. For entrée try the *ikan billis* – fried whiting in *sambal* – followed by a

---

Top Five Carlton & Fitzroy Eats

- **Ladro** (below)
- **Madame Sousou** (opposite)
- **Abla's** (left)
- **Mario's** (opposite)
- **Tiamo** (opposite)

---

piquant creamy laksa. Meals come in quick succession, so if you want to linger, let the obliging staff know. You can BYO wine or swill from the decent varieties on offer.

ICI Map pp206-08   *Café*

☎ 9417 2274; 359 Napier St, Fitzroy; dishes $7-12;
☺ breakfast & lunch

This small bluestone café is a cosy oasis situated behind the fast pace of Brunswick St and well worth finding for superb coffee and the unique breakfast menu. Try Moroccan spiced couscous with yogurt and almonds, or French toast with mixed berries and caramel *marscapone*, or just relax with the paper as the morning travels through the roundabout outside. Ici has dinner plans, too, pending council approval.

JIMMY WATSON'S Map pp206-08 *European*

☎ 9347 3985; 333 Lygon St, Carlton; mains $19-27;
☺ lunch Mon-Sat, dinner Tue-Sat

Jimmy Watson's is a Lygon St stalwart, dependably feeding students, families and business folk over two Watson generations. The humble interior of this classic bistro leads to a popular courtyard 'beer garden' – a misnomer, given that dry-and-dry is the most beerlike beverage on offer (no less tasty). Wine is the speciality here, with some serious options available from the dusty cellar. The egalitarian menu includes vegetarian dishes such as baked cheese pudding, as well as grills such as roo fillet with orange and mint couscous.

LADRO Map pp206-08   *Italian/Pizzeria*

☎ 9417 7575; 224a Gertrude St, Fitzroy; pizza $12-20;
☺ dinner Wed-Sun

Simple, inexpensive and probably the best pizza you'll ever have. Not one shred of processed ham will be found here. Chunks of spicy sausage sit in melted mozzarella among fennel on traditionally thin bases. Toppings are suited for pizza lovers possessing a more adventurous palate. Communal dining is the culture at Ladro where you book for a seat, not a table. Bookings essential.

MADAME SOUSOU Map pp206-08 *Italian*

☎ 9417 0400; 231 Brunswick St, Fitzroy;
mains $18-27; ☺ **breakfast, lunch & dinner**

Elbow your dinner partner out of the way to get the soft-leather banquette seat. The polished concrete floors, copper trimmings and aged posters give the impression you're in for some French dining. Not so; Sousou is sublime Italian, with organic produce used wherever possible. Your heavy cutlery is as substantial as the robust risotto fungi. Stick around for a *digestif* and perhaps a cigar from the humidor.

MARIOS Map pp206-08 *Café*

☎ 9417 3343; 303 Brunswick St, Fitzroy; dishes $7.50-18;
☺ **breakfast, lunch & dinner**

Breakfast, accepted as one of the best, can be ordered all day. Waiting for a table is part of the ritual so grab a superb coffee and position at the bar window for a moment spent checking out the Fitzroy scene. Marios' waiters run a tight ship with terrific service and speedy customer turnover; the wait is never long.

MRS JONES Map pp206-08 *Modern Australian*

☎ 9347 3312; www.mrsjones.com.au;
312 Drummond St, Carlton; 2-course meal $35;
☺ **breakfast Sat & Sun, lunch Friday, dinner Tue-Sat**

Diners are offered a choice of three entrees and three mains, which change weekly and can be reviewed on the website before booking. Sides and wine cost extra with the set two-course meal. This is innovative dining, with exceptional standards in flavour and presentation.

NEWTOWN SC Map pp206-08 *Café*

☎ 9415 7337; 180 Brunswick St, Fitzroy; breakfast $5-10;
☺ **breakfast, lunch**

Newtown's resident cat is an expert at dodging the many pairs of trendy shoes constantly shuffling through this small space. Morning takeaway caffeine fixes (one of the city's best) and delicious pastries such as the Portuguese custard tarts, lamingtons and *rugelach* – a scroll topped with pecans and caramel – are popular. Order the famous baked beans with feta, if you manage to find a seat.

PIREAUS BLUES Map pp206-08 *Greek*

☎ 9417 0222; 310 Brunswick St, Fitzroy; mains $12-23;
☺ **lunch & dinner**

Authentic, home-cooked Cretan dishes are served from this warm and lively restaurant with busy tables seating mainly parties of four

or larger. Pireaus Blues is one of the best Hellenic dining experiences in this city, home to the world's third-largest Greek population. Make room, after delicious char-grilled meats and seafood, for *loukoumades* (warm doughnuts drenched in honey and walnuts).

SHAKAHARI Map pp206-08 *Vegetarian*

☎ 9347 3848; 201 Faraday St, Carlton; mains $14-15.50;
☺ **lunch Mon-Sat, dinner daily**

Shakahari gives vegetarianism a good name. Its limited seasonal menu reflects both Asian and European influences, with dishes made from all-natural prime ingredients. Established over 20 years ago, Shakahari takes itself seriously, which is mirrored in its at-times earnest atmosphere. If the weather is in your favour, ask to be seated in the palm-fringed courtyard. The curries, *tagines* and noodle dishes are heroic, whatever the setting.

TIAMO Map pp206-08 *Italian*

☎ 9347 5759; 303 Lygon St, Carlton; mains $11-16;
☺ **breakfast, lunch & dinner**

From 7am, Tiamo's front window displays men sitting at the bar, downing espressos and chatting in Italian with the waiters. The dark and atmospheric interior has attracted local thespians, artists and Italophiles since the 1960s. Tiamo is licensed and recommended for lunch and dinner. Expect value for money and generous portions of simple and traditional cuisine at this treasured trattoria.

Cheap Eats
BABKA BAKERY CAFE

Map pp206-08 *Bakery/Café*

☎ 9416 0091; 358 Brunswick St, Fitzroy; dishes $7-15;
☺ **breakfast & lunch Tue-Sun**

The heavenly aroma of cinnamon and freshly baked bread is a good incentive to hang around if waiting for a table or takeaway coffee. Pastries are sweet, buttery and warm, much like the smiles and service from the waitresses. A Russian influence is present with borscht (a traditional beetroot and potato soup) on the menu. Babka encompasses the wholesome values of 1950s nostalgia.

BRUNETTI Map pp206-08 *Roman Pasticceria*

☎ 9347 2801; 194-204 Faraday St, Carlton;
café dishes $3-7, restaurant mains $12-23;
☺ **breakfast, lunch & dinner**

Owner and pastry chef Giorgio Angelé migrated to Australia after entering the country as the pastry chef for the 1956 Italian Olympic team. Brunetti is famous for its exceptional coffee and authentic Roman patisserie. Traditional European cuisine can also be experienced here, but alfresco coffee and *biscotti*, tiramisu or delicious *graffe* (custard filled donuts) is the way locals regularly visit.

RETRO CAFE Map pp206-08 *Café*
☎ 9419 9103; 413 Brunswick St, Fitzroy; mains $14-23; breakfast, lunch & dinner
Littlies love this candy-coloured café, with its separate kids' menu, toy box and water wall. There's something for all ages, be it a risotto, stack of meat or a burger. Reasonable prices make Retro a popular choice, especially for families and especially on weekends.

ROSAMONDE Map pp206-08 *Café*
☎ 9406 2839; rear 191 Smith St, Fitzroy, enter from Charles St; dishes $5-8.50; breakfast & lunch
Keep your eyes open for this tiny café with no sign. Rosamond offers a selection of baguettes, cakes and fruit salads, and is a popular hangout for the artists from the nearby Gertrude St studios who congregate to discuss upcoming shows over coffee or herbal tea.

VEGIE BAR Map pp206-08 *Vegetarian*
☎ 9417 6935; 380 Brunswick St, Fitzroy; dishes $3-15; lunch & dinner
You may wonder if the entire population of Melbourne is vegetarian as you wait for a table at this popular café. This is definitely not the place for a romantic rendezvous, but you could make some new acquaintances at one of the communal tables. Bring an appetite – the portions are as healthy as the dishes themselves.

PARKVILLE & NORTH MELBOURNE
This area might lack the glamour and popularity of other inner suburbs, but there are some great local places worth haunting if you find yourself hungry in the area's quiet, semi-industrial streets. Errol St has the highest number of choices. See the boxed text, p68, for transport options from the city.

AKITA Map p209 *Japanese*
☎ 9326 5766; cnr Courtney & Blackwood Sts, North Melbourne; mains $12-24; lunch & dinner Mon-Fri
Akita might be a little off the beaten track but it's considered one of the best Japanese restaurants in town. The à la carte menu is succinct, with sublime sushi and *sashimi*, but it's the specials board that attracts everyone's attention. Akita is licensed, with a small wine list rounded out by beer and sake, or you can BYO. Bookings are essential.

COURTHOUSE DINING ROOM
Map p209 *Modern Australian*
☎ 9329 5394; 86-90 Errol St, North Melbourne; mains $22-26; lunch Mon-Fri, dinner Mon-Sat
This new-fashioned pub is another notch in the gentrification belt enclosing the inner city. There's no sign of the sticky carpets and smoke-stained walls of yesteryear. Instead, Courthouse is all dark wood and linen. The menu echoes the elegant surrounds and reflects world influences from Thai to Eurocentric.

DON CAMILLO'S Map p209 *Italian*
☎ 9329 8883; 215 Victoria St, North Melbourne; dishes $4-14; breakfast & lunch daily, dinner Thu & Fri
The terrazzo floor at this classic 1950s Italian café-restaurant was one of the first to be laid in Melbourne. Not much has changed, save for the photos of footballers adorning the walls; many of whom have been spotted eating a high-protein egg breakfast here. A couple of blocks up from the Queen Victoria Market, Don Camillo's serves traditional Italian: soup, pasta, seafood and meat dishes.

INNER NORTH
The dappled streets of the city's north have a surprisingly high number of cafés and restaurants. The northern end of Brunswick St, in North Fitzroy, has a number of interesting options that sate the area's savvy young families. Eating options in Rathdowne St, North Carlton, are characterised by an easy-paced refinement. See the boxed text, p70, for details of transport options.

HIBISCUS Map p210 *Modern Australian*
☎ 9497 8101; 167 St Georges Rd, North Fitzroy; mains $16-19; breakfast & lunch Tue-Sun, dinner Tue-Sat
Informal and clean-cut Hibiscus comfortably sates the similarly characterised locals. The sparse, modern interior reflects the elegant restraint of owner/chef Steve Rogers' menu. There's a pure quality to the dishes: flavours are clean and subtle. Share a range of small plates, such as hazelnut-crumbed goats cheese with spiced eggplant, or baby octopus, chorizo and polenta croutons. Mains generally include a few pastas, plus succulent meat dishes.

I CARUSI Map p210 — *Italian/Pizzeria*
☎ 9386 5522; 46a Holmes St, Brunswick East; pizza $14-18; ☾ dinner Tue-Sun

Find out how pizza became so popular by tasting the definitive version. I Carusi does thin, crisp crusts without too much adornment. Synergic combinations of toppings, as well as basic classics, are at the centre of all tables here. I Carusi is BYO and fills up fast, so book ahead or come early.

MATTEO'S Map p210 — *Italian*
☎ 9481 1177; 533 Brunswick St, North Fitzroy; mains $28; ☾ lunch Sun-Fri, dinner daily

A plush interior, starched linen, impeccable service, impressive wine list and outstanding modern Italian-Australian cuisine are the ingredients that make Matteo's one to bookmark. Degustation menus (including vegetarian) and platters to share round out the offerings at this warm and welcoming restaurant.

MOROCCAN SOUP BAR
Map p210 — *North African/Vegetarian*
☎ 9482 4240; 183 St Georges Rd, North Fitzroy; dishes $10-14; ☾ dinner Tue-Sun

The alcohol-free Moroccan Soup Bar delivers its menu verbally; offerings consist of authentic recipes served up in marvellously Maghreb surrounds. Pay close attention to hear the choice of three soups and nine mains, which might be vegetables and quince on couscous, a *tagine* or chickpea bake.

PINNACLE Map p210 — *Bistro*
☎ 9489 3044; 251 St Georges Rd, North Fitzroy; mains $14-18; ☾ dinner

The Pinnacle reaches new heights in offbeat dining. The wedge-shaped building lends a warped *Alice in Wonderland* quality to the interior, which is adorned with kitsch trinkets. Try the Bo Peep lamb cutlets or Little Chihuahuas (mini frankfurts with cheese and mustard). There's also a cosy bar area, beer garden and lounge area that's stellar for a drink after seeing a show at the **Storeroom** (p134) across the road.

RATHDOWNE STREET FOODSTORE
Map p210 — *Café*
☎ 9347 4064; 617 Rathdowne St, North Carlton; dishes $11-24; ☾ breakfast, lunch & dinner

Classical music softly mingles with the dreamy scent of freshly baked bread in this calming, sun-soaked room. Breakfast on buttermilk pancakes and lavender-infused ice cream with exceptional coffee, or choose gourmet-quality

risotto for lunch or dinner. The delicious menu changes to suit seasonal produce. Foodstore provides a dining experience with class and care without intimidation.

ABBOTSFORD & RICHMOND

Experience a slice of Vietnam, without the pricey airfare, by taking a walk down Victoria St, Richmond. Packed with authentic Vietnamese restaurants and grocers, Victoria St is perennially popular for excellent dishes at bargain prices. Otherwise, interesting dining options are sprinkled across the area. See the boxed text, p71, for transport options.

PEARL Map p212 — *Modern Australian*
☎ 9421 4599; 631-633 Church St, Richmond; mains $28-34; ☾ breakfast Sat & Sun, lunch & dinner daily

Oh, so fine! If you only come out of your shell for one occasion, make it Pearl. The stylish, minimalist dining room with impeccable service is confidently refined without pretence. Foodies love the adventurous menu, especially the watermelon salad with tomato jelly and feta. Pearl comes replete with a jovial bar area, where svelte young things rah-rah until late.

PUBLIC HOUSE Map p211 — *Modern Pub*
☎ 9421 0187; 433-435 Church St, Richmond; mains $17-24; ☾ lunch Fri-Sun, dinner daily

It's more than the alcohol at Public House that is intoxicating. The heady atmosphere is infectious at this bustling modern pub. From the stylish, comfortable surrounds (by architectural firm Six Degrees) to the menu – centred on small plates for sharing – it's built for socialising. Tapas-style dishes typically contain Spanish influences, but also include Mediterranean and Middle Eastern flavours.

RICHMOND HILL CAFE & LARDER
Map p211 — *Mediterranean*
☎ 9421 2808; 48-50 Bridge Rd, Richmond; breakfast $8-16, dinner $28; ☾ breakfast & lunch daily, dinner Tue-Sun

Equal parts produce store, larder, café and restaurant, Richmond Hill Cafe & Larder does it all well. That's what you'd expect from celebrity chef/restaurateur/author Stephanie Alexander. The large, open, unfussy space is perfect for the popular breakfasts, lunches and evening dishes – all imbued with simplicity and style.

Cheap Eats
HA LONG BAY

Map p211   *Vietnamese*
☎ 9429 3268; 82 Victoria St, Richmond; mains $7-14;
☾ breakfast, lunch & dinner

In a long stretch of same-same restaurants, Ha Long is outstanding for its friendly service and cheery surrounds. The extensive menu includes all your Vietnamese favourites: rice and noodles done every way, with a choice of meats and vegetables. Dishes are as sprightly and colourful as the décor.

MINH MINH Map p211   *Southeast Asian*
☎ 9427 7891; 94 Victoria St, Richmond; mains $8-16;
☾ lunch & dinner

A smart fit-out and fine Thai, Lao and Vietnamese dishes distinguish Minh Minh. You can't beat the crispy fried calamari with lemon grass and chilli, and the springiest spring rolls in Victoria St. Service is high-camp and friendly. Tables are crammed cheek-by-jowl, with two or more sittings per night.

NEW YORK TOMATO Map p211   *Café*
☎ 9429 0505; cnr New & York Sts, Richmond; mains $8-12; ☾ breakfast & lunch

This place is so laid-back you'd think you were in someone's backyard; well…you are, actually. At the rear of a modern townhouse, the owners transformed the garage space and downstairs, added a communal table and invited the neighbourhood in. Try the berry porridge in brown sugar, and, for lunch, the pumpkin and chickpea fritters or tandoori chicken *pide*.

SOUTH YARRA, TOORAK & PRAHRAN

It's perpetually peak hour along Chapel St, with diners and drinkers converging from all corners for a piece of the action. The typically more sedate South Yarra end gives way to the bohemian Prahran scene as you head south. See p73 for transport options from town.

BLAKES CAFETERIA

Map p212   *Modern Australian*
☎ 9510 3900; 132a Greville St, Prahran; mains $20-25; ☾ breakfast & lunch daily, dinner Mon-Sat

Nude light bulbs draped from the stainless steel rafters are characteristic touches of this

stylish café frequented by Greville St groovers. The pert menu includes KFQ (Kentucky fried quail) and pan-fried squid with papaw. Blakes doesn't take bookings, but has a vibey bar next door for waiting patrons.

BOTANICAL Map pp214-15 *Modern Australian*
☎ 9820 7888; 169 Domain Rd, South Yarra; mains $23-34; ☾ breakfast, lunch & dinner

Capacious and chic, the Botanical is the darling of South Yarra. Its iconic location opposite the Botanical Gardens, bold menu and innovative approach won it the *Age Good Food Guide*'s Restaurant of the Year (2004). Indicative menu items include truffle and mushroom omelette with prawn, and tuna *sashimi* with *wasabi* custard.

DA NOI Map p212   *Italian*
☎ 9866 5975; 95 Toorak Rd, South Yarra; mains $25-34; ☾ lunch Fri-Sun, dinner daily

Da Noi has captured the imagination of diners with its exciting Sardinian dishes and constantly changing seasonal menu. The spontaneous kitchen might reinterpret the chef's special three times a night. Just go with it; it's a unique experience it seems many are keen to know. Bookings are advised.

DAVID'S Map p212   *Chinese*
☎ 9529 5199; 4 Cecil Pl, Prahran; mains $17-25; ☾ lunch daily, dinner Fri & Sat

The eponymous owner is also a Chinese herbalist and runs a nearby teashop. Don't be surprised to find sprinklings of health-giving ingredients such as ginseng and wolfberries among the mostly Shanghainese dishes. David's is licensed, but you might want to go with the health theme and stick to the enormous array of exotic teas also on offer.

JACQUES REYMOND

Map p212   *Modern Australian*
☎ 9525 2178; 78 Williams Rd, Prahran; 2-course menu $68; ☾ lunch Thu & Fri, dinner Tue-Sat

This is serious dining on a grand sumptuous scale. Frock up for the glamorous occasion with its striking Victorian-mansion setting. The set menu is the best way to appreciate the complex dishes, which might include oysters and foie gras with cucumber, spaghettini and brains. Quite a mouthful.

Cheap Eats

ORANGE Map p212 — *Café/Bar*
☎ 9529 1644; 126 Chapel St, Prahran; mains $14-23;
⏲ breakfast & lunch daily, dinner Wed-Sun

Orange straddles the café/bar label with ease, its well-worn vinyl banquettes cushioning fashionable bums for early breakfasts (from 7am) and late-night beverages (open until 2am Thursday to Sunday). Serving good coffee during the day, at night Orange slows its grinders and replaces teaspoons with bar coasters, and chooses Screamin' Jay Hawkins over Nina Simone LPs.

WINDSOR CASTLE Map p212 — *Pub*
☎ 9525 0239; 89 Albert St, Windsor; mains $16;
⏲ lunch Thu-Sun, dinner daily

You know you've arrived when you see the pink elephants walking across the roof. Pub retro favourites are given a modern spin, or dished up plain and simple, such as fish fingers with mushy peas. Dine in the chocolate-velour interior or spacious beer garden, especially on a Sunday when the Castle is most popular.

ST KILDA

Fitzroy St is one of the city's most famed and popular eating strips, for both foodies and funsters. Serious dining options mix it with casual choices and downright basic pub food (see the Esplanade Hotel, p128). Acland St is renowned for its fine European delicatessens and cake shops, and the traditional Sunday promenade, which includes a spell at impossibly delicious window displays. An avalanche of cafés, bars and restaurants also smothers the street.

See the boxed text, p75, for transport options from the city.

BEDOUIN KITCHEN
Map p213 — *Middle Eastern*
☎ 9534 0888; 103 Grey St; mains $15-25;
⏲ breakfast, lunch & dinner

With its smattering of expensive furniture stores and warehouse apartments, the inter-

section of Grey and Inkerman Sts will soon be as upwardly mobile as the rest of St Kilda. The young executives are going to love the Bedouin Kitchen, a dark and moody Middle Eastern and North African canteen serving *mezze* platters, claypots and roast pigeon.

BLUECORN Map p213 — *Modern Mexican*
☎ 9534 5996; 205 Barkly St; mains $12-25;
⏲ lunch Sat & Sun, dinner daily

Despite promoting itself as a 'real' Mexican restaurant, most dishes at Bluecorn are liberally doused in the salsa, sour cream and guacamole you'd expect of a suburban Taco Bell. The locals don't seem bothered by the lack of authenticity, however, as Bluecorn is perennially packed out.

CAFE A TAGLIO Map p213 — *Italian/Pizzeria*
☎ 9534 1344; 157a Fitzroy St; pizza $5-6, mains $13-18;
⏲ lunch & dinner

Line up at the glass cabinet to select your sliver of heaven: thin-crust pizza. The hard work done, sip a glass of wine or down a beer while your potato and leek or mushroom and gorgonzola slice is heated. A range of mains grace the blackboard menu, including a tender barbecued calamari salad.

CAFE DI STASIO Map p213 — *Italian*
☎ 9525 3999; 31a Fitzroy St; mains $27-38;
⏲ lunch & dinner

White-jacketed waiters, a jazz soundtrack and subdued lighting provide moody ambience at di Stasio (not to mention the original Bill Henson photograph gracing the back wall). But it's

Eating – St Kilda

the sublime Italian food, such as handsome meat dishes, that has kept this place at the top of the dining food chain for over 15 years.

CARLISLE WINE BAR
Map pp200-01 *Italian*
☎ 9531 3222; 137 Carlisle St, Balaclava; mains $14-27; breakfast Sat & Sun, lunch Thu-Sun, dinner daily

The Carlisle Wine Bar represents the changing face of East St Kilda. Nestled between the old-school Russian bakeries and Jewish delis of Carlisle St this chic bar and restaurant offers seasonal, Italian-style fare in comfortable surrounds. The bar gets rowdy come Friday and Saturday nights. The wine list won 'one glass' in 2003's Wine List of the Year awards.

CICCIOLINA
Map p213 *Modern Mediterranean*
☎ 9525 3333; 130 Acland St; mains $17.50-27; lunch & dinner

There's no shortage of wannabes hoping for a spot here. Cicciolina's back bar is where spunky diners go to wait in expectation of their equally spunky dishes, such as snapper with a champagne and saffron velouté. The boutique wine list and casual but attentive atmosphere are a sheer delight. Cicciolina doesn't take bookings, so expect a stint in the back bar first. The sultry smoky bar has more elegance than its political namesake. The huge leather booths and exceptional wine list may make it hard for you to move on anywhere else.

CIRCA, THE PRINCE
Map p213 *Modern European*
☎ 9536 1122; 2 Acland St; mains $25-35; breakfast, lunch & dinner

The décor at the Prince's renowned dining room is as silky and indulgent as the food. Groovy and refined at the same time, it's the best place in Melbourne for combining a credit card and diet blowout. Or halve the cost and stop by for the classiest, cosiest breakfast in the 'hood.

CLAYPOTS Map p213 *Claypot/Seafood*
☎ 9534 1282; 213 Barkly St; meals $10-15, $70 for a stingray to share; lunch & dinner

Claypots offers the kind of warming comfort food that you crave on wintry Melbourne evenings. It's great value for generous amounts of seafood and if there are a few of you, order some dishes to share. Bookings aren't accepted but staff will often find a way to squeeze you in somehow.

Top Five St Kilda Eats
- **Stokehouse** (opposite)
- **Tolarno** (opposite)
- **Pelican** (below)
- **Circa, the Prince** (left)
- **Bala's** (opposite)

DONOVANS
Map p213 *Modern Mediterranean*
☎ 9534 8221; 40 Jacka Blvd; dishes $24-35; lunch & dinner

Clomp across the hardwood floor of this up-market beach-house-style restaurant and try to snaffle a window seat for divine bay views, made cosier by a crackling log fire. This is country-style cooking with panache, such as chicken and tarragon pie or barbecued fish. With its beach-side position and dignified atmosphere, Donovan's commands dining respect.

MELBOURNE WINE ROOM
Map p213 *Italian*
☎ 9525 5599; 125 Fitzroy St; mains $24-33; dinner Tue-Sat, front bar lunch Fri-Sun, dinner daily

In the iconic George Hotel, the refined Wine Room is like the cone of silence compared to the heaving front bar next door (where bar meals are also available). Naturally for a wine room, there's a stellar selection on offer. Critics have acknowledged the service here as the city's best, although the Wine Room's overall reputation for superfine food is sliding.

PELICAN Map p213 *Mediterranean*
☎ 9525 5847; cnr Fitzroy & Park Sts; tapas $6-10, mains $18-23; breakfast, lunch & dinner

St Kilda's groovy young things love Pelican. Its idiosyncratic design (by the ubiquitous Six Degrees team) makes the most of its corner position with a wraparound terrace. Tapas are the heroes here; order pickled octopus or fried cheese balls while watching the Fitzroy St circus in full swing. Pelican's casual ambience sits well with breakfasters, too; especially champagne breakfasters.

SOUL MAMA Map p213 *Vegetarian*
☎ 9525 3338; St Kilda Sea Baths, Shop 10, 10 Jacka Blvd; mains $10-15; lunch & dinner

Dine on delicious vegetarian food while gazing out over Port Phillip Bay. If lining up to choose your food seems like too much work, you can ask your waiter to make a selection for you. This stylish, popular restaurant is a place where your nonvegetarian friends will also feel comfortable.

STOKEHOUSE Map p213 *Modern Australian*
☎ 9525 5555; 30 Jacka Blvd; mains upstairs $27.50-32, dishes downstairs $10-20; ☺ lunch & dinner

You'll be utterly stoked by the fine dining and quintessential St Kilda seaside views upstairs at the Stokehouse. The exceptional seafood and service that never misses a beat live up to their respectable reputations. Downstairs is downmarket, with a frenetic atmosphere and simple menu with antipasto, burgers, fish and chips, and gourmet pizza.

TOLARNO Map p213 *Bistro*
☎ 9525 0200; 42 Fitzroy St; mains $10-27; ☺ lunch & dinner

When the bustle of Fitzroy St becomes too much, head across to TV-chef Iain Hewitson's Tolarno bistro and experience old St Kilda. Originally established in 1967 by Georges and Mirka Mora, Tolarno offers à la carte dining,

or you can eat comfort food more casually in the front bar. Look out for Mirka's murals while you're there.

Cheap Eats
BAKER D CHIRICO Map p213 *Bakery/Café*
☎ 9534 3777; 149 Fitzroy St; dishes $2-15; ☺ breakfast & lunch

Melbourne isn't short of bakery/cafés, but the Baker's kill-your-granny-for-them loaves and pastries put it way ahead of the competition. Go in the morning for a coffee, a rhubarb Danish, a sugar doughnut oozing custard or all of the above. For lunch, try silver beet and olive calzone or a sandwich on *casalinga*, all wrapped up in a chic greaseproof paper collar.

BALA'S Map p213 *Asian*
☎ 9534 6116; 1e Shakespeare Grove; dishes $2.50-12; ☺ lunch & dinner

Bala's is always crowded, but with hearty, tasty mains available for less than $12 (and snacks for under $2) it's not surprising. Eat at one

Baker D Chirico, St Kilda (above)

of the few tables in the shop, or grab some takeaway and head down to the beach. The home-made lassis are great too, if you can fit one in.

MONARCH Map p213 *Cakes*
☎ 9534 2972; 103 Acland St; $1-15; ⏰ 7am-10pm

Coming home from a day in Acland St without a slab of ricotta cheesecake, some shortbread or a wedge of plum cake from Monarch is virtually illegal in Melbourne. If you've enjoyed one of its traditional European-style cakes on the footpath over a cup of coffee, you may possibly be excused.

WALL TWO 80 Map pp200-01 *Café*
☎ 9593 8280; rear 280 Carlisle St; dishes $5.50-9; ⏰ breakfast & lunch

Sit outside with your dog against the eponymous wall, or congregate with friends around the big table inside. You may think you've come just for coffee, but try resisting the smell of the toasted *pides* or the sight of the cakes once you're there. On hot days, the *granitas* are perfect.

SOUTH MELBOURNE & ALBERT PARK

Seaside and historic South Melbourne, home to a thriving produce market, home-wares stores, advertising agencies and video production houses, has plenty of good cafés and restaurants. Park, Clarendon and Coventry Sts are the most popular areas.

With its wide footpaths and classic Victorian architecture, leafy Albert Park has a number of fine casual cafés around Bridport St and Victoria Ave, a strip known as Dundas Pl.

See the boxed text, p78, for transport options from the city.

ISTHMUS OF KRA Map pp214-15 *Asian*
☎ 9690 3688; 50 Park St, South Melbourne; mains $16-28; ⏰ lunch & dinner

This classy establishment specialises in Thai and Nonya cuisines. You could try the house speciality, roast duck in red curry, or perhaps a superb Northern Thai laksa. If you take some friends, you can choose from one of three banquet options. Eat in the cool, lush courtyard in summer or inside, under the gaze of Hanuman, the monkey god. It's a good idea to book.

KAMEL Map pp214-15 *Café*
☎ 9696 5924; 19 Victoria Ave, Albert Park; dishes $5.50-$21; ⏰ breakfast, lunch & dinner Tue -Sun

A range of *mezze* dishes with North African and Middle Eastern inspiration are on offer here. There are plenty of great choices but, whatever you do, don't miss the zucchini-and-mint fritters. There's a well-priced wine list and a snug lounge area for a quiet drink. Bask over breakfast in the sunny courtyard; settle in and order the mushrooms with feta.

LA MADRAGUE Map pp214-15 *French*
☎ 9699 9627; 171 Buckhurst St, South Melbourne; mains $17-32; ⏰ lunch & dinner

La Madrague has been tucked away in an unlikely side street for over 25 years. The signature dish is the *confit canard*; try it with a little Krug rosé or, if you're not so flush, an Australian wine from the well-balanced selection of local and international wines. This is traditional French food, so be prepared for offal'n'all.

MISUZU Map pp214-15 *Japanese*
☎ 9699 9022; 3-7 Victoria Ave, Albert Park; mains downstairs $11-20, upstairs $25-30; ⏰ lunch & dinner

The ground floor is a popular café, with a more exclusive restaurant upstairs. Mizuzu's menu includes whopping noodle, rice and curry dishes, divine tempuras and takeaway options from the mouth-watering sushi bar. Sit outside under lantern-hung trees, or inside surrounded by murals and dark wood. Pop next door to Umami for a drink and sample sake from a vast selection.

MONTAGUE FOOD STORE
Map pp214-15 *Café*
☎ 9682 9680; 406 Park St, South Melbourne; dishes $4-15, Mon-Fri; ⏰ breakfast & lunch

This sunlit café has a friendly, low-key atmosphere. The Montague serves a range of breakfasts and lunches, incorporating its own breads, jams and relishes. The *croque-monsieur* will keep you going for days or if you insist on a healthier option, the wattle seed granola is really good. Filled baguettes, salads, cakes and daily specials round out the selection.

O'CONNELL'S Map pp214-15 *Pub*
☎ 9699 9600; cnr Montague & Coventry Sts, South Melbourne; mains $16-30; ⏰ lunch & dinner

Equal parts local pub and great restaurant, meet in O'Connell's bar for predinner drinks, or settle in for the evening – the same menu is available across the whole place. The dining room is a little posher, but welcoming and comes with an extensive wine list. The food is Modern Australian – try the cracking O'Connell's burger or fried zucchini flowers.

WILLIAMSTOWN

Williamstown has an abundance of cafés and restaurants, most of them spread along Nelson Pl and most of them providing honest fare to fuel the influx of day-trippers and weekend visitors. You wouldn't necessarily cross town for the food offerings alone, but waterfront dining is part of the experience here. See the boxed text, p79, for transport from the city.

PARADE DELI & FINE FOODS
Map p216   *Café*
☎ 9397 6177; 8 Douglas Pde; dishes $6-12;
☷ breakfast & lunch

Part deli, part café, this is a local fave providing superb deli produce, as well as dishes prepared from the ingredients in the cabinets. Pull in for a coffee or light lunch of focaccia, or grab a hunk of cheese and some salami to nosh down on the waterfront at Commonwealth Reserve.

REMVI BY THE BAY Map p216   *Greek*
☎ 9397 1818; 125 Nelson Pl; mains around $15;
☷ lunch Sun, dinner Tue-Sun

This is one of Williamstown's newer additions, which quickly won over the locals with its classic Greek food. Expect traditional favourites, such as lamb dishes and calamari, as well as those perennial ingredients of oregano and feta.

Bubble Tea

Bubble teashops are bursting onto almost every street corner in Footscray. These bright cutesy stores sell a staggering variety of bubble tea. The uniting ingredients are tea, sugar, milk and 'bubbles', which are little balls made from sago. Choose a flavour, stab the heat-sealed lid with the extra wide straw and start sucking up sweet iced-tea – the conduit for little gummy balls that shoot into your mouth like minicannonballs. You have to experience bubble tea once in your lifetime.

SIREN'S Map p216   *Modern Australian*
☎ 9397 7811; Beach Pavilion, Esplanade; mains $23;
☷ lunch & dinner

This Art Deco bathing pavilion propped right on the bay has been converted into a smart bar and bistro and a more formal restaurant. The seafood-oriented restaurant menu leans towards Mediterranean flavours, such as barramundi with capers and Spanish onion. The bistro menu features a range of tapas ($4 to $8) and gourmet pizzas ($15 to $19).

STRAND SEAFOOD RESTAURANT
Map p216   *Seafood*
☎ 9397 7474; 1 The Strand; mains $25-30;
☷ breakfast, lunch & dinner

The bobbing boats on the bay just outside and views to the city are the Strand's biggest drawcard. The menu covers a range of seafood dishes that won't win any prizes for imagination. But hey, it's the view you're paying for here.

INNER WEST

The villagelike atmosphere of Yarraville has spawned a number of cafés and restaurants that are starting to grab the attention of more than the locals. Particularly popular during the day, Yarraville's cosy scene makes a good adjunct to a visit to the West. Hopkins Rd in Footscray has numerous of Vietnamese restaurants rivalling Victoria St, Richmond for quality and choice. See the boxed text, p81, for transport options from the city.

BO DE TRAI Map pp200-01   *Vegetarian*
☎ 9689 9909; 94 Hopkins St, Footscray; mains around $10; ☷ breakfast, lunch & dinner

You've never tasted wontons this good, not to mention the tofu with chilli and lemongrass. There's a fair selection of imitation meat dishes, like the lamb claypot, which is a favourite of mock-meat lovers. Run by a Buddhist temple, Bo De Trai's tasty fare will get you closer to Nirvana.

CAFE FIDAMA Map pp200-01   *Café*
☎ 9687 0133; 34 Ballarat St, Yarraville; mains $15-20;
☷ breakfast, lunch & dinner

Rich and smooth chocolate-coloured surrounds are enough to make you melt at Yarraville's hottest café-restaurant. Book a table to wake up to pancakes and omelettes, or for a lunch or dinner of fancy pasta. Warm and welcoming service at this local gem will make you smile.

YARRAVILLE HOTEL
Map pp200-01   *Pub*
☎ 9687 2012; 58 Ballarat St, Yarraville; dishes around $13; ☽ lunch & dinner Mon-Sat

A genuine local where there's sport on the telly and everyone knows everyone, the Yarraville Hotel is a refreshing change from the tricked-up bistros of most inner-city pubs. Walk through the toilets to the back bistro with its typically laconic menu, such as roast and gravy or fish and chips. Bookings advised.

Drinking

Drinking

Melbourne celebrates the sanctioned drug of alcohol with gusto. It's the social lubricant in a highly sociable city. Typically, there is a variety of ways to enjoy the same simple act of having a drink, from the obvious at a sexy city bar to a tipple while at the movies.

But it's not just alcohol that sates the city's thirst; Melbourne has a few other curious drinking habits, too. Apart from coffee – for which Melbourne is the capital – Melburnians have been utterly seduced by juice. Vividly-coloured juice bars are everywhere pumping out their perky panaceas, serving dually as the enemy and the antidote of night-time indulgences. Don a pair of sunglasses and steel your seedy self for the bright surrounds. Bottled water is another daytime phenomenon. Although Melbourne has some of the world's best-quality drinking water, a bottle of commercially produced water is almost an accessory.

Traditionally, the pub was the prime place for Melburnians to wet their whistle. In the last decade, two competing regional breweries bought out many of the city's pubs to ensure dominance for their brands of brews, and things started to go awry. Pokie machines were also installed in many pubs, transforming the once quiet local into an alienating gambling den. A more recent resurgence in pub culture has brought discerning pot drinkers back to pubs, with many reverting to old-style aesthetics offering excellent food and/or live music.

George Hotel (p123)

That other drinking institution, the svelte city bar, continues to evolve. The bar scene is classy, dirty, boutique, egalitarian, retro, yet progressive all at the same time. Tired of the electronic-lounge theme, Melbourne's bars have responded by trashing the lounge room and moving out to the garage to rock. Find them – and you do have to search for them – in the city's laneways and alleys, behind unassuming doorways, down in basements and up flights of stairs. If you're staying for a while, consider buying the *Bar Secrets Melbourne* deck of cards available at bookstores. Shuffle the deck and pick a card – each has a rundown (and map) of what you can expect to find. See also www.melbournepubs .com.au for reviews of the city's pubs, bars and clubs.

It has to be said that categorising a venue is very difficult: bars do food, cafés turn into bars, and most bars have DJs and dance floors to shuffle about on. Club venues – where you go when the bars close, which is generally 1am weekdays and 3am Friday and Saturday – are listed on p130.

Top Five Bar-Cafés

Loads of Melbourne's bars also do great food. Here are a few of the best places where you can experience the city's stellar bar and café scene in the one venue.

- **Borsch, Vodka & Tears** (p122)
- **Cookie** (opposite)
- **Phoenix** (p120)
- **Transport** (p120)
- **Ume Nomiya** (p121)

CENTRAL MELBOURNE

Evening creatures jostle each other through unlikely locations in search of the next best thing. While different drinking strips pitch their own distinct style, and most of the best spots in the CBD are hidden from the unknowing eye, it's sometimes good to know where you're going and what you may find.

Most places are within walking distance of Flinders Street Station, but if you want to get there more quickly, see the transport network maps (pp217–18) for details on trams and trains nearest your chosen venue.

THE EAST

CHERRY Map pp202-04
☎ 9639 8122; 103 Flinders Lane, enter from Duckboard Pl; ☽ Tue-Sat
There's nothing 'pop' about this baby. If you love rock and roll – more like Joan Jett than Britney – then you warrant a piece of this cherry pie. Whether you're carving your name under the red-lit bar or playing air guitar on the elevated stage, remember to rock hard or go home.

COOKIE Map pp202-04
☎ 9663 7660; 252 Swanston St; ☽ nightly
What wins a place Bar of the Year? It could be Cookie's prime locale, with balconies overlooking Swanston St. The parquet walls, attractive staff, perverse collection of music – mostly on vinyl – and 16m marble bar might have something to do with it. Stellar cocktails, such as the fizzy Betel Bliss, and 10 beers on tap are further considerations. Still not sold? It does amazing Thai food, too.

CROFT INSTITUTE Map pp202-04
☎ 9671 4399; 21-25 Croft Alley; ☽ Mon-Sat
If you can find it, you're halfway there; just remember you need to go through 'Payne' to find the cure at this Melbourne institution. Prescribe yourself a beaker of house-distilled vodka in the downstairs laboratory or jerk around like Mr Hyde on the dance floor-cum-gymnasium bar upstairs.

DING DONG LOUNGE Map pp202-04
☎ 9662 1020; 18 Market Lane; ☽ Tue-Sun
One glance at the alleyway signage of Ding Dong and you'll get the idea: no frills or flowers, just flowing drink and rock and roll. Guitar-neck beer taps aren't as tacky as you'd think. Featuring live music in a space the size of your mum's garage, this is the perfect spot if you wanna let it all hang out.

DOUBLE HAPPINESS Map pp202-04
☎ 9650 4488; 21 Liverpool St; ☽ Mon-Sat
This stylish hole in the wall has no sign, but has become a landmark in its own right. The tongue-in-cheek interior features an array of Chinese socialist propaganda posters, while the names of the fusion cocktails are taken from infamous moments in communist history.

GIN PALACE Map pp202-04
☎ 9654 0533; 190 Little Collins St; ☽ nightly
If you love martinis, then this is your castle. With a drinks list to make your liver quiver, Gin Palace is the perfect place to grab a soft couch or secluded alcove, sip, and take it slow. Its seductive lighting, velvet drapes and cushioned nooks give it a top first-date rating.

Drinking – Central Melbourne

Culture in a Cup

Coffee is a cultural conduit in Melbourne. The humble espresso and its public consumption have reinvigorated community life and are at the centre of much of the city's socialising. Lingering over a coffee is sacred, whether with a newspaper, or with friends or colleagues.

Coffee in Melbourne is some of the best in the world. The city's many boutique and big-name roasters bestow the same care upon their beans as the vintners upon their grapes, aiming for balance of body and flavour. Everyone has a personal favourite, which is further complicated by matching it with the right grind, machine and barista. Add to this the ambience of the café, and you've got a lot of variables influencing personal preference.

Melburnians are coffee literate, discerning between particular roasters. And more Melbourne roasters are particular about their bean buying, offering Fair Trade coffee, for which set rates are paid for beans purchased from countries such as East Timor that are exploited by the world coffee market.

Coffee culture in this city is steeped in a tradition of Italian chic and has a long bohemian association. The liberalisation of liquor laws in the 1980s allowed cafés to serve alcohol, which saw patronage increase by 150% and entrenched the café into Melbourne society day and night.

See the Eating chapter (p100) for reviews of some of Melbourne's best cafés.

LOOP Map pp202-04

☎ 9654 0500; 23 Meyers Pl; ☺ Mon-Sat

Seriously blurring any contrast between bar and art space, Loop is the perfect theatre to observe the latest in esoteric visual media. Featuring a large double screen and scattered projectors, find yourself a dark seat or a spot at the bar and watch the 'Video Jockeys' display their wares.

MELBOURNE SUPPER CLUB Map pp202-04

☎ 9654 6300; level 1, 161 Spring St;
☺ nightly till 6am

The perfect spot to celebrate in style or merely indulge for the sake of it. Recline on the leather cushion of a Chesterfield, browse the wine encyclopaedia and allow yourself to be pampered with 'couch service'. Sommeliers will cater to any liquid desire and light supper requirement.

MEYERS PLACE Map pp202-04

☎ 9650 8609; 20 Meyers Pl; ☺ nightly

A landmark on its namesake, this drinking hole is the first-born child of a family of Melbourne bars designed by architectural firm Six Degrees. Using recycled materials and an eye for comfort, you're bound to feel right at home. Make sure you tune in to the foreign news broadcast via the toilet cubicles to keep you up to date while you're out late.

MISTY Map pp202-04

☎ 9663 9202; 3-5 Hosier Lane; ☺ Tue-Sat

One of Melbourne's originals, Misty is how a 1970s film-set designer might have imagined a millennium bar. Misty retains its hip status, with cool inner-city kids packing in to revel in its quiet, confident vibe. *Wasabi* peas and *wasabi*-spiked Bloody Marys will make you misty-eyed.

PHOENIX Map pp202-04

☎ 9650 4976; 82 Flinders St;
☺ nightly, till 4am Fri & Sat

Offering split levels of yellow hues, zebra carpet and dimly lit alcoves, Phoenix is the perfect inner-city nest. Contemporary bar snacks and late closing on weekends ensure its popularity with locals who know best. Distinctive food, such as crocodile-fillet tapas, makes for some pretty snappy bar snacks.

TROIKA Map pp202-04

☎ 9663 5461; 106 Little Lonsdale St; ☺ Tue-Sat

Troika has a loyal bunch of followers who get on board for the intimate, gimmick-free surrounds. It's about decent drinks and good

tunes, with booths and bar stools set close – conducive to conversation. If conversation is waning, the walls are adorned with art works to comment on.

RIVER DISTRICT

TRANSPORT Map pp202-04

☎ 9658 8808; Federation Sq; ☺ nightly

A modern pub conveniently located across the road from Flinders Street Station, Transport is the perfect spot to stop and watch Melburnians midtransit. A voyeur's paradise from any angle, whether you prefer a view of the Yarra River and its gliding water traffic, the hustle and bustle of St Kilda Rd trams and motors or the foot brigade of Federation Square. Just remember to look up and check out the beer's departure from the transparent elevated keg room. (See the boxed text, p40, for a profile of Transport founder Paul Mathis.)

THE WEST

BOND BAR Map pp202-04

☎ 9629 9844; 24 Bond St; ☺ Wed-Sat

With curves in all the right places, this slick basement bar has every detail covered, from wood furnishings to lush brown and cream tones. Eclectic sounds add a little groove to the swank. Cigar aficionados kick back, but never draw back, in the Cigar Lounge, while others kick-start in the Powder Room.

ROBOT Map pp202-04

☎ 9620 3646; 12 Bligh Pl; ☺ Mon-Sat

If you ever got caught up in Japanese Manga mania or you just feel like a sushi handroll washed down with a crisp Asahi, check out Robot. It has an all-welcome door policy, and animated movies screen free on Tuesday.

RUE BEBELONS Map pp202-04

☎ 9663 1700; 267 Little Lonsdale St; ☺ nightly

For such a small space this bar's reputation is gigantic. Offering affordable drinks, great coffee and an in-house vinyl collection, it's no wonder why. By day, grab yourself a slice of Brazilian bohemia and a salad roll to die for. By night, grab any space you can and contribute to the hubbub.

SCUBAR Map pp202-04

☎ 9670 2105; 224-228 Queen St; ☺ Thu-Sun

As you descend along polished pine panels to the plush warmth below, this underground bunker is almost reminiscent of a Swedish sauna. Featuring two bars, plenty of comfort and a pool table, submerge yourself. Just don't feed the fish.

TONY STARR'S KITTEN CLUB
Map pp202-04

☎ 9650 2448; level 1, 267 Little Collins St; ☽ nightly
Ascend the lime-green stairs to the split-level world of Tony Starr. First stop, the Galaxy Lounge with its '50s-inspired cocktail-hour décor, open kitchen and weekend live cabaret. Or, company depending, climb the stairs again and stretch out and purr in the pink plushness of the Lovers Lounge.

CARLTON & FITZROY

Fitzroy has an eclectic drinking scene. It has the highest density of pubs of any suburb, its cafés take on the night crew by parking the coffee machine and driving the bar, and its many bars are supplemented with entertainment – live music, film screenings and/ or literary readings. For transport options from the city see the boxed text, p66.

BAR OPEN Map pp206-08
☎ 9415 9601; 317 Brunswick St, Fitzroy; ☽ nightly
Be warned, Bar Open closes around 3am, but that still gives you more time than most in the area to take advantage of its two levels. Relax and chat at the downstairs bar or, if there's no room, grab an empty keg as a seat in the courtyard. Then, if you feel like being entertained, there seems to always be something happening upstairs, be it an array of live music, installation art or spoken word. Brunswick St nightlife at its finest.

GERTRUDE'S Map pp206-08
☎ 9417 6420; 30-32 Gertrude St, Fitzroy; ☽ Tue-Sat
With a roster of DJs and cosy classic-film nights, Gertrude's is a find. Effortlessly dashing, its amiable interior and deftly prepared drinks are loved by locals. Supplement this with bistro-style food and there's little more you could ask for from a bar. Gertrude's is generous and genuine.

LAMBSGO BAR Map pp206-08
☎ 8415 0511; 136 Greeves St, Fitzroy; ☽ nightly
If you love beer you'll love Lambsgo. From the exterior, you could imagine it might contain any type of cosy fairy-tale inhabitant, and maybe that's not far from the truth. For after sampling

the spellbinding selection of over 110 different imported beers, you may never want to return home. Haunt the modest beer garden or poolroom and you'll find such treats as Kwak beer, a brew served in a glass with a bulbous bottom so it can't balance without hand or stand; and Delirium Tremens, a high-alcohol beer adorned with pink elephants. And if washing the hops over the chin gets you a little peckish, Lambsgo even lets you dial for pizza. Cheers!

OLD BAR Map pp206-08
☎ 9417 4155; 74 Johnston St, Fitzroy; ☽ Tue-Sun
A lounge atmosphere with fantastic music, this is where DJs go on their nights off to enjoy the best tracks that are off the beaten track. It's nothing flash, but that's why it's loved. There's always a need for affordable drinks and an uncontrived ambience.

POLLY Map pp206-08
☎ 9417 0880; 401 Brunswick St, Fitzroy; ☽ nightly
Ornate and regal décor swirled with the character of an eccentric grandmother. Think well-worn antique couches, red velvet drapes, blood-red hues dipped in gold and a cocktail list that'll make you want to lipstick stain every glass. Polly is affordable and elegant.

UME NOMIYA Map pp206-08
☎ 9415 6101; 197 Gertrude St, Fitzroy; ☽ Tue-Sun
Meaning 'drinking house' in Japanese, Ume Nomiya is the perfect place to do just that. Locals have the option of buying a whole bottle

---

Fitzroy Pubs

Serving as the neighbourhood's lounge room, Fitzroy's pubs are more than just beer-swilling hubs. They also dish up great pub grub to line your stomach. Some recommendations:

- **Builders Arms** (Map pp206-08; ☎ 9419 0818; 211 Gertrude St) Old-school grunge; gay Thursday night.
- **Napier Hotel** (Map pp206-08; ☎ 9419 4240; 210 Napier St) Favoured by young locals.
- **Rainbow Hotel** (Map pp206-08; ☎ 9419 4193; 27 St David St) Jumping pub, with regular live music (see p129).
- **The Standard** (Map pp206-08; ☎ 9419 4793; 293 Fitzroy St) Gorgeous beer garden; 11pm closing.
- **Union Club** (Map pp206-08; ☎ 9417 2926; 164 Gore St) Mixed crowd with loyal following.

of their favourite to be kept behind the bar for their lips only. Whether you're in the mood to sip sake while sampling the authentic Japanese menu, or just wanting to hang at the bar with a cold crisp beer, *kanpai*!

YELZA Map pp206-08
☎ 9416 3977; 245 Gertrude St, Fitzroy; ⏰ Wed-Sun
A celebrated marriage of pub meets Liberace's lounge room, Yelza drips 17th-century extravagance and grace. Beautifully lit and dressed in red and gold, it's tempting not to explore any further than the front bar. Alas, this would be foolish, as the beer garden beyond, set with a separate bar and DJ console, is a definite hot spot during the warmer months – especially for enjoying one of the hearty meals on offer.

ABBOTSFORD & RICHMOND

While not a drinking hub, there are a few places worthy of a visit in Abbotsford and Richmond, particularly before a gig at the Corner Hotel (p127), or after the footy. See the boxed text, p71, for transport options from the city.

DER RAUM Map p211
☎ 9428 0055; 438 Church St, Richmond; ⏰ Tue-Sun
Meaning 'the room' in German, Der Raum has plenty of room for its Germanic beers. It takes drinks seriously and stocks many of the finest. Grab a stein and croon along to the '50s-inspired musical selection, but don't swing too wide, for this room is cosy.

GREAT BRITAIN Map p211
☎ 9429 5066; 447 Church St, Richmond; ⏰ nightly
This big corner pub does the dingy local thing with panache. Noted for its own brand of beer called 'Piss' and a low-alcohol version called 'Piss Weak', there are few other pubs where you can ask for a pot of 'Piss' without anyone batting an eyelid. The GB also serves up oysters and will call-in a pizza from across the road.

THE VIC Map p211
☎ 9421 3922; 281 Victoria St, Abbotsford; ⏰ nightly
The masses of regulars who eat at Victoria St's restaurants have been crying out for a post-prandial bar. Finally, they have the Vic. Prop at the window with a *digestif amaro*, or head further back, slouch in a couch and undo the top button to make room for a cleansing beer.

SOUTH YARRA, TOORAK & PRAHRAN

This area is a hedonist's haven. The bar scene is predominantly loungey, inviting long nights in casual surrounds. Plenty of clubs will see you through well into the next day; see p130 for clubs listings. See also the boxed text, p73, for transport options from the city.

BACK BAR Map p212
☎ 9529 7899; 67 Green St, Prahran; ⏰ Tue-Sun
Tucked behind the street frontage of Tusk Café on Chapel St, Back Bar is a cosy evening parlour with lavish décor. Take a spell on a settee and repudiate any knowledge of the outside world till late.

BLUE BAR Map p212
☎ 9529 6499; 330 Chapel St, Prahran; ⏰ nightly
A narrow and dimly lit sanctum away from the bustle of Chapel St, Blue Bar is a tunnel designed for total liquid salvation. Its linear architecture and street-smart clientele are contrasted with the sprawl of couches and microwave pizzas sleeping further within.

BORSCH, VODKA & TEARS Map p212
☎ 9530 2694; 173 Chapel St, Prahran; ⏰ nightly
Ever seen *Au Chocolat*, when Juliette Binoche spins the plate and can tell exactly which chocolate will satisfy her customer best? Well, at BVT the savvy staff has an uncanny knack in doing just the same, minus the plate spinning. The unsurpassed range of imported vodkas can be daunting, so don't be afraid to ask for some advice. And before it ends in tears, soak it up with some traditional Polish cuisine, or return in the morning for a big bowl of borscht (beetroot broth) – the perfect hangover cure.

CANDY BAR Map p212
☎ 9529 6566; 162 Greville St, Prahran; ⏰ nightly
What starts the day as a café lunch venue turns into a DJ lounge bar in the evenings. Sunday is gay night and every Monday night you can try your luck with transvestite-hosted bingo.

DADA BAR Map p212
☎ 9533 8888; 160 Greville St, Prahran; ⏰ Thu-Sun
Commanding a street corner complete with footpath tables and fishbowl windows, it's sometimes difficult to distinguish exactly

Prince of Wales Hotel (below)

who's watching whom. Whether you'd rather see or be seen, DaDa is defiantly on display. DJs play till late, and a café-style menu keeps the customers coming during the day.

GREVILLE BAR Map p212
☎ 9529 4800; 143 Greville St, Prahran; 🕲 Tue-Sat

With park-side windows and amiable wood panelling spanning the bar, Greville Bar specialises in a superb wine list. Take your place at the window and watch others scurry home, then allow the evening menu to save you from having to move far.

LA LA LAND Map p212
☎ 9533 8972; 134 Chapel St, Prahran; 🕲 nightly

When the sun goes down and you're left needing a little liquid rejuvenation, you always have La La, the relaxing land of open fires, snug couches and flowing drink. Nuzzle yourself into a corner with a bottle of wine, fondue and a friend or two.

ST KILDA

It's impossible to list the huge number of options here. You need only to come, follow the throngs and join the queues. If you prefer a slower pace, choose one of the many casual offerings. And for a pot of beer with stellar views, head to the Esplanade Hotel (p128). Transport options from the city are in the boxed text, p75.

GEORGE PUBLIC BAR Map p213
☎ 9534 8822; basement, 127 Fitzroy St; 🕲 nightly

The GPB, as it's known by the locals, is under the George Hotel. Turn down the stairs when you see the blackboard A-frame displaying the GPB's thought for the day, then think beer on tap, a huge counter meal or a game of pool.

MINK Map p213
☎ 9536 1199; 2b Acland St; 🕲 nightly

March down the dimly lit concrete stairs and you can soak in the glory of socialist Russia, while also soaking in the vodka. And with over 80 different distilled delights to choose from, storming the vodka list could prove too much for just one comrade. If you're sharing good company why not retreat behind the red curtain to your own private booth.

PRINCE OF WALES Map p213
☎ 9536 1177; 2 Acland St; 🕲 nightly

An institution, the POW features twilight street seating, a gay pub room with a disco jukebox and dollar pots on a Monday night. On Saturday night, upstairs in the Band Room, One Love straddles the bar-club category. When things heat up, the garage doors open out onto the huge balcony, and there's a little DJ booth in the little ladies' room.

VELUDO Map p213

☎ 9534 4456; 175 Acland St; ⏰ nightly

A dark and sultry way to lose a few hours, especially during the cooler months when you can couch it next to a roaring open fire. Food runs till late.

Entertainment

Entertainment

Melburnians enthusiastically participate in the city's vivid arts and cultural scene. The variety of entertainment options available could have you wondering whether anyone actually works. Melburnians work hard at enjoying themselves, with layers of choices from conspicuous commercial endeavours to esoteric ventures motivated by necessity rather than financial gain. You could be a tourist of every subscene imaginable in Melbourne, dropping in on a one-off, feminist-inspired wet–T-shirt performance piece, or seeing a comedic Melbourne-made short film. There's a willing audience for everything – albeit a specialised one.

Of course, there's also a huge range of universal options, such as going to a heaving nightclub, hearing a symphony and being carried along by a theatrical drama.

It's difficult not to notice the Crown Casino & Entertainment Complex (p59), conspicuously occupying a lengthy stretch of the southern bank of the Yarra River. With cinemas, restaurants, nightclubs, gaming tables and tenpin bowling, you could stay tucked away in this city within the city for days, even weeks.

The best source of what's-on information is the *Entertainment Guide (EG)*, published every Friday in the *Age* newspaper. It lists everything from music and cinema screenings to spoken-word events. Cyberphiles should see **City Search** (www.melbourne.citysearch.com.au) for up-to-date listings and reviews. *Beat* and *Inpress* are free music and entertainment magazines, each with reviews, interviews and a comprehensive gig guide. They're available from pubs, cafés and venues.

For information on attending sporting events and matches see the Sports, Health & Fitness chapter (p138).

Tickets & Reservations

HALF TIX Map pp202-04

☎ 9650 9420; Melbourne Town Hall, cnr Little Collins & Swanston Sts; ☽ 10am-2pm Mon & Sat, 11am-6pm Tue-Thu, 11am-6.30pm Fri

If you're after cheap tickets, visit the Half Tix counter, which sells half-price tickets to shows and concerts on the day of the performance. Half Tix accepts cash payments only.

TICKETEK Map pp202-04

☎ 13 28 49; www.ticketek.com.au; 225 Exhibition St; ☽ 9am-5pm Mon-Fri, 9am-1pm Sat

Ticketek is a ticket agency representing some headline acts, also sporting events and big productions. It takes phone bookings, with credit card payment. You can also book over the Internet, or visit a street outlet, including **Rod Laver Arena** (Map p205; Batman Ave) and the **Princess Theatre** (Map pp202-04; 163 Spring St) during office hours.

TICKETMASTER7 Map pp202-04

☎ 1300 136 166; www.ticketmaster7.com; Theatres Bldg, Victorian Arts Centre, 100 St Kilda Rd; ☽ 9am-9pm Mon-Sat

This is the main booking agency for major theatre and sports events, as well as headline concerts. Besides taking bookings by phone and over the Internet, Ticketmaster7 has a number of city outlets (Map pp202–04) open during office hours, including **Myer** (level 5, 275 Lonsdale St) and **Telstra Dome** (Gate 2, Bourke St, entry via Spencer St).

MUSIC

See p26 for a rundown on Melbourne's diverse music scene.

PUB VENUES

It's hard enough trying to label individual bands as playing within a particular genre, let alone Melbourne venues as hosting one

Transport

The Neighbourhoods chapter (p50) lists transport options for each neighbourhood. See also the transport network maps (pp217–18) to check the best way to travel to listed venues.

genre in particular. Each draws from such a diverse range of influences that they're difficult to box. The listings here are general venues that might stage rock and roll one night, a comeback attempt by a fading '80s star the following night and DJs the next.

Shows generally start between 9pm and 10pm. Entry charges vary wildly depending on the act. Expect to pay anywhere from nothing to $30. Check the *EG* section or street press to find out who's playing what and where. Also tune into radio station 3RRR (102.7FM) on Wednesday from 4pm to 7pm for the *Incoming* show featuring new Australian music and gig information; the website (www.rrr.org.au) also has an up-to-date gig guide.

ARTHOUSE Map p209
☎ 9347 3917; cnr Elizabeth & Queensberry Sts, North Melbourne

The Arthouse, at the Royal Artillery Hotel, is the place to bang yer head. Hardcore punk and metal, as well as ska, plays Wednesday to Saturday: mohawks and big wallet chains welcome. Sunday sees acoustic sets.

CORNER HOTEL Map p211
☎ 9427 9198; www.cornerhotel.com; 57 Swan St, Richmond

With an old-school public bar serving pub grub, the Corner is your classic band venue: dark, sticky carpet and no attitude. It's about music, and the Corner is the venue of choice for many midlevel alternative acts such as Peaches and Francoiz Breut.

CORNISH ARMS Map p210
☎ 9380 8383; www.cornisharms.com.au; 163a Sydney Rd, Brunswick

Cornish Arms is a big, friendly venue hosting performances by local talents you're unlikely to have heard of, but who are likely to have had some success in the Australian music scene. There's some form of entertainment nightly, be it music, comedy or cabaret. Sunday afternoon sessions are popular with young families.

DING DONG Map pp202-04
☎ 9662 1020; www.dingdonglounge.com.au; 18 Market Lane

This rock-and-roll bar (see p119) also stages touring and local bands. Luke Roberts, (formerly at the **Tote**, p129), who books the bands here, is responsible for bringing us the White Stripes and Dirt Bombs, among others. Check the website for upcoming rockers.

DUKE OF WINDSOR Map p212
☎ 9510 1062; 179 Chapel St, Prahran

The Duke recently reinvented itself as a band venue, and is increasingly attracting excellent bands and, with them, increasing numbers of patrons. Any night between Wednesday and Saturday should give you something to look at and rock to.

Headline Acts

For big-name local and international acts, the city's main venues include the following. Book tickets through one of the agencies listed in Tickets & Reservations (opposite).

Forum Theatre (Map pp202-04; www.marrinertheatres.com.au; 150-152 Flinders St) One of the city's most atmospheric film and theatre venues. The Arab-inspired exterior – replete with gargoyles – has an equally interesting interior, with the southern sky rendered on the domed ceiling.

Hamer Hall (Melbourne Concert Hall; Map pp202-04; www.vicartscentre.com.au/melbourneconcerthall; Victorian Arts Centre, 100 St Kilda Rd) The concert hall is well known for its excellent acoustics, with a décor inspired by Australia's mineral and gemstone deposits.

Palais Theatre (Map p213; ☎ 9537 2444; www.palaistheatre.com; Lower Esplanade, St Kilda) Standing gracefully next to Luna Park, the Palais is a St Kilda icon. Not only is it a beautiful old space, but it also stages some pretty special performances. It's always worth checking out who's playing here.

Rod Laver Arena (Map p205; www.mopt.com.au; Batman Ave) A giant, versatile space used for headline concerts and sporting events, with a huge sunroof.

Sidney Myer Music Bowl (Map p205; www.vicartscentre.com.au/sidneymyermusicbowl; Kings Domain) This beautiful amphitheatre in the park is used for a variety of outdoor events, from the Tropfest film festival (p30) to the New Year's Day rave Summerdayze.

EMPRESS HOTEL Map p210

☎ 9489 8605; 714 Nicholson St, North Fitzroy

The Empress continues to grace the Melbourne music scene with its presence. This quintessential Fitzroy pub was one of the first to book Silverchair. It stages a variety of genres from folk to unplugged rock every night of the week. Monday to Wednesday and Sunday are free, admission Thursday through Saturday costs between $6 and $8. The Empress also serves decent counter meals.

ESPLANADE HOTEL Map p213

☎ 9534 0211; www.theesplanadehotel.com.au; 11 The Esplanade, St Kilda

The good ol' reliable Espy is still staging rockin' live music nightly from one or all of its four stages. The front stage is free, with larger acts and a regular comedy night in the back Gershwin Room. A night at this legendary pub is like attending the last party at a mansion that's been earmarked for demolition. Due to its prime location and crumbling grandeur, the Espy's future is constantly under threat from developers. Built in 1880, it was once grand seaside accommodation; the actress Sarah Bernhardt stayed here back in 1891. Today the Espy is part of the city's pub-rock psyche.

The excellent Espy Kitchen out the back does decent grub at very reasonable prices. There are many worse ways to spend a night than at the Espy: come early to take in the sunset over St Kilda from the front balcony.

EVELYN HOTEL Map pp206-08

☎ 9419 5500; www.evelynhotel.com; 351 Brunswick St, Fitzroy

Playing mostly local acts, the Evelyn also pulls some biggish-name international performers. The Ev doesn't discriminate by genre; as long as it's quality music it gets a look-in here. Both one-off gigs and band residencies feature from Tuesday to Sunday at this long-running, well-respected venue.

GREEN ROOM Map pp202-04

☎ 9620 5100; basement, 33 Elizabeth St

In the basement of the Flinders Station Hotel, the Green Room has been rescued from its previous incarnation as a pokie joint and recently transformed into an oddly shaped band room. Wednesday is karaoke night, with bands playing Thursday to Saturday – entry fees apply. Green Room recently celebrated its first birthday with a supergroup featuring members from Warped, Bored and Bloodsucking Freaks.

GREYHOUND HOTEL Map p213

☎ 9534 4189; cnr Carlisle St & Brighton Rd, St Kilda

This small, sweaty hotel holds absolutely no pretensions. It's one of the few Melbourne pubs that hasn't been refurbished, and is an original all right, doing drag on Saturday night, karaoke on Sunday and bands from Thursday to Saturday.

Esplanade Hotel (above)

PONY Map pp202-04
☎ 9654 5917; 68 Little Collins St

Bands thump away upstairs (from Wednesday to Saturday), above the low ceilings and smoky din. You can also saddle up for the long haul, with Pony open downstairs until 7am Friday and Saturday night.

PRINCE BANDROOM Map p213
☎ 9536 1166; www.princebandroom.com.au; 29 Fitzroy St, St Kilda

The Prince Bandroom (upstairs) at the Prince of Wales has been part of the live music scene for over 20 years. The giant blackboard out the front tells you who's playing on any given night. Recent faves include Teenage Fanclub and Black Rebel Motorcycle Club.

RAINBOW HOTEL Map pp206-08
☎ 9419 4193; www.therainbowhotel.com; 27 St David St, Fitzroy

There's a mixed bag of music every night, and there has been for over 12 years at this Fitzroy icon. Struggling with noise complaints, the Rainbow has undergone some soundproofing renovations, using funds raised by local musicians donating their talents and time. It's a tiny band space, and you often have to look over the bar, but it has a long and loyal following. Monday night, hear Paul Williamson's Hammond Combo – a jazz outfit going into its 13th year of residency in this spot.

RETREAT Map p210
☎ 9380 4090; 280 Sydney Rd, Brunswick

Retreat to the big grassy beer garden, or stay inside for the mixed line-up of live music every night. Monday to Thursday is generally blues, roots and acoustic. Friday and Saturday the DJs move in. Sunday-afternoon acoustic sessions are also popular.

ROB ROY Map pp206-08
☎ 9419 7180; 51 Brunswick St, Fitzroy

The respectable Rob Roy is the sort of venue you can pop into any night of the week and be happily entertained by whoever's playing. The kitschy décor is reminiscent of your grandmother's lounge room. Entry fees are extremely affordable, sometimes free.

By the by, staff have reported spooky sightings and things that go bump in the night.

TOTE Map pp206-08
☎ 9419 5320; 71 Johnston St, Collingwood

Last time we were here, the band was swinging from the rafters, dripping in sweat. The Tote has been belting out alternative music seemingly forever: the carpet is threadbare and the mosh area is literally a pit. There's live music in the back room from Tuesday to Sunday, or select a track from the Tote's jukebox loaded with alternative faves.

TOWN HALL HOTEL Map p209
☎ 9328 1983; 33 Errol St, North Melbourne

The Town Hall is an unfussy North Melbourne local. Typical of this area, bands are from the city's musical fringe. Live music is staged free in the front room from Thursday to Saturday. There's a beaut beer garden and meals are also available.

JAZZ

BENNETTS LANE Map pp202-04
☎ 9663 2856; www.bennettslane.com; 25 Bennetts Lane

Bennetts Lane has been a quintessential part of the Melbourne music scene for years. Attracting the cream of local talents, as well as regular international acts, this is the perfect pad if you love a good toe-tap to contemporary jazz. Prince chose to play a secret jazzy set here for a privileged few during his 2003 tour of Australia. Just remember, if you go please don't light up; this is a nonsmoking venue.

DIZZY'S Map p211
☎ 9428 1233; www.dizzys.com.au; 90 Swan St, Richmond

Occupying Richmond's old post office building, Dizzy's has a variety of jazz artists playing from Wednesday and Thursday at 8pm, and Friday and Saturday from 9pm. The first Saturday of every month, from 5.30pm to 7pm, there's a 'cry baby' session for young families. Dizzy's is a smoke-free venue.

MANCHESTER LANE Map pp202-04
☎ 9663 0630; www.manchesterlane.com.au; 234 Flinders Lane, enter from Manchester Lane

This classy establishment caters to an older crowd, playing free music nightly of the big-band and boogie-woogie variety. There's a semiformal restaurant here, perfect for a pre-show meal.

NIGHT CAT Map pp206-08
☎ 9417 0090; 141 Johnston St, Fitzroy; ☽ Thu-Sun

The Night Cat is a barn-sized space with a '50s aesthetic, two bars, a stage (for patrons!) and a black-and-white checked dance floor backed by some stellar musicians. Music is generally in the Latin jazz and/or funk vein. Bands usually start around 10.30pm and play three sets to around 1.45am. There's a $5 door charge Friday and Saturday.

CLASSICAL

Following are a few of the city's main players. These groups play at various venues across town. Check their websites or the local press for venues and concert dates.

MELBOURNE CHORALE
www.melbournechorale.com.au
Melbourne Chorale's two choirs perform a diverse range of music, from classical oratorio works such as Handel's *Messiah*, to modern works, sometimes commissioned by the choir. They perform both a cappella and with orchestras at various venues across town; usually in one of the city's cathedrals.

MELBOURNE SYMPHONY ORCHESTRA
MSO; www.mso.com.au
Averaging 130 performances a year, the MSO has a loyal following. It was good enough for the Three Tenors, Frank Sinatra and Ray Charles when each toured to Australia. The MSO performs regularly at **Hamer Hall** (see the boxed text, p127).

MUSICA VIVA
www.mva.org.au
Musica Viva stages ensemble music from around the world and locally. Musica Viva performs on average once a month at **Hamer Hall** (see the boxed text, p127) and includes preshow talks. Its Ménage concert series, where pioneering new music is performed in informal venues, is specifically aimed at 18 to 35 year olds.

OPERA

If you're visiting from Europe, you could be excused for looking sideways at opera performances in a city where footy replaces opera as the majority of the population's preferred form of entertainment. But, you'd be sorry. Australia, and Melbourne specifically, has nurtured some internationally acclaimed opera singers and stages world-class productions.

CHAMBER MADE Map p209
☎ 9329 7422; www.chambermade.org.au; Arts House, North Melbourne Town Hall, cnr Queensberry & Errol Sts, North Melbourne
Founded in 1988, Chamber Made productions showcase contemporary music/theatre written locally as well as abroad. Performances aren't that frequent but all works are broadcast more regularly on ABC radio (105.9FM).

OPERA AUSTRALIA
www.opera-australia.org.au
The national opera company performs with some regularity at Melbourne's **Victorian Arts Centre** (p61). OzOpera, the company's education and access arm, tours regionally and to schools. Check the website for upcoming performances, as well as tips and recommendations for first timers.

CLUBBING

Melbourne's club scene could keep you from seeing daylight for days. When one club closes, usually at 7am, another opens for the recovery.

Most clubs have specific nights dedicated to a certain style, but they go on and off quicker than a record, so check street press for the latest. You could also try www.club vibes.com for local reviews of the city's clubs.

Generally, clubs start to get going once the bars close around 1am; the majority of clubs close between 5am and 7am. Cover charges range from $10 to $15.

Commercial Rd, Prahran has a number of clubs (mostly gay), and King St in the city has a cluster of big sloppy clubs.

ALIA Map pp206-08
☎ 9486 0999; 83 Smith St, Fitzroy; ⊗ Thu-Sun
Kind of a bar, kind of a club. Alia's big curvaceous counter, wraparound windows and soft lounges comprise the bar; the funky tunes

---

Gay-Friendly Options
- **Boutique** (opposite)
- **Builders Arms** (see the boxed text, p121) Thursday night
- **Candy Bar** (p122) Sunday night
- **Prince of Wales** (p123) Especially Monday night
- **Yelza** (p122) Every second Sunday

make up the club. Friendly and unpretentious, you'll find it upstairs, through the doorway next to **Yelza** (p122) on Gertrude St.

AREA 61 Map p213
☎ 9537 1999; www.area61.com.au;
61 Fitzroy St, St Kilda; ☺ Thu-Sun
Everything looks good through the upstairs water wall, down to the dance floor below. Area 61 is a relatively small club catering for about 300 boisterous backpackers. Sunday night, things get a bit dirtier, and uplifting hard house is pumped out to those who are still going.

BOUTIQUE Map p212
☎ 9525 2322; 132a Greville St, Prahran; ☺ Thu-Sun
You might overhear a toilet-cubicle conversation about the cute guy/girl the girl/boy washing their hands has been watching here. This crowd is hearing Boutique's '80s music for the first time, and loving it. A number of rooms cater to your whim, be it dance, chill or drinking at a bar. Boutique is gay friendly, too.

COMMERCIAL LOUNGE Map p212
☎ 9529 2088; 138 Commercial Rd, Prahran;
☺ Wed-Sun
It's lucky dip at Commercial Lounge. A changing roster means you never know what you'll find. Friday is generally alternative rock, and Saturday's Groovalicious plays hip-hop and house. Daytime recoveries are another feature of this two-storey place with a relaxed dress code.

DOUBLE O Map pp202-04
☎ 9654 8000; Sniders Lane; ☺ Fri & Sat
Down the end of Sniders Lane, Double O plays sneaker-busting beats till dawn. The downstairs room is simply furnished in vinyl, while upstairs the dance area is subtly lit. Expect hip-hop and drum and bass.

FFOUR Map pp202-04
☎ 9650 4494; level 2, 322 Little Collins St; ☺ Thu-Sat
This stark all-nighter is also popular earlier with the after-work drinkers. It's a futuristic space with harsh lighting that can be a tad alienating. As can the glass-walled VIP enclosure for those on the A list.

FIRST FLOOR Map pp206-08
☎ 9419 6380; 393 Brunswick St, Fitzroy; ☺ Tue-Sun
This whole floor is one capacious space divided into a number of separate areas. First Floor is soft centred, and the service is attentive and friendly.

HONKYTONKS Map pp202-04
☎ 9662 4555; Duckboard Pl; ☺ Wed-Sun
The archetypal lost-up-a-laneway, at-the-top-of-a-dark-staircase bar/club. Down the back, past the grand piano holding the DJ decks, are unhindered panoramic views over the MCG. The exceptionally well-stocked giant bar is a feature in itself. A number of small separate spaces will keep you comfortable all night. Honkys also hosts some stellar touring acts.

Melbourne Shuffle *Dj mt raum (aka Tony Macvean)*

Visitors to Melbourne are usually aware of the city's status as a sporting mecca, its reputation as the country's cultural capital and its thriving café, bar and restaurant scene. But perhaps less well known is Melbourne's contribution to international dance and nightclub culture, the Melbourne Shuffle.

For those in the scene, the Shuffle is recognised around the world as the distinctive and impressive way of Melbourne clubbers. For the uninitiated, it may seem like a hybrid of a disjointed twist and a wedding reception chicken dance. However, for the young nightclubbers who take their Shuffling seriously, it is recognised as an underground art form – and Melbourne's own.

While the Shuffle has various forms, to properly Shuffle the feet are all important. The basic step involves shuffling the feet inwards and outwards using a swift heel-and-toe movement, all in time to 150-plus bpm. The arms are clucked up and down or thrust from side to side, while the upper body provides supporting rhythm. Expert Shufflers will throw in a few full-circle spins or a jump for added kudos. Serious aficionados of the Shuffle even go to the length of sprinkling talcum powder on the dance floor to assist.

The Shuffle is a style particularly favoured by younger ravers and most commonly seen in Melbourne's hard house and techno venues, and big outdoor events such as Summerdayze (held at the Sidney Myer Music Bowl on New Year's Day). The Shuffle's halcyon days as an art form were earlier this decade, with 'Shuffle Showdowns' much-hyped events in the scene.

Some are now saying that the Shuffle has begun its inevitable demise; however, its legacy will remain. All those who have spent time in Melbourne's clubs over the past 10 years hold the Shuffle dear to their heart, and the influence of the Shuffle on their moves will continue to be unmistakable.

LAUNDRY Map pp206-08

☎ 9419 7111; 50 Johnston St, Fitzroy; ☾ nightly

The Laundry happily mixes everything from live music and DJs to film and karaoke. There are pool tables downstairs, plus two stages for performances.

LOUNGE Map pp202-04

☎ 9663 2916; upstairs, 243 Swanston St; ☾ Wed-Sat

The Lounge is an easy option and often provides the setting for a cracker night that might feature Latin rhythms, soul grooves or hip-hop. It's open till 6am. Lounge also does reasonably priced meals (see p103).

ONESIXONE Map p212

☎ 9533 8433; 161 High St, Prahran; ☾ Wed-Sat

Known for its hilariously exclusive door policy, space is a commodity here. So, if you consider yourself one of the beautiful set, hope that the person behind the peephole does too. Snaffle a couch or a pouf, or have a jiggle on the small dance floor. Chances are it isn't dawn yet, it's just the bright lights emanating from the fish tanks set into the wall. Friday is house till 9am before the recovery takes over, running all the way through to 11am Sunday.

Q BAR Map p212

☎ 9804 7800; basement, 257 Toorak Rd, South Yarra; ☾ Thu-Sun

Q Bar is a safe option: no hardcore air punchers here. It's a friendly, middle-of-the-road place, with pool tables down one end and a small dance floor down the other. Q Bar attracts people from all walks.

REVOLVER Map p212

☎ 9521 5985; www.revolverupstairs.com.au; 229 Chapel St, Prahran; ☾ nightly

Upstairs at Revolver is like an enormous lounge room. With 54 hours of nonstop music from Friday to Sunday, it's like a revolving door of DJs that keeps the shag-pile rugs downtrodden. The front room is also used for a variety of film screenings and hosting heaps of bands. Out the back there's even a Thai restaurant.

Top Five Clubs

- **Best newcomer** – Boutique (p131)
- **Best all-rounder** – Seven (right)
- **Most enduringly funky** – Honkytonks (p131)
- **Most like a giant lounge room** – Revolver (above)
- **Tightest door policy** – Onesixone (above)

ROBARTA Map p213

☎ 9534 9041; 109 Fitzroy St, St Kilda; ☾ Thu-Sun

Two-storey Robarta has a number of rooms running off rooms that teem with 20-somethings looking for a possie. The mostly commercial music shifts up a gear once the surrounding bars close around 3am.

SEVEN Map pp214-15

☎ 9690 7877; www.sevennightclub.com; 52 Albert Rd, South Melbourne; ☾ Thu-Sun

Seven has four rooms, each with its own distinct music style and décor. Expect an energetic young crowd whooping it up to extended versions of mainstream dance tracks. Seven also hosts touring local and international DJs by the likes of Nick Warren and Dimitri from Paris.

VIPER ROOM Map p212

☎ 9827 1771; 373 Chapel St, South Yarra; ☾ Thu-Sun

The later it gets, the harder the doof-doof. This small club has two bars open until 7am Friday and Saturday.

CINEMA

Cinema tickets generally cost between $13 and $15, with concessions for students and seniors (proof required). The city centre's mainstream-cinema strip is around the intersection of Bourke and Russell Sts. Art-house cinemas are so plentiful that they outnumber mainstream cinemas. Melbourne has a healthy film-going culture, with most people seeing a film at least monthly. It's also a great excuse to eat ice cream; if you haven't tried the choc-top (see the boxed text, p133) they alone are worth going for.

ASTOR Map p213

☎ 9510 1414; www.astor-theatre.com; cnr Chapel St & Dandenong Rd, St Kilda

This classic screens all the classics in absolutely stunning Art Deco surrounds. The Astor is a bit of magic: the candy-bar staff appear to have stepped out of a noir set, and the Astor cat makes celebrity appearances now and then. This cinema is well known for a superb line-up of films that have attained classic or cult status. Its double features screen nightly and it has some of the city's best choc-top ice creams.

AUSTRALIAN CENTRE FOR THE MOVING IMAGE Map pp202-04

ACMI; ☎ 9663 2583; www.acmi.net.au; Federation Sq

ACMI's cinemas screen an incredibly diverse range of films. It programmes regular events and festivals for film genres and audiences, as well as screening one-offs. Check the website for information on what's coming up.

CINEMA EUROPA Map p212
☎ 1300 555 400; level 1, Jam Factory, Chapel St, Prahran

This is the less commercial arm of Village, screening highly acclaimed foreign and documentary films. It's also licensed and has an exceptionally classy snack bar with good coffee.

CINEMA NOVA Map pp206-08
☎ 9347 5331; www.cinemanova.com.au; 380 Lygon St, Carlton

Apart from its stellar film selection of art house, documentary and foreign films, Nova has bargain Monday screenings; sessions before 4pm cost $5 and $7.50 after 4pm.

GEORGE CINEMAS Map p213
☎ 9534 6922; www.palace.net.au; 135 Fitzroy St, St Kilda

Fully licensed, the George is relatively small, but integral to local film culture. It's a venue for the St Kilda and Short Film Festivals, and VCA film and television graduate screenings.

IMAX Map pp206-08
☎ 9663 5454; www.imax.com.au; Melbourne Museum, Carlton Gardens

As is the norm with IMAX, you can expect a spectacle on a grand scale here, with a selection of 2-D and 3-D movies specially made for these giant screens.

KINO Map pp202-04
☎ 9650 2100; www.kinodendy.com.au; Collins Place, 45 Collins St

Kino outgrew its previous location in Collins Place and has had a fancy expansion. Quality

Open-Air Cinema

Between December and March, the open-air **Moonlight Cinema** (Map pp214-15; www.moonlight.com.au; Royal Botanic Gardens, entry through Gate F on Birdwood Ave) screens classic, art house and cult films. **Open Air Cinema** (Map p205; Sidney Myer Music Bowl, entry through Gate 1, Kings Domain, Lithgow Ave) has a similar theme. Ticket prices are much the same as standard cinemas and bookings are handled by **Ticketmaster7** (☎ 1300 136 166; www.ticketmaster7.com). BYO rug, picnic basket and wine for a night with the stars under the stars.

art-house films screen in its comfy licensed cinemas. It offers a seniors special: the first session from Tuesday to Friday costs $6.50, including morning tea.

LUMIERE Map pp202-04
☎ 9639 1055; www.lumiere.com.au; 108 Lonsdale St

So it isn't the city's most comfortable cinema, but it's worth the numb bum to see films the rest of the city's cinemas won't show. It seems conservatives camp outside the Lumiere, looking for something about which to complain to the censorship board. Attempts to ban films in this city only serve to promote them, with film-goers making a statement about who can and can't tell them what they should see.

SUN THEATRE Map pp200-01
☎ 9362 0999; www.suntheatre.com.au; 8 Ballarat St, Yarraville

Opened in 1938, this glorious Art Deco cinema is a gem. It features four screens and original club seating reupholstered in suede. It's licensed and has exemplary-quality sound and screens.

Choc-Tops

The choc-top is a chocolate-dipped ice cream specific to Australian cinemas. Choc-tops were traditionally limited to vanilla ice cream, but the palette has more recently been extended to flavours such as berry and chocolate. Because the majority of choc-tops are handmade at each cinema, they have distinctive characteristics that identify them as belonging to certain cinemas. For example, the **Astor** (opposite) choc-top is popularly known as the 'big-top', and considered one of the city's best. Mainstream cinemas such as Village and Hoyts have their delicious choc-tops outsourced. The only ones to use dairy whip and waffle cones, they're made by the Wonka-esque factory in one of Melbourne's outer suburbs, which guards the world's only choc-top-making machine.

The choc-top is a cultural institution, like eating a pie at the footy and fairyfloss at the fun park; it is perennially crunched at cinemas across town. No matter what the weather outside, it's always ice-cream weather at the movies.

THEATRE

There is no distinct theatre district in Melbourne, with individual companies and theatres spread across town. Tickets generally start at about $20 for independent theatre productions, and usually cost from $30 to $40 for mainstream theatre. See p28 for more on Melbourne's thriving theatre scene.

LA MAMA Map pp206-08
☎ 9347 6948; 205 Faraday St, Carlton

La Mama is historically significant to Melbourne's theatre scene. This tiny, intimate forum produces new Australian works and experimental theatre, and has a reputation for developing emerging playwrights. See the boxed text, p28, for a profile of La Mama's artistic director, Liz Jones.

MELBOURNE THEATRE COMPANY
Map pp202-04

MTC; ☎ 9684 4500; www.mtc.com.au; Victorian Arts Centre, 100 St Kilda Rd

Melbourne's major theatrical company performs at the Victorian Arts Centre. The MTC stages around 15 productions each year, ranging from contemporary and modern (including many new Australian works) to Shakespearean and other classics.

PLAYBOX Map pp214-15
☎ 9685 5111; www.playbox.com.au; 113 Sturt St, South Melbourne

The Playbox theatre company has been a resident of the atmospheric CUB Malthouse since 1990. Dedicated to performing works by emerging Australian playwrights, the company is instrumental in touring works, taking innovative Australian theatre to a wider audience.

RED STITCH Map pp200-01
☎ 9533 8083; www.invincible.net; rear 2 Chapel St, St Kilda

This is an independent company of actors staging new international works often previously unseen in Australia. The tiny black-box theatre, opposite the Astor – down the end of the driveway – is a cosy, intimate space.

STOREROOM Map p210
☎ 9486 5651; www.thestoreroom.com.au; upstairs, rear Parkview Hotel, cnr St Georges Rd & Scotchmer St, North Fitzroy

Buy a drink from the bottle shop on your way upstairs to the theatre. The Storeroom is a venue for local companies, staging high-quality, professional fringe theatre. It features a diverse range of works from both Australia and overseas.

THEATREWORKS Map p213
☎ 9534 3399; www.theatreworks.org.au; 14 Acland St, St Kilda

Theatreworks is a community theatre dedicated to supporting a range of arts practitioners. It's been around for 24 years and recently launched an initiative to provide affordable theatre space to innovative and emerging artists.

DANCE

Melbourne's dance scene is a long way from being strictly ballroom. It's dominated by a few companies specialising in traditional ballet performances as well as genre-busting modern pieces – see also p29.

AUSTRALIAN BALLET Map pp202-04
☎ 1300 369 741; www.australianballet.com.au; State Theatre, Victorian Arts Centre, 100 St Kilda Rd

Based in Melbourne and now more than 40 years old, the Australian Ballet performs traditional and new works at the Victorian Arts Centre. See p29 or visit the website for more details.

Entertainment – Theatre

CHUNKY MOVE Map pp214-15
☎ 9645 5188; www.chunkymove.com;
111 Sturt St, Southbank
The state's contemporary dance company performs at its sexy newish venue behind the Australian Centre for Contemporary Art. See p29 for more on Chunky Move.

DANCEWORKS Map pp202-04
www.danceworks.com.au; Victorian Arts Centre,
100 St Kilda Rd
A contemporary dance company that incorporates new music styles in its performances, which are held at different locations, depending on the context of the show.

KAGE PHYSICAL THEATRE Map p209
☎ 9328 2474; www.kagephysicaltheatre;
Arts House, North Melbourne Town Hall,
cnr Queensberry & Errol Sts, North Melbourne
This modern dance company explores the nexus between theatre and dance. Narrative

is played out without dialogue, using music, design and movement to tell the story. This is witty and innovative stuff, well worth a look. Check *EG* or the company's website for performance details.

COMEDY

Melbourne prides itself on being the home of Australian comedy and isn't shy about turning the jokes on itself. The perennial International Comedy Festival (see p11) tickles the entire city, turning it into one sprawling comedy venue. Local comedians join forces with international acts (many coming from the Edinburgh Festival) to perform in pubs, clubs, theatres and on the city streets.

Melbourne has a few regular comedy venues and nightspots where stand-up comics stand or fall. Look in the *EG* section of the *Age* for weekly gigs or try the following venues.

Malthouse Theatre, home of Playbox (left)

COMIC'S LOUNGE Map p209

☎ 9348 9488; www.thecomicslounge.com.au;
26 Errol St, North Melbourne

There is stand-up every night of the week here. Admission prices vary, but are usually between $8 and $12. Monday night features 12 local comedians and is recorded by community TV – Channel 31. Tuesday is kind of an open-mic night, where aspiring comics have their eight minutes of fame (or shame).

LAST LAUGH COMEDY CLUB

Map pp202-04

☎ 9650 1977; www.comedyclub.com.au;
Athenaeum Theatre, 188 Collins St

The Last Laugh is open Friday and Saturday year-round, with additional nights in summer. This is professional stand-up, featuring local and international artists. Dinner/show packages are available – booking recommended. The club is a venue for acts during the Comedy Festival.

Sports, Health & Fitness

Sports, Health & Fitness

Australians in general, and Melburnians in particular, love their sport, especially when it comes to watching it. Screaming at a football match is the chosen way to vent a week's worth of work frustration. Preferring brains to brawn, the increasingly sedentary lifestyles of professional folk don't make Melburnians the fittest bunch on earth.

That said, Melbourne has its fair share of gym zealots, joggers and outdoor lifestylers eager to have the best possible body from which to hang their designer clothes. Temperate weather and the many gardens and parks provide multiple options to participate actively in city life.

During the late '90s, it seemed most Melburnians were obsessed with the attainment of 'wellness' – a term bandied about to encompass alternative, health-giving therapies such as aromatherapy, massage and meditation. These days such practices are widely accepted, and the focus has shifted from promoting inner wellbeing to showing off one's external assets. Common parlance recognises the 'metrosexual' as a city dweller, male or female, who regularly visits a beautician and/or solarium. Eyebrow waxes, body peels, manicures and facials are part of many people's health and fitness regimes.

Japanese Bath House, Collingwood (p142)

WATCHING SPORT

No matter what time of year, there's always some sporting spectacle on offer in Melbourne, be it the Melbourne Cup, Australian Formula One Grand Prix or **Commonwealth Games** (www.melbourne2006.com.au). See p16 for more on Melbourne's No 1 passion: watching sport.

Tickets & Reservations

You'll need to book tickets through Ticketek (p126) or Ticketmaster7 (p126). A booking fee will be charged by the agency and added to your total bill.

FOOTBALL
Australian Rules

If you're in town between April and September you should try to see a match, as much for the spectacle of the barracking as for the game. The **Australian Football League** (AFL; www.afl.com.au) runs the nationwide competition, and while there are teams based in Geelong, Perth, Adelaide, Sydney and Brisbane, Melbourne is still the game's stronghold.

For most games, you can buy tickets from the ground on match day: entry costs between $14 and $20.

Transport

Refer to the train and tram network maps on pp217–18 for details on the best way to negotiate your way around town. The transport boxes in the Neighbourhoods chapter (p50) also list specific tram numbers and train lines from the city to a particular neighbourhood.

MELBOURNE CRICKET GROUND

Map p205

MCG; ☎ 9657 8888; www.mcg.org.au; Brunton Ave
Melbourne's coliseum, the MCG, regularly pulls crowds of 50,000 to 80,000. The 'G' is the jewel in the sporting precinct's crown (see also p63).

OPTUS OVAL Map p210

☎ 9387 3777; Royal Pde, North Carlton
The last surviving suburban ground, Optus Oval, in **Princes Park** (p70) has been Carlton's home venue and training base since the club entered the VFL (Victorian Football League) competition in 1897. With a 35,000 capacity, some AFL games are played here.

TELSTRA DOME Map pp202-04

☎ 8625 7700; www.telstradome.com.au; Docklands
Melbourne's newest sporting oval, Telstra Dome, boasts a retractable roof and state-of-the-art facilities. It has poached many events from the MCG's sporting and entertainment calendar. **Tours** (adult/child $13/5) are offered on weekdays; check the website or phone for details.

Rugby

Rugby union has been slow to catch on in this town where Australian Rules rules. Despite this, the MCG and Telstra Dome attract huge crowds to international matches. Visit www.rugby.com.au to find out when the Australian team, the Wallabies, is playing and where.

Rugby league attracts a moderate following with around 8000 fans a match showing up to watch **Melbourne Storm** (www.melbournestorm.com.au) – the only Melbourne side in the National Rugby League. Home matches are played at **Olympic Park** (Map p205; ☎ 9286 1600; www.mopt.com.au; Batman Ave).

April to September is the season for both codes.

Soccer

Although it receives but a smidgen of the media coverage dedicated to Australian Rules, soccer has a huge fan base in Melbourne, with the Italian, Croatian and Greek communities being particularly avid followers of the game. The national soccer league season commences in October and finishes in May.

For details on home matches and venues contact the **Victorian Soccer Federation** (☎ 9682 9666; www.soccervictoria.org.au).

CRICKET

Melbourne's summer sport: international Test matches, one-day internationals and the state competition are all played at the **MCG** (p63). General admission to international matches is around $28 and reserved seats start at about $37; finals cost more. Tickets can usually be bought at the venue on match days, except for potential sell-out matches (such as the ever-popular Boxing Day Test).

HORSE RACING

Every Saturday they're racing at either Flemington, Caulfield, Moonee Valley or Sandown. The *Age* and *Herald Sun* newspapers publish what's happening around the fields every Friday. For a long-term calendar visit the website of **Racing Victoria** (www.racingvictoria.com.au).

The Melbourne Cup, watched by 700 million people in over 170 countries, is the feature event of Melbourne's Spring Racing Carnival, which runs through October and finishes with the Cup in early November. The carnival's major races are the Cox Plate, the Caulfield Cup, the Dalgety, the Mackinnon Stakes and the Holy Grail itself, the Melbourne Cup. Apart from these races, Derby Day and Oaks Day feature prominently on the spring racing calendar.

The two-mile (3.2km) Melbourne Cup, always run on the first Tuesday of November at Flemington Racecourse, was first staged in 1861. The Cup (a public holiday in Victoria) brings the whole of Australia to a standstill for the three-or-so minutes during which the race is run. Serious punters and fashion-conscious racegoers (spending an estimated $54.5 million on clothes and accessories) pack the grandstand and lawns of the racecourse. The city's once-a-year gamblers each make their choice or organise Cup syndicates with friends, and the race is watched or listened to on TVs and radios in pubs, clubs, TAB betting shops and houses across the land.

FLEMINGTON RACECOURSE

Map pp200-01

☎ 1300 727 575; www.vrc.net.au;
400 Epsom Rd, Flemington
Home of the Victoria Racing Club and the Melbourne Cup, Flemington has regular race meets. During the **Spring Racing Carnival** (p12), Flemington's roses bloom, the lawns are manicured and the bars are groomed for the thousands who come at this time of the year.

MOTOR SPORTS

Melbourne hosts the **Australian Formula One Grand Prix** (☎ 9258 7100; www.grandprix.com.au /cars) in March at Albert Park Lake, and the **Motorcycle Grand Prix** (www.grandprix.com .au/bikes) on Phillip Island in October.

TENNIS

For two weeks each January, **Melbourne Park** (Map p205; ☎ 9286 1244; www.mopt.com .au; Batman Ave) hosts the **Australian Open tennis championships** (www.ausopen.org). Top players from around the world come to compete in the year's first of the four Grand Slam tournaments.

BASKETBALL

The **National Basketball League** (www.nbl.com .au) follows the American model of showiness, with cheerleaders and quick motivational music grabs, but without the number of followers. Melbourne's league teams are the **Tigers** (www.sportal.com.au/tigers.asp) and the Victoria Giants. The season runs from October to March.

OUTDOOR ACTIVITIES

Even if you've never canoed, cycled or sailed before, they are super ways to see the city and its surrounds. Melbourne's landscape is flat as a tack, so cycling can be as leisurely as you like. Traversing the city's waterways offers a unique perspective on equally unique surrounds.

CANOEING

Yarra Bend Park (p72) stretches 12km north of Richmond. Most popular with walkers, you can also trade your sneakers for some oars. **Studley Park Boathouse** (Map p211; ☎ 9853 1972; www.studleyparkboathouse .com.au) hires two-person canoes for $22 per hour. Further out, try **Fairfield Boathouse** (Map pp200-01; ☎ 9486 1501; www.fairfield boathouse.com), which rents a variety of leisure craft, including replicas of the Thames craft used in the 19th century – unique to the southern hemisphere. Prices per hour range from $12 to $26. Both boathouses have cafés to reward you after all that exertion.

CYCLING

You're cycling beside the river through a grove of trees, bellbirds are chiming, rosellas are swooping low over the path, and the tangy aroma of hops from the brewery is mingling with the chocolatey smell from the biscuit factory. You're somewhere in the country, miles from Melbourne, right? Wrong, you're on the Main Yarra Trail, one of Melbourne's many inner-city bike paths constructed along the riverside green belts.

Melbourne has a growing network of bike lanes, which make a great way to actively appreciate this lush city. Maps are available from the visitor information centre at Federation Square (Map pp202–04) and **Bicycle Victoria** (☎ 8636 8888; www.bv .com.au). The series includes the Main Yarra Trail (38km), off which runs the Merri Creek Trail (19km); the Outer Circle Trail (34km); the Maribyrnong River Trail (22km); and the western beaches. At least 20 other long urban cycle paths exist, all marked in the Melway *Greater Melbourne Street Directory*. In addition, **VicRoads** (www .vicroads.vic.gov.au) has printable maps of Melbourne's cycle paths on its website.

Wearing a helmet while cycling is compulsory in Melbourne.

Cyclist, St Kilda

Bike Hire

A number of places hire good bikes; a deposit (or credit-card imprint) is often required. Take some form of photo ID with you.

Bicycles Now (Map pp214-15; ☎ 9696 8588; 100 Park St, South Melbourne) Day hire $59 plus $8 for a helmet and lock.

Hire a Bike (Map pp202-04; ☎ 0412 616 633; Princes Bridge, Southbank) Day hire $35, including helmet and lock.

St Kilda Cycles (Map p213; ☎ 9534 3074; www.stkilda cycles.com.au; 11 Carlisle St, St Kilda) Day hire $20, including helmet and lock.

GOLF

According to **AusGolf** (www.ausgolf.com.au), Victoria has the country's best and most famous golf courses.

You will need to book if you're going to play on a weekend. Green fees at a public course cost around $20 for 18 holes, and most courses have clubs and buggies for hire. Some good public courses close to town include the following.

ALBERT PARK Map pp214-15
☎ 9510 5588; www.golfvictoria.com.au; Queens Rd, driving range Aughtie Dve, Albert Park; ☉ dawn-dusk
This 18-hole championship golf course is situated on the fringes of **Albert Park Lake** (p78) by the Australian Formula One Grand Prix racing circuit, just 2km from the city.

ROYAL PARK Map p209
☎ 9387 3585; Poplar Rd, Parkville; ☉ dawn-dusk
Near the zoo, you'd do well to book a round at this nine-hole course.

YARRA BEND Map p211
☎ 9481 3729; Yarra Bend Rd, Fairfield; ☉ dawn-dusk
Yarra Bend is the best public course for views over the Yarra River and you have 27 holes in which to enjoy them; bookings essential.

IN-LINE SKATING

Although many people scoot along on semi-motorised or puff-powered scooters, you can still enjoy a scenic skate along the foreshore. The best paths are those around Port Phillip Bay, particularly the stretch from Port Melbourne south through St Kilda to Brighton.

ALBERT PARK IN-LINE SKATES
Map pp214-15
☎ 9645 9099; 179 Victoria Ave, Albert Park; ☉ 10am-7pm Mon-Fri, 9am-7pm Sat & Sun
Walk in with your passport for identification purposes and roll out with skates and padding for $7 per hour. There's also a day rate of $20.

ROCK'N'ROLL'N' SKATE SHOP Map p213
☎ 9525 3434; Suite 3, 22 Fitzroy St, St Kilda; ☉ 10am-7pm Mon-Fri, 9am-7pm Sat & Sun
Skates and padding for one/two/three hours cost $8/15/20. Overnight hire, with pick up after 5pm and return before noon, is $15, and 24-hour hire is $25.

LAWN BOWLS

Bowling clubs opened their doors to non-members in the last few years, gaining a wave of youthful followers. These new proponents of lawn bowls appreciate the social atmosphere, and that you can play in bare feet, slippers or thongs, with a drink in one hand. A game costs between $5 and $10.

NORTH FITZROY BOWLS Map p210
☎ 9481 3137; www.fvbowls.com.au; 578 Brunswick St, North Fitzroy; ☉ daily
This centre, officially known as the Fitzroy Victoria Bowling & Sports Club, has lights for night bowls, barbecues and a beer garden. The dress code is neat-casual, with slippers or thongs. Phone to make a booking and for opening times, which vary day to day.

ST KILDA BOWLING CLUB Map p213
☎ 9537 0370; 66 Fitzroy St, St Kilda; ☉ noon-sunset Tue-Sun
The only dress code is no shoes. This club provides bowls and a bit of friendly instruction for first timers; *boules* is also available.

SAILING

Melbourne's two main ocean races are the Melbourne to Devonport and Melbourne to Hobart events, held annually between Christmas and New Year. The Melbourne to Hobart race goes around Tasmania's wild western coast; the more famous Sydney to Hobart event runs down the eastern coast.

Hobsons Bay Yacht Club (Map p216; ☎ 9397 6393; www.hbyc.asn.au; 268 Nelson Pl, Williamstown) welcomes volunteers Saturday and Sunday. In summer, you can join a boat with the **Royal Melbourne Yacht Squadron** (Map p213; ☎ 9534 0227; Pier Rd, St Kilda) from Wednesday to Sunday ($11).

You can sail on glorious **Albert Park Lake** (p78) with **Jolly Roger School of Sailing** (Map pp214-15; ☎ 9690 5862; www.jollyroger sailing.com.au; Aquatic Dve; ☺ 9am-5pm), which has been run by the same family since 1882. Boat hire starts at $55 per hour. Rowboats and aquabikes are also available for $22 per half-hour.

SURFING

The closest surf beaches to Melbourne are those on the **Mornington Peninsula** (p176) and **Bellarine Peninsula** (p169), both about an hour's drive from the city.

WINDSURFING & KITESURFING

Elwood, just south of St Kilda, is a popular sailboarding area. **RPS – the Board Store** (Map pp200-01; ☎ 9525 6475; www.rpstheboard store.com; 87 Ormond Rd, Elwood) hires gear and offers tuition. A one-hour introductory lesson in kitesurfing costs $75. A three-hour introductory course in windsurfing costs $129. All gear is included, and courses are weather-dependent.

HEALTH & FITNESS

There's no need to stop your health and beauty regime because you're away from home. In fact, Melbourne is a great place to cultivate a regime if you don't have one already.

ALTERNATIVE THERAPIES

Whether you're into rebirthing, reflexology or Reiki, there's a therapist for you. See the Yellow Pages for full listings. The **Southern School of Natural Therapies** (Map pp206-08; ☎ 9416 1448; www.southernschool.com; 39 Victoria St, Fitzroy) offers subsidised natural health care at the college's clinic.

GYMS

Not happy with your body shape? Attending one of the city's innumerable gyms will help you sculpt it into the desired shape. Many gyms are open only to members, but offer

yoga and Pilates classes to the general public. The women-only **Fernwood Fitness Centre** (Map p213; ☎ 9534 8088; www.fernwoodfitness .com.au; 203 Fitzroy St, St Kilda) charges $15 for a casual visit. **Fitness First** (Map p212; ☎ 9425 9888; 560 Church St, Richmond) has excellent facilities and charges $18 for a casual visit.

JOGGING

Melbourne has some great routes for runners. Favourites include the Tan track around the **Royal Botanic Gardens** (p60) and the path around **Albert Park Lake** (p78); both circuits are approximately 5km. The bicycle tracks beside the Yarra River and along the bay are also good.

PLACES FOR PAMPERING

Day spas are the perfect way to take a holiday from yourself; let someone else look after you for a while.

GEISHA Map pp202-04

☎ 9663 5544; www.geishaonline.com; 1st fl, 285 Little Collins St; ☺ 11am-7pm Tue & Wed, 11am-8pm Thu
This Japanese-style hair and relaxation centre supplies *yukata* (belted cotton robes) and slippers, and offers massage and hair treatments, plus tearooms and relaxation packages. Bookings essential.

JAPANESE BATH HOUSE Map p211

☎ 9419 0268; 59 Cromwell St, Collingwood; ☺ noon-11pm Tue-Fri, noon-8pm Sat & Sun
You can scrub yourself silly at Melbourne's only traditional Japanese bathhouse. The communal space has a shower area, hot tub and steam room. Shiatsu massage is also available; bookings required.

MAN, WHAT A FUSS Map pp202-04

☎ 9642 3860; 5 McKillop St; ☺ 10am-6pm Mon-Fri
Buffing up takes on a whole new meaning here, where facials reinvigorate tired skin. Men unite for a hair treatment, massage, manicure or pedicure.

SWIMMING

Depending on where you're from, the term 'grab your bathers' may sound a bit odd. 'Bathers' means a swimming costume, so grab yours and head to one of Melbourne's super public pools.

Melbourne Sports & Aquatic Centre (below)

FITZROY SWIMMING POOL Map pp206-08
☎ 9417 6493; Alexandra Pde, Fitzroy; adult/concession $3.80/2.20; ⊙ Nov-Mar

A community action group saved the glorious Fitzroy pool when the council tried to close it, citing high up-keep costs as the rationale. Locals love catching a few rays between laps up in the bleachers or on the lawn; there's also a toddlers' pool.

HAROLD HOLT SWIM CENTRE
Map pp200-01
☎ 8290 1678; 9 High St, Glen Iris; adult/concession $4/3; ⊙ year round

There's an indoor pool and a 50m heated outdoor pool open daily, as well as the high-diving platform and a shaded grassy area. The swimming centre is named in honour of Harold Holt, the Australian prime minister who went missing at Portsea surf beach – presumed drowned.

MELBOURNE CITY BATHS Map pp206-08
☎ 9663 5888; 420 Swanston St; adult/concession $4/3.20; ⊙ year round

This 25m indoor pool is a city institution. Squash courts are also available for hire, and there's a gym, spa and sauna. See also p56.

MELBOURNE SPORTS & AQUATIC CENTRE Map pp214-15
☎ 9926 1555; Albert Rd, Albert Park; adult/concession $5.50/4.10; ⊙ year round

In the parklands of Albert Park the Aquatic Centre features a 75m lap pool. Work done, go play in the wave pool and on the water slide.

PRAHRAN AQUATIC CENTRE Map p212
☎ 8290 9140; 41 Essex St, Prahran; adult/child $3.50/1.80; ⊙ Oct-Apr

The 50m heated outdoor pool is surrounded by a little lawn – to be avoided by those with self-confidence issues. There's piped music above and below water, as well as a café.

RICHMOND RECREATION CENTRE
Map p211
☎ 9205 5032; Gleadell St, Richmond; adult/concession $3.80/2.20; ⊙ 6am-9pm Mon-Thu, 6am-8pm Fri, 8am-6pm Sat & Sun

This 50m pool doesn't have the chlorine cloud that clogs the air in many indoor pools. It's fresh and clean, and a hub of activity. Part of the pool is often given over to water-aerobics classes, so you can pace your stroke to disco beats.

TENNIS

Grab a mate and some sneakers for a hit of tennis. The **East Melbourne Tennis Centre** (Map p205; ☎ 9417 6511; cnr Simpson & Albert Sts, East Melbourne) charges between $18 and $26 for court hire (including racquets); it costs more on weekends and after 4pm. **Melbourne Park** (Map p205; ☎ 9286 1244; Batman Ave), venue of the Australian Open, has 23 outdoor and five indoor courts for $20 per hour, plus $5 for a racquet.

YOGA

Iyengar yoga looks deceptively easy. This strenuous form of yoga increases your body's flexibility and suppleness. Classes are generally one hour long and cost between $14 and $17. The **Action School of Yoga** (Map pp206-08; ☎ 9415 9798; www.actionyoga.com; level 1, 275 Smith St, Fitzroy) is an excellent school. The **St Kilda Iyengar Yoga School** (Map p213; ☎ 9537 1015; www.skys.com.au; 11/82 Acland St, St Kilda) is opposite Luna Park.

Shopping

Shopping

Melbourne and its inner-city suburbs offer comprehensive shopping opportunities, embracing brave design and chic aesthetics. Outlets stock the best and most eclectic from around the world, as well as home-grown goods that mix it with the best of them.

Melburnians, it seems, are addicted to the soft rustle of wrapping tissue paper and high gloss of shopping bags. They're savvy shoppers, and know and love quality products.

We've included just a smattering of the city's multitude of speciality stores, focusing on those with a particularly Melbourne bent, be they city institutions or distinctly Melbourne designer stores. Melbourne's

changing weather conditions can play havoc with your choice of attire; for a daily weather and fashion forecast visit www.michigirl.com.au.

Opening Hours

Most shops open between 9.30am and 10am and close between 5.30pm and 6pm Monday to Wednesday and Saturday. Late-night shopping sees most stores close at 9pm on Thursday and Friday. On Sunday, stores open around 11am and close about 4pm. In the following listings, we've quoted opening hours if they vary from these general times.

Consumer Taxes

A 10% federal tax on goods and services (GST) is automatically added to almost everything you buy in Australia. Visitors to Australia are entitled to a refund of any GST paid on items over $300 from one supplier, bought within 30 days of departure from the country. You can organise a refund at the designated booth located past customs at Melbourne Airport. Contact the Australian Customs Service (☎ 1300 363 263; www.customs.gov.au) for details.

Bargaining

While Melburnians love a bargain, bargaining is not the norm, unless you're at a car-boot second-hand market. If you find yourself buying a whole new wardrobe from one store, it probably wouldn't hurt to ask if it could throw in an extra shirt, or knock a little off the total.

CENTRAL MELBOURNE

The purchasing potential in Melbourne's CBD runs the gamut from exquisite boutique shopping in its cobbled lanes to the department-store bustle on main thoroughfares.

The city's main department stores, Myer and David Jones, are both on the Bourke Street Mall. Other all-in-ones include QV (p58), Melbourne Central (p56), Southbank (p61), the Crown Casino & Entertainment Complex (p59) and Australia on Collins (260 Collins St). The real magic of Melbourne shopping lies in its strip shopping, so you'd do well to come out from under the covers and explore the city's lanes and secret streets. Walking is the best mode of transport. For public transport routes about town, see the transport network maps (pp217–18).

THE EAST

ARCHITEXT Map pp202-04 *Books*
☎ 9650 3474; www.architext.com.au; 41 Exhibition St
Even if you're not looking for a text about houses built on cliffs, this shop is dang swanky. Architext covers the gamut of design and architecture-related titles, including environmental architecture, urban design, photography, theory, journals and magazines. It also stocks the best range of Melbourne-specific books: look for titles by author Philip Goad or photographer John Gollings.

CHIODO Map pp202-04 *Men's Clothing*
☎ 9663 0044; basement, 114 Russell St
Chiodo subverts classic male fashion, so that army-style khaki shirts are deliciously embroidered with pink tulips. A business shirt will be perfect except for that inside-out piece, designed to reference the construction of garments. Chiodo is clever, cheeky and chic, and accessorises with fab local designers.

COUNTER Map p205 *Art & Craft*
☎ 9650 7775; www.craftvic.asn.au; 31 Flinders Lane;
🕑 11am-5.30pm Tue-Sat
The retail arm of Craft Victoria, Counter has a range of handcrafted, locally made jewellery, ceramics, textiles, wood and glass. We're not talking ashtrays and frilly tissue-box covers either; this is classy stuff. What better Melbourne memento than an original piece from Craft Victoria? Add a notch to your karma belt, too, for supporting local artists.

EG ETAL Map pp202-04 *Jewellery*
☎ 9663 4334; 185 Little Collins St
With a collection of pieces from over 40 local and overseas designers, this unique retail space holds many little treasures. It's a place where

Clothing Sizes
Measurements approximate only, try before you buy

Women's Clothing

Aus/UK	8	10	12	14	16	18
Europe	36	38	40	42	44	46
Japan	5	7	9	11	13	15
USA	6	8	10	12	14	16

Women's Shoes

Aus/USA	5	6	7	8	9	10
Europe	35	36	37	38	39	40
France only	35	36	38	39	40	42
Japan	22	23	24	25	26	27
UK	3½	4½	5½	6½	7½	8½

Men's Clothing

Aus	92	96	100	104	108	112
Europe	46	48	50	52	54	56
Japan	S		M	M		L
UK/USA	35	36	37	38	39	40

Men's Shirts (Collar Sizes)

Aus/Japan	38	39	40	41	42	43
Europe	38	39	40	41	42	43
UK/USA	15	15½	16	16½	17	17½

Men's Shoes

Aus/UK	7	8	9	10	11	12
Europe	41	42	43	44½	46	47
Japan	26	27	27½	28	29	30
USA	7½	8½	9½	10½	11½	12½

fishing wire and metal piping are precious metals, and where aesthetics and meaning are given equal consideration, with symbolic pieces preferred over the purely contrived.

LE LOUVRE Map pp202-04 *Women's Clothing*
☎ 9654 7641; 74 Collins St
Behind the couturier's classic and enigmatic façade, moneyed women are measured up for the likes of Westwood, Givenchy, Stella McCartney and Galliano. Society lady Lillian Wightman founded this treasure in 1935; it has now been handed on to her daughter, Georgina Weir.

RIVER DISTRICT

AUSTRALIAN CENTRE FOR THE MOVING IMAGE Map pp202-04 *Gallery Shop*
ACMI; ☎ 8663 2573; ground fl, Federation Sq
ACMI has the best range of postcards (most derived from past ACMI exhibitions) and Lomo cameras, including the Flash Action Sampler: 'more than a photograph, but not quite a movie'. It's also stocked with hard-to-get DVDs

Shopping – Central Melbourne

such as Matthew Barney's *The Order* from the *Cremaster Cycle*, screen-printed Ts, plus books, bags and stationery, all with some screen reference.

CITY HATTERS Map pp202-04 *Milliner*
☎ 9614 3294; 211 Flinders St

For those dapper gentlemen thinking of attending the Melbourne Cup, stop at City Hatters next to Flinders Street Station before taking the train to Flemington Racecourse. Top that outfit with a bowler, fur felt, pork pie or that Australian icon, the Akubra. You can also pick up a simple cap to keep the sun off your face.

THE WEST

ALICE EUPHEMIA Map pp202-04 *Clothing*
☎ 9650 4300; 241 Flinders Lane

The staff here really know their product: offbeat clothing, jewellery and accessories. That's because the staff are also the designers, which is handy when you're not quite sure which bit of gorgeously printed or otherwise embellished fabric is supposed to drape where.

BASEMENT DISCS Map pp202-04 *Music*
☎ 9654 1110; www.basementdiscs.com.au; 24 Block Pl

Apart from being music specialists, supplying an exemplary range of CD titles across all genres, Basement Discs has regular in-store performances by big-name touring and local acts. Descend the long narrow staircase to the basement for a browse; you never know who you might find playing.

BERNARD'S MAGIC SHOP
Map pp202-04 *Children's*
☎ 9670 9270; 211 Elizabeth St

Australia's oldest magic shop (open since 1937), Bernard's sure knows a good fake dog poo, whoopee cushion or fly-in-the-ice-cube when it sees one. But, practical jokes aside, there are items for the practising magician, such as rope and card tricks, as well as instructional videos.

BETTINA LIANO
Map pp202-04 *Women's Clothing*
☎ 9654 1912; 269 Little Collins St

Pour yourself into a pair of itsy-bitsy jeans, for which Bettina Liano is famous. Designs are very 'now', so you probably won't want to be wearing them tomorrow. But, hey, you'll look pretty fabulous for a moment.

FOREIGN LANGUAGE BOOKSHOP
Map pp202-04 *Books*
☎ 9654 2883; 259 Collins St; ✣ closed Sun

Read Paulo Coelho in Spanish, pick up a Scrabble board in French, or perhaps some tapes in Russian for those long car journeys. The Foreign Language Bookshop has more than texts to help you learn German grammar or Japanese kanji; it's a den of surprises, and stocks a range of international magazines.

GENKI Map pp202-04 *Clothes & Accessories*
☎ 9650 6366; shop 5, Cathedral Arcade, 37 Swanston St; ✣ closed Sun

Stocking funky imported Japanese clothing for men and women, accessories, and its own T-shirts with slogans such as 'I Love Kissing' and 'I Love Frisbee', Genki is a haven for all things cute, pink and quirky. You'll also find next-big-thing labels from London and New York.

SCANLAN & THEODORE
Map pp202-04 *Women's Clothing & Accessories*
☎ 9650 6195; 285 Little Collins St

If you want to purchase Melbourne's finest, this is it. Mixing glamour and luxury, these special garments become part of you, making you feel how you always want to feel: gorgeous! The best of Aussie design, mixed with European accessories from Jamin Peuch and

City Hatters (above)

Pampering Products

Aesop (Map pp202-04; ☎ 9639 2436; www.aesop .net.au; 35 Albert Coates Lane) This Melbourne-based company has a range of sublime plant-based skin, hair and body preparations that eschew the girly image. Look also for its store in **St Kilda** (Map p213; ☎ 9534 9433; 2 Acland St).

Aveda (Map pp202-04; ☎ 9654 2217; www.aveda .com; shop 318, Australia on Collins, Collins St) Botanical preparations for the skin and hair, as well as a range of make-up.

Kleins (Map pp206-08; ☎ 9416 1221; www.kleins perfumery.com.au; 313 Brunswick St, Fitzroy) Stocks hundreds of lines; if you can't get it here, you can't get it.

Lush (Map pp202-04; ☎ 9654 8665; www.lush.com .au; 153 Swanston St) You don't really need the address; follow your nose to the outlet, which stocks handmade soaps and bath bombs.

So Hum (Map p209; ☎ 9329 1170; 139 Queen Victoria Market) A range of cruelty-free, vegetable-based products and essential oils.

Alessandro Dell' Acqua; it's the stuff of fashion aficionados' dreams. Scanlan also has an outlet in **South Yarra** (566 Chapel St).

CARLTON & FITZROY

No Melbourne shopping jaunt worth its weight in credit cards would be complete without a visit to Brunswick St, Fitzroy. The street holds a diverse range of retail outlets straddling grunge and glamour with aplomb. Gertrude St also warrants a look, as does Smith St – the stretch between Johnston St and Alexandra Pde is lined with sporty-type clearance outlets.

Lygon St, Carlton has a number of sophisticated clothing stores that make for great distractions between coffees.

For transport options from the city, see the boxed text, p66.

BOOKS FOR COOKS Map pp206-08   *Books*
☎ 8415 1415; 233 Gertrude St, Fitzroy

Want to learn to make the classic Aussie three-course meal – party pies, rissoles and a lamington? You're sure to find the recipe here, among a selection of new and out-of-print kitchen titles. For a list of tantalising books, see the boxed text, p41.

BRUNSWICK STREET BOOKSTORE
Map pp206-08   *Books*
☎ 9416 1030; 305 Brunswick St, Fitzroy

Upstairs, in a recent addition to this enduring and loved bookstore, is a specialised selection of well-sourced art literature, from books on skateboard stickers to Caravaggio. A large, white ottoman gives this space a gallery feel and a place for people to browse the pages of the display books. Downstairs is stocked with recent releases, classic contemporary titles and a smattering of theory.

CRUMPLER Map pp206-08   *Bags & Stuff*
☎ 9417 5338; www.crumpler.com.au; cnr Gertrude & Smith Sts, Fitzroy

Crumpler had humble beginnings, making bags specifically for Melbourne's bike couriers. Their products impressed everyone, so it made more. The bags are durable, practical and have unique designs, and they're now sold all over the world. Situated among some of the city's quirkiest shops is this flagship outlet that also familiarised us with bag names such as Scrote, Snauros and Company Embarrassment.

DEAKIN TOYS Map pp206-08   *Children's*
☎ 9419 1871; 155 Brunswick St, Fitzroy;
🕙 10am-6pm Thu-Sat, 10am-4pm Sun

If you hear yourself saying 'they don't make 'em like they used to', come here, where they do. Wooden puzzles, mobiles, trucks and puppets are hand-whittled and hand-painted with loving detail. The makers also run the shop floor and will duck into the on-site workshop to paint your name on your purchase. With every buy you also get a bean that just might sprout into the clouds given the magic of this store.

JASPER Map pp206-08   *Caffeine Dealer*
☎ 9416 0921; www.jaspercoffee.com;
267 Brunswick St, Fitzroy

All coffee paraphernalia and accompaniments such as delicious gourmet chocolates and biscuits are sold here. You can also sample famous blends as you sit in the caffeine-embellished surrounds of the store. Jasper also has an outlet at **Prahran Market** (p74). Indulge in one of its Fair Trade blends and 10% from the sale will go towards buying medical equipment for the people of East Timor. Coffee with a conscience.

KLEINS Map pp206-08   *Perfumery*
☎ 9416 1221; www.kleinsperfumery.com.au;
313 Brunswick St, Fitzroy

Experiencing the hedonic scent of Kleins is like stepping into a luxury spa. Imported products from France as well as fine lotions created locally are found in an abundance of boxes covering the walls. Kleins also brews its own brand of perfume, with fragrances changing to suit the season. Melbourne women enjoy hours in here sampling everything before deciding what to buy.

DOUGLAS & HOPE

Map pp206-08   *Clothing & Cushions*
☎ 9417 0662; 181 Brunswick St, Fitzroy
Along with New Zealand label Karen Walker and popular local designer Gorman, Douglas & Hope carries its own range of quilts and cushions. Made in Melbourne from pieces of vintage fabric, the quilts are so soft and dreamy that it's hard to resist curling up on them and going to sleep in the store.

LITTLE SALON Map pp206-08 *Precious Things*
☎ 9419 7123; 71 Gertrude St, Fitzroy
Part art gallery, part retail outlet, this little store is an aesthete's heaven. Wearable art, such as bags made from seat belts, knitted corsages and button bracelets, shares space here with pieces for your wall or shelf. Everything is locally made and extremely well priced.

MAX WATTS INDUSTRIA

Map pp206-08   *Ex-industrial*
☎ 9417 1117; 202 Gertrude St, Fitzroy
This is the place to go if you want to deck your lounge out like a classroom, or your bedroom like a hospital ward. Globes, desks, ancient surgical equipment, microscopes, it's all here. Poking around Industria is a fascinating way to spend an afternoon.

MELBOURNE CLEANSKIN COMPANY

Map pp206-08   *Wine*
☎ 9347 9233; www.melbournecleanskins.com.au;
350-352 Drummond St, Carlton
Melbourne Cleanskin does a roaring trade from suffering students in search of an occasional treat, as well as the local professional well aware of the excellent quality. 'Cleanskin' wines are simply those bearing no maker's labels, with product from all over Australia and New Zealand priced under $15. Tastings are held after 5pm Friday and all day on Saturday.

NORTHSIDE Map pp206-08   *Records*
☎ 9417 7557; 236 Gertrude St, Fitzroy;
⏰ 11am-6pm Mon-Thu, 11am-7pm Fri, 11am-5pm Sat
Northside stocks everything from straight-up funk through to Bollywood soundtracks, much

of it on vinyl. When you've finished choosing your music be sure to look at the walls – the interior won the Dulux Colour Grand Prix in 2003. Northside will also track down rare albums on request.

POLYESTER Map pp206-08   *Books & Music*
☎ 9419 5223; www.polyester.com.au;
330 Brunswick St, Fitzroy
If Charles Manson had a personal library, Polyester Books would be it. Specialising in literature, magazines and audiovisual materials on topics from satanic cult sex to underground comics and everything in between, Polyester Books detests censorship. Its pride in its product and outspoken stance have staff working hard to find new and interesting titles, almost impossible to source anywhere else.

Don't expect to find the latest boy band on the shelves across the road at **Polyester Music** (☎ 9419 5137; 387 Brunswick St, Fitzroy). Shop here instead for titles in the genre of Australian and international independent artists. As long as you know what you're talking about, you'll be treated with respect and dodge the kind of attitude associated with music boffins.

Deakin Toys (p149)

QUEEN Map pp206-08   *Clothing & Accessories*
☎ 9416 4964; 71 Smith St, Fitzroy;
☺ 11am-6pm Mon-Sat, noon-5pm Sun

One of a number of independent clothing stores in the area, Queen offers a range of bags, jewellery and clothes that you won't see on the backs of every second person you pass. The store has its own label but also stocks other Melbourne designers.

READINGS Map pp206-08   *Books*
☎ 9347 6633; www.readings.com.au;
309 Lygon St, Carlton

A favourite among Melbourne book lovers for its inviting atmosphere, eclectic range of literature, CDs and DVDs, and well-educated staff. Readings has a unique supply of Australian poetry and fiction and hosts regular in-store events with local and international literary speakers and musicians. The event calendar is posted on the website.

ST LUKES Map pp206-08   *Art Supplies*
☎ 9486 9992; 225 Gertrude St, Fitzroy;
☺ 10am-6pm Mon-Fri, 10am-5pm Sat

The art supplies available at St Lukes are almost too beautiful to use. Pick up a sketchbook, a travel watercolour kit, or perhaps some gold leaf. If you have a spare $259 you can buy a beautiful, fully articulated giraffe drawing mannequin. The window sometimes doubles as a miniature gallery for local artists.

TRAVELLERS BOOKSTORE

Map pp206-08   *Books*
☎ 9417 4179; 294 Smith St, Collingwood

Stocks everything you need for advice on weekends away to round-the-world journeys. With a good selection of books and maps, the staff are friendly and happy to help with any travel tips. Has a travel agency in store.

VEGAN WARES

Map pp206-08   *Shoes & Accessories*
☎ 9417 0230; www.veganwares.com;
78 Smith St, Collingwood

Vegan Wares makes shoes from microfibre rather than leather so they're perfect for people who eschew animal products but still want something durable, comfortable and fashionable on their feet. The footwear comes in a broad range of styles for men and women – it even makes ballet shoes – and can be made to order. Belts and wallets are also available.

Top Five Melbourne Mementos

- **Cardigan** – Melbourne's weather commands layering. You may as well do it in local-designer style; for males, **Chiodo** (p147); females, **Scanlan & Theodore** (p148).
- **Coffee** – it's a conspicuous thing in Melbourne; try **Jasper** (p149).
- **Music** – because every holiday needs a soundtrack; buy a local artist's CD (see p26) from a local outlet such as **Polyester** (opposite).
- **Visual art** – check the city's commercial galleries (p96) or **Counter** (p147).
- **Wine** – Australian wines are up there with the world's best; try the **Melbourne Cleanskin Company** (opposite).

WUNDERKAAMER

Map pp206-08   *Ex-industrial*
☎ 9348 0048; 155 Elgin St, Carlton; ☺ 11am-6pm Tue-Fri, noon-5pm Sat

Wunderkaamer is the sort of place where mad scientists might come to shop – it sells taxidermied animals, bugs in jars, antique scientific and surgical tools and carnivorous plants, among other things. Spend some time looking though the Cabinet of Wonders in the corner; each drawer contains a new surprise.

ZETTA FLORENCE

Map pp206-08   *Archival Stationery*
☎ 9416 2236; www.zettaflorence.com.au;
197 Brunswick St, Fitzroy

Zetta Florence specialises in long-term preservation for photographers and artists, as well as Australia's national archives. Its impressive showroom has been artistically arranged to display practical products, such as binders, folios and designer archive boxes, alongside exquisitely bound notebooks, quality papers and gorgeous cards.

ABBOTSFORD & RICHMOND

Bridge Rd, Richmond is renowned for off-the-rack bargains, and lined with clearance outlets and seconds stores. Church St is a haven for designer-furniture stores, with the likes of Space and Poliform, while Swan St is a mishmash of retail shops and supermarkets. See the boxed text, p71, for transport options from the city.

DIMMEYS Map p211 *Emporium*
☎ 9427 0442; 140 Swan St, Richmond

Fancy it ain't, but Dimmeys is legendary for its iconic Richmond dome and its TV face – a moustachioed ex-footballer. The huge emporium sells everything cheap, from undies to things for the shed, and the window displays prove that Dimmeys doesn't take itself too seriously (even male mannequins wear bras during the lingerie sell out).

PASSIONFRUIT – SENSUALITY SHOP
Map p211 *Sex Shop*
☎ 9421 3391; 404 Bridge Rd, Richmond; ⏱ 10am-6pm Mon-Wed, 10am-10pm Thu-Sat, noon-6pm Sun

Passionfruit takes the seedy out of sex shops. A huge range of sensual oils, books, lingerie and toys are openly displayed in warm, welcoming surrounds. There are no blacked-out windows or stained overcoat wearers here. It's a playful, light-hearted acknowledgement of human intimacy, and…um, needs.

RG MADDEN
Map p212 *Home wares & Accessories*
☎ 1800 815 662; 597 Church St, Richmond

This large, sleekly outfitted store props local and international designers side by side. Whatever your designer want, it's likely you'll find a solution here. Alessi key ring? Hi-tech doll's house? Banana lounge? RG Madden's sharp range of home wares, furniture, jewellery, bags, stationery and electronic gadgetry will bamboozle even the most seasoned browser.

SOUTH YARRA, TOORAK & PRAHRAN

OK shoppers, let's get serious. The perennially popular Chapel St is busting at the seams with Australia's leading fashion designers. While most of us can't afford to deck out a wardrobe with these exclusive offerings, you can't afford to miss it. Tiny

Armadale

In the market for some handsome antiques, commercial art, a lush carpet or just a little something in gold? High St, Armadale can oblige. This is chichi central, surpassing Toorak Rd for extravagant old-school offerings.

Greville St surpasses its size in shopping appeal, with a high density of speciality stores, from retro to underwear. See the boxed text, p73, for information on transport from the city.

CHAPEL BAZAAR Map p212 *Second-hand*
☎ 9529 1727; 217-223 Chapel St, Prahran

From Noddy egg cups to 1950s couches and yellowing lace; as long as it's retro, it earns a space at this giant undercover market. Permanent stallholders sell off their hoarded treasures at marked prices. Even if you walk out empty handed, you'll have a whole new appreciation for shag carpets and paisley.

COLLETTE DINNIGAN Map p212 *Clothing*
☎ 9827 2111; 553 Chapel St, South Yarra

Looking for an Oscar frock? Look no further. New Zealand–born, Australian-claimed, internationally renowned Collette Dinnigan has dressed Oscar attendees and celebrities aplenty – Naomi Watts and Halle Berry to name a couple – for their slinky saunter. Signature delicate lace gowns and underwear, as well as shimmering satin pieces, celebrate the feminine form.

DINOSAUR DESIGNS
Map p212 *Home wares & Jewellery*
☎ 9827 2600; 562 Chapel St, South Yarra

Polyester resins previously only used for industrial purposes have been brightly coloured and whipped into figurative shapes for the home and body. Founded nigh on 10 years ago, Dinosaur Designs is inspired by robots, prehistoric images and tattoo designs when creating its unique range of home wares and contemporary jewellery.

ELLIN AMBE Map p212 *Clothing*
☎ 9827 8022; 511 Chapel St, South Yarra

Melbourne designer Di Clarke has been making stylish duds for her Chapel St boutique for over 10 years under the pseudonym Ellin Ambe. Her line of handsome garments for women is teamed with overseas designer accessories, by the likes of Rossi, Tribu and Mogil.

FAT 272 Map p212 *Clothing & Accessories*
☎ 9510 2311; 272 Chapel St, Prahran

Über-cool young designs such as Gorman and I Peck Your Pun line up with Fat's own label. The clothing may not make the international fashion catwalks, but that's the point. Individual bags and accessories complete the offerings. Fat has another store in Fitzroy,

Fat 52 (Map pp206-08; ☎ 9486 0391; 52 Johnston St) with a similar range, but minus the built-in-the-floor water feature.

HANDWORKS Map p212   *Art & Craft Supplies*
☎ 9533 8566; 244 Chapel St, Prahran

The range of sequins, feathers, papers, tiles and other mediums will have you craftily bedazzling your backpack in no time. Kewpie dolls and disco balls for your rear-view mirror need little further adornment but, then, you could create an interesting lampshade out of them; Handworks has wire lampshades, too.

KILL CITY Map p212   *Books*
☎ 9510 6661; 226 Chapel St, Prahran

There's a murderer on every shelf here. For new release or second-hand crime books, Kill City has the most comprehensive range in the city. From true crime to classic whodunnits, read between the lines to find out why they dunnit.

OWL Map p212   *Funky Things*
☎ 9510 6077; 30 Chatham St, Prahran

Other Worldly Lives (OWL) scours the globe collecting everyday items with an original bent. It stocks a range of Lomo and Holga cameras, ace stationery and Afro-Ken – the dog doll with a huge interchangeable Velcro afro wig. You might also pick up a designer alarm clock or coat hooks.

ST KILDA

As you'd expect from a suburb entirely centred on leisure, St Kilda has its fair share of interesting boutiques and home-wares stores. The big three – Acland, Fitzroy and Barkly Sts – should keep you trawling gleefully for days. The suburb's east, Carlisle St (over Brighton Rd), is more local, but no less urbane. See the boxed text, p75, for transport options from the city.

COSMOS Map p213   *Books & Music*
☎ 9525 3852; shop 1/112 Acland St

The shelves at Cosmos are laden with a wide range of books including art, architecture, cookery and fiction. Floor space is tight; squeeze past the specials tables and make your way to the back of the store, which carries a range of CDs.

DOLLHOUSE Map p213   *Clothing*
☎ 9525 3520; 23 Carlisle St

With racks of accessories, jewellery and clothing in all shades of black, make Dollhouse your first stop if you're looking for the perfect thing to wear to a hipper-than-thou party. That said, it's a surprisingly friendly store with chatty, interested staff who will help you acquire that layered Melbourne look with a minimum of attitude.

HOSS Map p213   *Clothing*
☎ 9537 0933; shop 3/135 Fitzroy St

The more paint splattered and frayed they are, the more you'll pay for the shirts, jeans and knitwear here. Hoss carries men's and women's labels such as Tsubi, Shem and Roy; although it has to be said that these small labels are more ubiquitous than edgy these days.

HUNTER GATHERER Map p213   *Clothing*
☎ 9593 8168; 82a Acland St

Into retro? Hunter Gatherer takes all the hard work out of trawling through numerous racks of mothball-scented clothes. Run by the welfare organisation Brotherhood of St Laurence, Hunter Gatherer filters through its 26-odd op shops to bring you the hippest second-hand gear. It also stocks its own label. All profits go to programmes to assist low-income families, the elderly and unemployed.

RAOUL RECORDS Map p213 *Music*
☎ 9525 5066; www.raoulrecords.com.au;
221 Barkly St
Specialising in soul-funk vinyl and new music (especially electronic, house and hip-hop), Raoul stocks only the best. It annually awards its own Best Record of the Year, with the HW Slack trophy – a tribute to the 'old St Kilda' when Raoul's neighbours comprised eclectic stores (such as the second-hand no-name premises with the proprietor's name, HW Slack, inscribed above the door) rather than this-minute fashion outlets.

SOUTH MELBOURNE & ALBERT PARK

While you wouldn't necessarily cross town for the shopping alone, the area's seaside location and restaurants are complemented by some typically refined retail options. Head for Dundas Pl in Albert Park. In and around the South Melbourne Market (p79) is a vibrant scene, as is South Melbourne's main shopping strip, Clarendon St. See the boxed text, p77, for transport details from town.

EMPIRE III
Map pp214-15 *Clothing & Accessories*
☎ 9682 6677; **63 Cardigan Pl, Albert Park**
Pretty vintage clothes, accessories, soft furnishings and furniture spill out the doors of Empire

III. Where else could you pick up a rose-printed quilt, a chandelier, a nightie and a sumptuous evening gown? Empire III also has its own range of girlie bags and purses created from vintage, floral fabrics.

HUSK Map pp214-15 *Clothing & Accessories*
☎ 9690 6994; **123 Dundas Pl, Albert Park**
A treasure trove of discerningly selected clothes from Australian and New Zealand designers hang alongside acute imported labels. Investigate further and you'll find jewellery, accessories, children's clothes, home wares and exotic bits and pieces. If you make it past all of these distractions, you'll find a café serving great food and teas from Husk's signature collection.

VICTORIAN TAPESTRY WORKSHOP
Map pp214-15 *Tapestries*
☎ 9699 7885; **262-266 Park St, South Melbourne; admission $4;** ⊗ **10am-3pm Mon-Fri**
Since its foundation in 1976, the Tapestry Workshop has been creating striking, contemporary work. If you visit during viewing hours or take a guided tour, you'll see the weavers at their massive looms, creating tapestries for public and private display. You could also buy a little something from the workshop's range of woven jewellery, yarns and small tapestries. **Tours** ($6) run at 2pm Wednesday and 11am Thursday; it's best to call to make a booking.

Sleeping

Sleeping

Melbourne's accommodation options cover all types and price ranges. In the mid- to upper-range categories, you can choose from hotels, motels, serviced apartments, B&Bs and self-contained accommodation (not serviced).

Many of the larger hotels offer breakfast. Many also have free parking, though others can charge up to $12 per day. Motels are usually more basic than hotels, but you can almost always drive to your door. Check-in for hotels and motels is around 1pm, checkout around 10am.

Melbourne's B&Bs are small and with a personal touch, and cater for those looking for a home-away-from-home experience, including a hearty home-cooked breakfast. There's a growing propensity for individually themed rooms at B&Bs, too.

For an equally intimate experience with a dash of style try a boutique hotel. They're synonymous with individuality and chic, and often occupy classic Victorian-era buildings.

Melbourne also has an ever-expanding range of self-contained apartments and serviced apartments. More spacious than regular hotels, with their own kitchen and laundry facilities, these accommodation options can be better value and more comfortable than an equivalently priced hotel, especially for people travelling in a group. Several companies manage blocks of apartments, and you're likely to be offered a better deal if you speak to head office rather than individual managers. Try **Apartments of Melbourne** (☎ 9280 1000; www .aom.com.au), **Punt Hill** (☎ 1800 331 529; www.punthill-apartments.com.au) or **Quest** (☎ 1800 334 033; www.questapartments.com.au).

On a budget level, backpacker hostels with communal facilities are the most obvious choice. For more privacy, stay in a budget hotel or guesthouse.

Price Ranges

The majority of our listings fall in the mid-range and upper price brackets. Mid-range hotels start at around $80 per double room. Anything that costs less qualifies for our Cheap Sleeps section. Prices listed are indicative and should be used as a guide only.

Size matters when it comes to room prices: you'll pay more for a bigger room or a bigger bed, and for additional touches, such as a spa bath. Hotels publish 'rack' (standard) rates, but on the rack is generally where they stay, as there are almost always special deals. Rates generally drop at the weekend, which is 'off-peak' for the majority of hotels that cater primarily to business clients. Most places offer cheaper rates during the week and for Internet bookings.

Note that during major festivals and events, accommodation in Melbourne is often scarce, and you can expect prices to rise substantially.

The price of a dorm bed varies depending on how many beds to a room: the more beds to a dorm, the less you pay per bed.

Reservations

You can book accommodation directly with the establishment, or through **Tourism Victoria** (☎ 13 28 42). Most places take reservations via their websites, or those of accommodation agencies (of which there are dozens). If you're coming during a major event, such as the Australian Grand Prix or Commonwealth Games, you'd do well to book accommodation well in advance.

Longer-term Rentals

For longer-term stays, there are plenty of places in the 'flats to let', or 'share accommodation' ads in the *Age* newspaper's Domain section on Wednesday and Saturday.

Top Five Melbourne Sleeps

- **Best Seaside** Prince (p165)
- **Great View** Sofitel Melbourne (p159)
- **Most Elegant Old-School** Windsor (p159)
- **Perfect Penny Pincher** Nunnery (p162)
- **Sexy Getaway** Hotel Lindrum (p158)

CENTRAL MELBOURNE

The centre of town is dense with accommodation option or everyone, from those on theatre-package deals to busy business folk. Staying in town obviously puts you in the thick of Melbourne's restaurants, bars and sights.

Transport

See the Directory chapter (p180) for transport information from the airport. If you're arriving from interstate by bus or train, you'll be dropped at Southern Cross Station (Map pp202–04) in Spencer St. See the public transport maps pp217–18 for routes around town.

THE EAST

ADELPHI HOTEL

Map pp202-04   *Boutique Hotel*
☎ 9650 2709; www.adelphi.com.au;
187 Flinders Lane; r $300-575
Smack in the heart of the city's fashion and arts district, Adelphi epitomises chic from top to bottom. One of Melbourne's best restaurants, **Ezard at Adelphi** (p102), resides in the basement and there's a superb rooftop bar with city views and the famous glass-bottomed open-air swimming pool extending over the street. Handsome, modern and minimalist rooms have the full range of facilities. This is one of our faves.

ALBERT HEIGHTS

Map p205   *Serviced Apartments*
☎ 9419 0955; www.albertheights.com.au;
83 Albert St, East Melbourne; apt $120-160
Staying here places you a short walk away from the city, Richmond and Fitzroy. Your comfortable apartment has a fully equipped kitchen, lounge area and bathroom. The small pool is set in the ferny courtyard.

CITY LIMITS Map pp202-04   *Motel*
☎ 9662 2544; www.citylimits.com.au;
20-22 Little Bourke St; r incl breakfast $145; Ⓟ
Well-designed rooms at City Limits make optimum use of limited space. The kitchenette means you can prepare food, but with breakfast included in the tariff and Chinatown 100m down the street, you probably won't spend too much time in it, except perhaps to make microwave popcorn while you watch TV.

GEORGE POWLETT MOTEL/
APARTMENTS Map p205   *Self-Contained*
☎ 9419 9488; www.georgepowlett.com.au;
cnr George & Powlett Sts; s/d $105/110; Ⓟ
The only thing that disturbs the tranquillity of East Melbourne is the footy. You are bathed in the glow of the MCG light towers and can hear the roar of the crowd from here. These older motel-style rooms have kitchenettes and are a short walk from town through the Fitzroy Gardens.

Swimming pool, Adelphi Hotel (above)

GEORGIAN COURT Map p205 *B&B*

☎ 9419 6353; www.georgiancourt.com.au;
21 George St, East Melbourne; r $80-135

Little rooms and big breakfasts are on offer in this stately mansion. The leafy, exclusive suburb of East Melbourne is characterised by imposing terraces, and is a fine place to stop: an oasis surrounded by the thriving areas of Richmond, Fitzroy and the city.

GRAND HYATT MELBOURNE

Map pp202-04 *Hotel*

☎ 9657 1234; www.melbourne.hyatt.com;
123 Collins St; r $195-500

Grand in both scale and aesthetics, the Grand Hyatt is Melbourne's biggest modern hotel. You could keep fit just moving between the swimming pool and rooftop tennis court, let alone actually swimming or playing a game of tennis. You won't be disappointed by any of the 580 luxuriously appointed rooms. The hotel features a cavernous foyer chiselled from Italian marble, plus everything you could ever want for.

HILTON ON THE PARK Map p205 *Hotel*

☎ 9419 2000; www.hilton.com; 192 Wellington Pde, East Melbourne; r $155-275

What a family…of hotels. International hotel standards are easily met at this link in the Hilton chain located beside the Fitzroy Gardens and MCG. This Hilton is not that pretty on the outside, but is pretty smart on the inside.

HOTEL GRAND CHANCELLOR

Map pp202-04 *Hotel*

☎ 9663 3161; www.ghihotels.com; 131 Lonsdale St; r $140-260

Any hotel with a rooftop pool scores extra points in this book. There's something exhilaratingly incongruous about swimming among high-rise city offices. The Grand Chancellor is close to the city's old theatres and bustling Chinatown at the eastern end of town.

HOTEL LINDRUM Map p205 *Boutique Hotel*

☎ 9668 1111; www.hotellindrum.com.au;
26 Flinders St; r $230-470

All class, Hotel Lindrum occupies a stand-out building overlooking Birrarung Marr and the railway line. This former pool hall is an intimate designer hotel with sleek well-appointed rooms. Supplemented by Felt restaurant, a bar and a smattering of memorabilia from the building's past, the Lindrum should be your hotel of choice if you value stylish individuality.

MAGNOLIA COURT Map p205 *B&B*

☎ 9419 4222; www.magnolia-court.com.au;
101 Powlett St, East Melbourne; r $135-250

This cheery B&B has two wings. The charming older section was formerly a ladies' finishing college dating back to 1862, while rooms in the new wing have a modern sameness about them. Take breakfast in the light-filled breakfast room, then soak in the heated outdoor spa.

MANHATTAN

Map pp202-04 *Serviced Apartments*

☎ 1800 681 900; www.aom.com.au;
57 Flinders Lane; apt $210-310

This is one of a group of serviced-apartment complexes run by the same company, and each complex is styled with an individual theme. As you've probably guessed by the name, the Manhattan is open-plan warehouse-style apartments with high ceilings and plenty of designer chic. The gymnasium, spa, and business and conference facilities keep the mostly corporate clients happy.

MERCURE HOTEL MELBOURNE

Map p205 *Hotel*

☎ 9205 9999; www.accorhotels.com.au;
13 Spring St; r from $130

One off the international-hotel production line, the Mercure holds no surprises, but offers dependable high-quality rooms and service. What distinguishes the Mercure is its location at the eastern end of town: a hop, skip and a jump away from the sporting precinct, Yarra River and Fitzroy Gardens.

OAKFORD GORDON PLACE

Map pp202-04 *Serviced Apartments*

☎ 9663 3317; www.oakford.com; 43 Lonsdale St; apt $120-160

You won't feel homesick while you have your own stylish apartment. Choose a studio or one- to three-bedroom apartment; all have fully equipped kitchens. Oakford also manages the **Oakford on Collins** (182 Collins St).

PARK HYATT Map p205 *Hotel*

☎ 9224 1234; www.melbourne.park.hyatt.com;
1 Parliament Sq, off Parliament Pl; r from $315

The Park Hyatt is reminiscent of an Art Deco ocean liner. Be your own captain of the deep-set bath. There's TV built into the marble wall. King-size beds are standard issue and each room oozes elegance. When you do finally leave the bedroom, there are banquet rooms, a ballroom, a cigar lounge, a tennis court, a gymnasium and a 25m lap pool to keep you entertained. The excellent Radii restaurant offers imaginative food in a fine-dining setting. Remember, you came to see the city, so you'll have to leave the premises at some point.

QUEST ON BOURKE

Map pp202-04 _Serviced Apartments_
☎ 9631 0400; www.questapartments.com.au;
155 Bourke St; apt from $195
Staying in a city apartment block can sometimes feel like you're sleeping at the office. At Quest on Bourke, however, you can open the windows and enliven the apartment with real air. These stylish apartments have kitchens and separate living areas, all designed with a nod to contemporary living. Quest manages a number of properties throughout the city and suburbs.

SOFITEL MELBOURNE Map pp202-04 _Hotel_
☎ 9653 0000; www.sofitelmelbourne.com.au;
25 Collins St; r from $260; P
The views of Melbourne are somehow better when you're wearing a fluffy white bathrobe and standing on the 49th floor of a building in the centre of town. This hotel provides both views and robes, with 365 lush rooms to choose from – one for every day of the year?

STAMFORD PLAZA Map pp202-04 _Hotel_
☎ 9659 1000; www.stamford.com.au;
111 Little Collins St; r from $240
The Stamford is composed entirely of suites – available with one, two or three bedrooms. All have kitchens, and bathrooms complete with a spa bath. Internet deals are standard here. Package deals include Romance & Seduction (think rose petals scattered across the bed, candlelight and soft music), and the Jet-Lag Recovery, including late checkout and a facial kit.

VICTORIA HOTEL Map pp202-04 _Hotel_
☎ 9653 0441; www.victoriahotel.com.au;
215 Little Collins St; s $56-92, d $78-155
This old timer is a city institution, offering a flexible range of comfortable accommodation in the heart of the city's designer-fashion and arts precinct. Choose from a room with shared facilities or en-suite bathroom.

WESTIN MELBOURNE Map pp202-04 _Hotel_
☎ 9635 2222; www.westin.com.au; 205 Collins St;
r from $290
This imposing hotel-mountain occupies the corner that was once the city square. It offers five-star accommodation overlooking Swanston St, the city's main north–south axis that carries heavy tram, pushbike and foot traffic.

WINDSOR HOTEL Map pp202-04 _Hotel_
☎ 9633 6000; www.thewindsor.com.au;
103 Spring St; r from $500
The Windsor is Melbourne's 'Grand Lady', and is indisputably the matriarch of Melbourne's hotels. There are other hotels more opulent, more luxurious and with better facilities, but there are some things you can't manufacture and a grand sense of history is one of them. Built in 1883 and restored during the 1980s, the Windsor epitomises old-world elegance. Beyond the top-hatted door attendant, the interior is all marble and mahogany, shaded lamps and potted palms. The suites have often accommodated the rich and famous, including the Duke of Windsor and Rudolf Nureyev.

High tea at the Windsor, One Eleven Spring Street, is famous. Tiered trays of scones, cakes and triangle sandwiches, served in flouncy surrounds make it a great place to take your granny. The restaurant offers special-occasion dining in an elegant atmosphere; very old-school.

RIVER DISTRICT

CROWN TOWERS Map pp202-04 _Hotel_
☎ 9292 6666; www.crowntowers.com.au;
8 Whiteman St; r/ste $320/600; P
Part of the enormous Crown Entertainment Complex on the Yarra's southern bank, this hotel has all the glam and glitz you would expect from a Disneyland for adults. The oversized rooms all have a built-in safe (good for those big wins at the nearby casino) and a TV above the spa.

SHERATON TOWERS SOUTHGATE

Map pp202-04 _Hotel_
☎ 9696 3100; www.luxurycollection.com;
1 Brown St; r from $260
Expect five-star flourishes here, with the added bonus of views of the city and Flinders Street Station. Located on the Yarra River, this elaborate hotel is perfectly positioned just minutes from the city's major sights.

THE WEST

ASTORIA CITY TRAVEL INN

Map pp202-04 _Motel_
☎ 9670 6801; www.astoriainternational.com;
288 Spencer St; r $100; P
While it won't win any design awards, the Astoria is honest accommodation close to Southern Cross Station at the city's western end. All rooms have TV and a sparkling bathroom, and laundry facilities are available.

ATLANTIS HOTEL Map pp202-04 *Hotel*
☎ 9600 2900; www.atlantishotel.com.au;
300 Spencer St; r from $135; **P**

Opened in 2002, the Atlantis is a modern addition to the city's increasingly popular western fringe. Across from Docklands and Southern Cross Station, rooms have been touched with the minimalist-chic wand.

BATMAN'S HILL pp202-04 *Hotel*
☎ 9614 6344; www.batmanshill.com.au;
66-70 Spencer St; r $155-175

In a heritage-listing building, Batman's rooms are comfortable, if a bit boxy, and include all the facilities you'd expect. You're conveniently near Docklands and Southern Cross Station here.

CAUSEWAY INN ON THE MALL
Map pp202-04 *Hotel*
☎ 9650 0688; www.causeway.com.au;
327 Bourke St Mall; r $165-195

So, you loved the city's bars and clubs tucked away in bustling laneways, now try the hotel. The dowdy Causeway is as neat as a pin; don't expect visiting rock stars here. Rooms have a minifridge and TV.

CITY SQUARE MOTEL Map pp202-04 *Motel*
☎ 9654 7011; www.citysquaremotel.com.au;
67 Swanston St; s/d $80/105

If you value being in the centre of town, then City Square is a good square deal. Rooms are fitted with all the basics (bathroom, TV and fridge) in basic fashion.

DUXTON HOTEL Map pp202-04 *Hotel*
☎ 9250 1888; www.duxton.com; 328 Finders St;
r $140-450; **P**

Rich wood panelling and columns soaring to the circular interior balcony feature in the foyer of this heritage-listed hotel. Built in 1913 as the Commercial Travellers Club, restorations have remained true to the Duxton's regal history. History lesson over, individual rooms are up-to-the-minute modern, with a sleek finish, contrasting with the ornate aesthetic of the building.

EXPLORERS INN Map pp202-04 *Hotel*
☎ 9621 3333; www.explorersinn.com.au;
16 Spencer St; r $120

Though the rooms aren't huge, they're comfy enough to receive a tired body after a full day of exploring the city. All rooms come with an en suite, and there is an honest bar and bistro on the ground floor.

GRAND HOTEL MELBOURNE
Map pp202-04 *Hotel*
☎ 9611 4567; www.sofitel.com.au; 33 Spencer St;
r $160-400

This grand Italianate building once housed the old Victorian Railways administration, and the sheer scale of the structure is daunting. Its rooms were originally offices, and have such high ceilings that loft-style mezzanines have been added. Much of the interior has been restored, and the new additions are spacious and in keeping with the original style.

HOTEL CAUSEWAY
Map pp202-04 *Boutique Hotel*
☎ 9660 8888; www.causeway.com.au;
275 Little Collins St; r $210-310

This is a gem. Art Deco elegance mixes it with modern rooms in one of the city's best streets. Each room has its own safe, and if you've been shopping along this strip, it's your new clothes you'll want to lock up. Sprawl out on the king-size bed to read your complimentary morning newspaper.

HOTEL ENTERPRIZE Map pp202-04 *Hotel*
☎ 9629 6991; www.hotelenterprize.com.au;
44 Spencer St; r $90-180; **P**

The Hotel Enterprize segregates the enterprising from the holiday-maker, with a separate business wing. You don't have to wear a suit to enjoy the extra comforts of this newly renovated section, you can laze about in either wing, experiencing the varying degrees of comfort, including the option of ISDN connections in your room, plus room service and extra TV channels.

KINGSGATE HOTEL Map pp202-04 *Hotel*
☎ 9629 4171; www.kingsgatehotel.com.au;
131 King St; r $70-100

Unfussy Kingsgate isn't fancy, but it's central, clean and comfortable. In the city's west, this hotel is within walking distance of Southern Cross Station and is a short tram ride to the city centre. Rooms are priced according to whether or not you can live without an en suite and/or colour TV.

LE MERIDIEN AT RIALTO
Map pp202-04 *Hotel*
☎ 9620 9111; www.lemeridien.com; 495 Collins St;
r $200-450; **P**

This international chain is distinguished by its elaborate twin façades dating back to 1891, which are more reminiscent of Venice than

Melbourne. Individually styled rooms overlook an enclosed central atrium that covers the original cobbled laneway between the two buildings. This laneway now houses stylish bars, cafés and restaurants.

PACIFIC INTERNATIONAL APARTMENTS

Map pp202-04   *Serviced Apartments*
☎ 1800 682 003; www.pacificinthotels.com.au;
318 Little Bourke St; apt $145-220

Staying in one of these modish apartments immediately places you in the groovy-city-dweller ranks. You have one up on them, though, as someone comes to clean your pad daily. The magnificent old building belies the modern interior, with one or two bedrooms in mezzanine loft-style configurations. It's located in one of the city's 'Little' streets, right in the centre of Central Melbourne.

PUNT HILL

Map pp202-04   *Serviced Apartments*
☎ 1300 731 299; www.punthill.com.au;
267 Flinders Lane; apt from $180

A company with a few inner-city properties manages these conservative, homey apartments. With fully equipped kitchens, you'll be baking scones and lamingtons in no time. Choose between a studio, and an apartment with one or two bedrooms. Flinders Lane is a charismatic Melbourne street, lined with fashion boutiques and designer stores.

SAVOY PARK PLAZA Map pp202-04   *Hotel*
☎ 9622 8888; www.parkplaza.com.au;
630 Little Collins St; r from $180

Opposite the Southern Cross Station, the Savoy was built in the 1920s and later became a police academy. A uniformed concierge lends a touch of the traditional to the contemporary–Art Deco aesthetic.

CHEAP SLEEPS

FRIENDLY BACKPACKER
Map pp202-04   *Hostel*
☎ 9670 1111; www.friendlygroup.com.au; 197 King St; dm/d incl breakfast $25/80

Friendly by name, friendly by nature: you get free breakfast and Internet access just for staying here. Rooms and facilities are clean, and there are plenty of organised trips and pub crawls. There's also satellite TV and video screenings.

GREENHOUSE BACKPACKER

Map pp202-04   *Hostel*
☎ 9639 6400; www.friendlygroup.com.au;
228 Flinders Lane; dm/s/d incl breakfast $27/60/78

Run by the same friendly folk as the Friendly, Greenhouse has a brilliant location close to Melbourne's historic laneways, cafés and restaurants, and is only a short walk from Flinders Street Station. It's spic-n-span, with chatty and helpful staff, good facilities and key-card security.

HOTEL BAKPAK Map pp202-04   *Hostel*
☎ 1800 645 200; www.bakpakgroup.com;
167 Franklin St; dm $21-25, s/d $55/60

A backpacker's bonanza, Hotel Bakpak is a sprawling place offering just about everything you could ask for, from the basement bar and small cinema to a rooftop entertainment area with stellar city views. There's also a resource centre, which assists in finding short- or long-term work.

MELBOURNE CONNECTION TRAVELLERS HOSTEL Map pp202-04   *Hostel*
☎ 9642 4464; www.melbourneconnection.com;
205 King St; dm $21-25, d $68

This little charmer follows the small-is-better principle, offering simple, clean and uncluttered budget accommodation in an intimate setting. The hostel has good kitchen and laundry facilities and a TV room.

CARLTON & FITZROY

Considering these areas' popularity for shopping, eating and entertainment, they're relatively light on sleeping options. There are enough attractions to keep you occupied for days here, so you may as well stay over for a night. Within walking distance of the city, these neighbourhoods are also well served by public transport; see the boxed text, p66, for options.

DOWNTOWNER ON LYGON

Map pp206-08   *Hotel*
☎ 9663 5555; www.downtowner.com.au;
66 Lygon St, Carlton; r around $150; Ⓟ

Fall into bed at the Downtowner after musing at the nearby Melbourne Museum or Old Melbourne Gaol and dining at one of Lygon St's many options. Rooms are neat and modern and some come with kitchens and balconies.

KING BOUTIQUE ACCOMMODATION

Map pp206-08   *Boutique Hotel*
☎ 9417 1113; www.kingaccomm.com.au;
122 Nicholson St, Fitzroy; r $150-195

Behind the imposing façade are warm stylish rooms and communal spaces with unique designer touches. With the Carlton Gardens at your doorstep, Fitzroy out the back and the city up the street, book ahead to snaffle one of the three individually styled rooms.

METROPOLE

Map pp206-08   *Serviced Apartments*
☎ 9411 8100; www.metropole.org; 44 Brunswick St, Fitzroy; studio/1-bedroom apt $195/225; **P**

Fans of Hitchcock's *Rear Window* will love the view from the balcony onto others' balconies. Apartments here are set around a central courtyard, with a small pool. All come equipped with fully fitted-out kitchens. The Metropole sits at the quiet end of frenetic Brunswick St, a five-minute tram ride from town.

ROYAL GARDENS APARTMENTS

Map pp206-08   *Serviced Apartments*
☎ 9419 9888; www.royalgardens.com.au; 8 Royal Lane, Fitzroy; 1-/2-/3-bedroom apt $198/258/330; **P**

These apartments are built around a manicured courtyard with a swimming pool. Carrying the garden theme through to the décor,

floral bed-covers bring a whole new meaning to the term 'flower beds'. All apartments have fully equipped kitchens and separate living spaces.

RYDGES CARLTON Map pp206-08   *Hotel*
☎ 9347 7811; www.rydges.com;
701 Swanston St, Carlton; r $160

A link in a chain of international hotels, Rydges regularly offers special package deals, so phone ahead to see what deal you can broker for one of its handsome rooms. It's close to Lygon St and the CBD, and facilities include a restaurant, bar and rooftop pool. Rydges also has hotels in the city and in North Melbourne.

CHEAP SLEEPS

CARLTON COLLEGE Map pp206-08   *Hostel*
☎ 9664 0664; www.carltoncollege.com.au;
95 Drummond St, Carlton; dm $15-21, s/d $42/50; **P**

These grand old Victorian terraces have been partitioned into neat little rooms for short-term stays. At Carlton College, kitchen and bathroom facilities are shared, as are the TV lounge and central courtyard.

NUNNERY Map pp206-08   *Hostel*
☎ 9419 8637; www.bakpakgroup.com; 116 Nicholson St, Fitzroy; dm $23-27, s/d $60/80

It seems old habits die fast at the Nunnery, with

Nunnery (above)

not a hint of lemon-lipped attitude to be seen. This fabulous place oozes atmosphere, with big comfortable lounges and communal areas. Apart from the main building there's also the Nunnery Guesthouse, which has larger rooms in a private setting (single $75, double from $100 to $110). Highly recommended.

PARKVILLE & NORTH MELBOURNE

On the main road into the city from Melbourne Airport, these areas have mostly motel accommodation. You're about 15 minutes by car from the airport here, and 10 minutes from the centre of town. North Melbourne also has a high proportion of backpacker accommodation. See the boxed text, p68, for transport options from town.

APOLLO OLD MELBOURNE
Map p209   *Hotel*
☎ 9329 9344; www.oldmelbourne.com.au;
5-17 Flemington Rd, North Melbourne; r $155-230; P
Quaint wrought-iron balconies, leafy surrounds and a cobbled courtyard could have you believing you've arrived in an earlier century. Set back from the main road frontage, the Old Melbourne has a range of facilities, including a swimming pool, gym and sauna. Standard rooms start at $155 and include breakfast; courtyard rooms with French doors opening onto a private balcony cost $175, including breakfast. Luxury spa rooms cost $230, plus $15 per person for breakfast.

ARDEN MOTEL Map p209   *Motel*
☎ 9329 7211; www.lygonst.com/ardenmotel;
15 Arden St, North Melbourne; r incl breakfast $83; P
Start the day consuming the print news with your continental breakfast, both included in the price of your room. Comfortable, if a tad dowdy, rooms come with or without a kitchen.

ELIZABETH TOWER Map p209   *Hotel*
☎ 9347 9211; www.elizabethtower.com.au;
792 Elizabeth St; r $150-215; P
Opposite Melbourne University, Elizabeth Tower is 1km from the city centre. This large impersonal hotel has stacks of floors, its own restaurant, bar and swimming pool. Rooms are well equipped: from minifridge to complimentary toiletries.

HOTEL Y Map p209   *Hotel*
☎ 9329 5188; www.hotely.com.au; 489 Elizabeth St; r $80-150
The Young Women's Christian Association (YWCA) runs this award-winning hotel. Clearly a good choice for young women, it's also a ripper for other demographics. The 'Y' is fitted with modern facilities, including a budget café, communal kitchen and laundry, and is close to the Queen Victoria Market.

RAMADA INN Map p209   *Motel*
☎ 9380 8131; www.ramadainn.com.au; 539 Royal Pde, Parkville; r $115-135; P
You can hear the lions roar at Melbourne Zoo from this low-rise motel. Close to Optus Oval, you can also hear the occasional football crowd roar on weekends. The Ramada is functional and unfussy.

CHEAP SLEEPS

CHAPMAN GARDENS Map p209   *Hostel*
☎ 9328 3595; www.yha.com.au; 76 Chapman St, North Melbourne; dm $20-27, s/d $50/58
This YHA-operated hostel consists of mostly twin-share rooms. It's relatively small and personal, with two communal kitchens and a subdued ambience.

QUEENSBERRY HILL Map p209   *Hotel*
☎ 9329 8599; www.yha.com.au; 78 Howard St, North Melbourne; dm $20-27, s/d with en suite $62/84; P
The jewel in YHA's crown, Queensberry Hill is a showpiece of backpacker culture. It provides large communal areas, including a rooftop patio with barbecues and city views. Kitchens and bathrooms are well equipped and clean, and loads of group-tour information is available.

STORK HOTEL Map p209   *Pub*
☎ 9663 6237; www.storkhotel.com; 504 Elizabeth St; s/d $43/58
Close to the Queen Victoria Market, this friendly old pub offers basic accommodation upstairs. The rooms are small, simple and brightly coloured with polished floors. Facilities include a laundry and adjoining restaurant.

SOUTH YARRA, TOORAK & PRAHRAN

Welcome to Stylish Central. In terms of accommodation, this fashionable area has many boutique hotels and B&Bs. It's assumed that you'll be dining out at one of the area's numerous restaurants and cafés, as well as shopping at its hot designer boutiques. For transport options from town, see the boxed text, p73.

ALBANY SOUTH YARRA
Map pp214-15 *Hotel*

☎ 9866 4485; www.thealbany.com.au; cnr Toorak Rd & Millswyn St, South Yarra; r $100-180; P
There are a number of sleeping options at the Albany. If you simply must have a room in the separate Mansion Wing, you can; if you'll settle for the standard rooms with a modern décor, then that's no problem either. A communal kitchen and laundry facilities are also available to guests.

COMO Map p212 *Hotel*
☎ 9825 2222; www.mirvachotels.com.au; 630 Chapel St, South Yarra; r from around $200
Located at the junction of the city's famous fashion streets, Como is typically stylish. The complimentary shoeshine may not be great for those strappy mules you just purchased, but it's nice to know the service is there. The 105 studios and penthouses come in 25 different shapes and sizes: you're bound to find one to fit.

HATTON Map pp214-15 *Boutique Hotel*
☎ 9868 4800; www.hatton.com.au; 65 Park St, South Yarra; r from $185; P
This stately old building is enjoying its luxurious reincarnation as a boutique hotel. Each of the 20 rooms contains personal touches, such as plunger tea and coffee; some rooms also offer roomy balconies from which to sip your just-plunged tea. Quality furnishings and fabulous bathrooms create a sophisticated ambience.

TILBA Map pp214-15 *B&B*
☎ 9867 8844; www.thetilba.com.au; cnr Toorak Rd & Domain St, South Yarra; r $154-220
The same family has run this charming little hotel for over 16 years. High ceilings, antique furnishings, lead-light windows and breakfast in the sun-filled dining room create a homey, cottagelike atmosphere. Rooms range from 'small' through to 'grand'.

TOORAK MANOR Map p212 *Boutique Hotel*
☎ 9827 2689; www.toorakmanor.citysearch.com.au; 220 Williams Rd, Toorak; r incl breakfast from $125; P
This gracious old mansion retains its preference for frills and flowing chiffon in the décor

of its period-style rooms. Each of the 12 rooms has an en suite, and there is a communal lounge and reading room, the perfect place to creak open a yellowing copy of *Wuthering Heights* perhaps?

CHEAP SLEEPS
CLAREMONT ACCOMMODATION
Map p212 *Guesthouse*

☎ 9826 8000; www.hotelclaremont.com; 189 Toorak Rd, South Yarra; dm/s/d $30/66/76; P
Light-filled and large, Claremont offers basic, budget accommodation with shared bathrooms. Continuing the budget theme, breakfast is an extra $2.

ST KILDA

St Kilda is one of Melbourne's liveliest suburbs. It lives up to its historical reputation as a recreational hub, offering exceptional dining and entertainment, as well as a range of accommodation to suit all types. Located on the foreshore, there's a frivolous seaside ambience to St Kilda that's infectious. For information on how to get here from town, see the boxed text, p75.

BISHOPSGATE Map p213 *B&B*
☎ 9525 4512; www.bishopsgate.com.au; 57 Mary St; r $145-195
Feeling a little French? Or perhaps you prefer the Orient? Rooms with individual motifs here will accommodate your thematic whim. Each lush room has an en suite and fireplace, and is large enough to manoeuvre though in a bustled dress – if you choose the Victorian-themed room.

CABANA COURT MOTEL Map p213 *Motel*
☎ 9534 0771; www.cabanacourtapartments.com; 46 Park St; s/d from $90/100; P
With the city's finest chefs at the helm of so many fantastic kitchens just up the street, you

---

Top Five Hotel Restaurants

- Circa, the Prince (p112)
- Ezard at Adelphi (p102)
- Radii, Park Hyatt (p158)
- Tolarno (p113)
- Windsor (p159)

Sleeping – St Kilda

may not use the fully equipped kitchens that come with these basic motel rooms. Cabana Court is located in a leafy St Kilda street, one block back from the beach.

COSMOPOLITAN Map p213 *Hotel/Motel*
☎ 9534 0781; www.cosmopolitanhotel.com.au; 6 Carlisle St; r $100-135, apt from $140; **P**
The Cosmopolitan offers a full range of accommodation, from basic rooms to apartments with en suite and kitchen. The fading 'modern' aesthetic of pastels and industrial carpet detracts little from the cheerful ambience.

CREST ON BARKLY Map p213 *Hotel/Motel*
☎ 9537 1788; www.crestob.com.au; 47 Barkly St; r $120; **P**
This large hotel/motel offers a variety of accommodation, from serviced apartments to rooms and suites. Professional and polite, Crest on Barkly caters equally for business clients and leisure seekers.

FOUNTAIN TERRACE Map p213 *B&B*
☎ 9593 8696; www.fountainterrace.com.au; 28 Mary St; s/d from $140/165
The seven rooms here are lavishly and lovingly appointed in honour of famous Australians, including Henry Lawson (author) and Caroline Chisholm (who worked to improve the lot of immigrants in the early 1800s). All have en suites and two have spas. Named after opera diva Nellie Melba, the Melba suite is the most lavish, with three rooms accessing the front veranda.

HOTEL TOLARNO Map p213 *Boutique Hotel*
☎ 9537 0200; www.hoteltolarno.com.au; 42 Fitzroy St; r from $115
In the heart of vivacious Fitzroy St, Tolarno's bright solid colours and retro furnishings are emblematic of late 1990s Melbourne style. You can choose a room with/without a balcony/en suite commensurate with the tariff. The downstairs bar/restaurant **Tolarno** (p113) is highly recommended.

NOVOTEL ST KILDA Map p213 *Hotel*
☎ 9525 5522; www.novotel.com; 14-16 The Esplanade; r from $150; **P**
This modern high-rise and its international-style interior could be anywhere in the world, but the surrounds are quintessentially St Kilda. Opposite the foreshore, the Novotel places you moments from St Kilda's hub: Fitzroy and Acland Sts, Luna Park and the Sunday Esplanade market. Amenities here are above reproach.

PRINCE Map p213 *Boutique Hotel*
☎ 9536 1111; www.theprince.com.au; 29 Fitzroy St; r $200-520; **P**
The Prrrrrince will have you purring: it's quixotic and exotic, yet lyrical and local. Rooms are stylishly sparse with elegant finishes. The Prince does everything well, from the bar, **Mink** (p123), to the bakery, **Il Fornaio** (see the boxed text, p42). The hotel's restaurant, **Circa** (p112), is one of Melbourne's best, just metres from the foreshore.

QUEST ST KILDA BAYSIDE
Map p213 *Serviced Apartments*
☎ 9593 9500; www.questapartments.com.au; 1 Eildon Rd; studio/1-/2-bedroom apt $140/155/200; **P**
These Quest apartments come fully equipped for the modern lifestyle with gym, pool and babysitting services. They also come with more traditional facilities, such as a kitchen. Located on a quiet leafy street, this is a welcoming and well-run apartment block.

CHEAP SLEEPS
ALL NATIONS Map p213 *Hostel*
☎ 9534 0300; www.allnations.com.au; 32 Carlisle St; dm $18-25, d$80-120
Cosy clean rooms belie the ugly '70s exterior. All rooms have en suite and TV, and there's free use of bikes and Internet. Reception is closed between noon and 5pm.

BASE Map p213 *Hostel*
☎ 9536 6109; www.basebackpackers.com; 17 Carlisle St; dm $22-28, r $85
The most recent addition to the Base chain of accommodation, this sassy, red-glass-fronted establishment opened in mid-2004. Sparkling new facilities include a bar, communal kitchen, lounge and dining areas, and Internet access.

CHARNWOOD MOTOR INN
Map p213 *Motel*
☎ 9525 4199; www.charnwoodmotorinn.com.au; 3 Charnwood Rd; s/d from $82/88; **P**
Part of the Budget chain of motels, you almost expect the neon signage to wink and buzz intermittently at this old-timer. It's bare and it's basic, but is in a quiet street within walking distance of all the St Kilda action.

OLEMBIA GUESTHOUSE Map p213 *Hostel*
☎ 9537 1412; www.olembia.com.au; 96 Barkly St; dm/s/d $25/46/78; **P**
Charming Olembia resembles a boutique hotel rather than a hostel. Excellent facilities include a

cosy lounge, dining room and courtyard. Rooms are small but spotlessly clean and comfortable, and all have washbasins and central heating (shared bathroom). Bookings are advised.

WARWICK BEACHSIDE
Map p213   *Budget Hotel*
☎ 9525 4800; www.warwickbeachside.com.au;
363 Beaconsfield Pde; units $77-110; ℗
Opposite St Kilda beach, this 1950s-style complex offers a range of holiday flats. They're far from fancy, but have all the basics in clean seaside surrounds.

SOUTH MELBOURNE & ALBERT PARK

The majority of accommodation options in this area are chain hotels geared towards business travellers who'll appreciate the golf course and lake opposite. It's close to lively St Kilda and a short distance from town (see the boxed text, p78, for transport options). The residential pockets of these areas are on the foreshore offering inner-city beachgoers a treat.

BAYVIEW ON THE PARK
Map pp214-15   *Hotel*
☎ 9243 9999; www.bayviewonthepark.com.au;
52 Queens Rd; r from $130
The Bayview is both wedding and wheelchair friendly. This big impersonal hotel opposite Albert Park Lake might be just what you're looking for. There's a public golf course just across the road, and many rooms have views over the lake (for a premium).

CARLTON CREST HOTEL
Map pp214-15   *Hotel*
☎ 9529 4300; www.carltonhotels.com.au/melbourne/;
65 Queens Rd; r from $120
The Carlton Crest functions as both a large tourist hotel, regularly offering special package deals, and a conference/business centre. Don't be chicken to cross busy Queens Rd: just

on the other side is the gorgeous Albert Park Lake. Don't expect any bargains come Grand Prix time in March.

EDEN ON THE PARK
Map pp214-15   *Hotel*
☎ 9250 2222; www.edenonthepark.com.au;
6 Queens Rd; r from $145; ℗
The garden in front of Eden is the attractive Albert Park Lake. Though dated, the Eden is well located and has 192 rooms and suites catering to a mostly business clientele. Some rooms have superb views, and all are supplemented with the hotel's swimming pool, café and cocktail lounge. Parking is included in the rates.

ROYCE HOTEL
Map pp214-15   *Boutique Hotel*
☎ 9677 9900; www.roycehotels.com.au;
379 St Kilda Rd; r from $190
Housed in a landmark Spanish Art Deco building, the Royce's successful mix of period details and stylish fit-out extends from the bathroom to the bed. Although located outside the city centre, its oh-so-groovy amberoom bar and restaurant, Dish, can make you feel as though you're at the centre of social activity anyway.

STATION PIER CONDOMINIUMS
Map pp214-15   *Serviced Apartments*
☎ 9647 9666; www.stationpiercondos.com.au;
15 Beach St; 1-/2-bedroom apt $275/300
These newish condos nestle in a residential area that looks like a page from a comic book. Bright, boxy buildings are packed in tight, separated slightly by landscaped gardens and boardwalks. Guests have access to a pool, sauna and tennis court.

CHEAP SLEEPS
NOMADS MARKET INN
Map pp214-15   *Hostel*
☎ 9690 2220; www.marketinn.com.au;
143 York St, South Melbourne; dm $19-23, d $58
In a converted pub, the Nomads Market Inn is located next to the South Melbourne Market. Your 'free beer on arrival' may not go down so well if arriving early in the morning, but the complimentary breakfast will.

Excursions

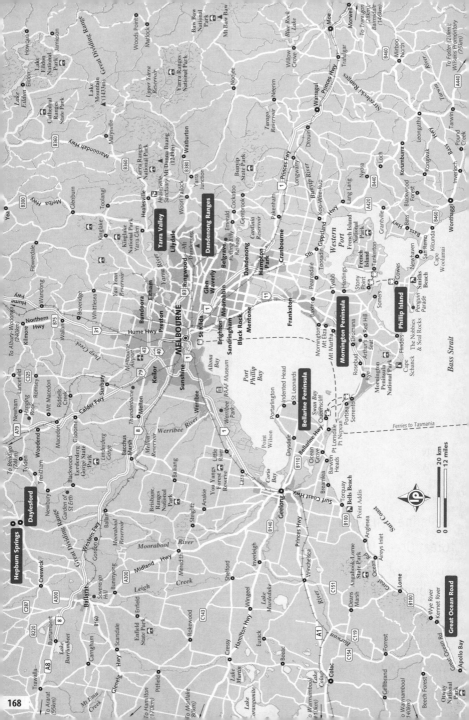

Excursions

You've seen the city, now see its backyard. Head in any direction and in no time you'll reach somewhere special. There are the beaches and coastal towns of the Mornington and Bellarine Peninsulas, where you can just sit on the sand and soak up the sun or cut up the waves with a surfboard. There are the cool forests, gorgeous gardens and bushwalks of the Dandenong Ranges. Some of Australia's finest wines are produced in the Yarra Valley region, with its hills gracefully streaked with grapevines. The native wildlife at Healesville Sanctuary and Phillip Island will confirm any suspicions you had that Australia's native animals are an odd bunch. The spectacular Great Ocean Rd contains long stretches of rugged cliffs and sheltered beaches, and cuts and curls through equally stunning rainforest.

Note that many of these places are popular holiday destinations, so if you're planning to stay overnight you should try to book accommodation in advance, especially during school-holiday periods. We've quoted high-season rates for places to stay. If you're travelling outside the high season or during the week, you may find cheaper rates.

NATURE
There are a number of options for anyone needing to get back to nature. If you're short on time, head to the **Dandenong Ranges** (p175). The cool fern forests of the national park line many walking trails.

The other option is to combine a little coast with your country by heading down the Great Ocean Rd to the **Angahook-Lorne State Park** (p171). A number of easy walks in ferny surrounds, combined with the cascading Erskine Falls, make for a superb escape.

TOWNS
For a boutique blend of the historical and the coastal, head to **Queenscliff** (below). From here you can catch a ferry across the bay (look out for dolphins) to **Sorrento** (p176), another historical town and site of the state's first settlement (albeit short-lived). There are loads of cafés and boutiques to keep you distracted.

Daylesford (p172) is a superb town with country spirit. It's long been a retreat for city folk, and is characterised by antique stores, cafés and some grand old buildings. It's also the day-spa capital, so if you're feeling shabby before you arrive, you won't by the time you leave.

WINE
Although there are wineries in just about every rural region of Victoria, those of the **Yarra Valley** (p173) would have to be the most well known. Whatever your preferred varietal or blend, there's a winery to suit. All have cellars for tastings, and most have restaurants, so you can stop in for some solid sustenance.

BEACHES
If you're hankering for some sand in your hair, salt on your skin, or a blustery beach walk, pack up the car and head for the **Great Ocean Rd** (p171). The winding road is as much a part of the experience as the coast itself. There are many beaches along this stretch but to get from one to the next you really need your own wheels. You can keep on driving for days if you have the time, or travel just over an hour out from Melbourne for a taste of the road's treasures.

BELLARINE PENINSULA
The sedate Bellarine Peninsula is where city-weary bodies go for a dose of revitalising sea change. Quiet bay beaches and the historical hub of Queenscliff attract weekenders and retirees alike. The peninsula forms the western side of Port Phillip Bay and is just beyond

the state's second-largest city, Geelong – sitting pretty on Corio Bay, and home to the Ford motorcar factory and an AFL team.

Stop halfway between Geelong and Queenscliff to pick your own strawberries at **Wallington Strawberry Farm**. When you're strawberried out, continue on to Queenscliff.

The serenity of **Queenscliff** belies its formative *raison d'être* as a settlement for sea pilots whose job it was to steer ships through the wildly treacherous Port Phillip Heads. Later, successful gold prospectors moved here, and by the 1880s the town became known as the 'Queen of the South'. Many of the era's elaborate buildings are still standing.

History buffs can visit **Fort Queenscliff**, built to protect Melbourne from the perceived threat of Russian invasion during the Crimean War. There's also a **Historical Museum** and a **Maritime Museum** in the town.

Train spotters will love the **Bellarine Peninsula Railway**, run by a group of like-minded enthusiasts. It has a collection of old locomotives and carriages, as well as working steam trains. The line was originally built when Fort Queenscliff was under construction; its purpose was to transport workers and materials from Geelong.

If you're feeling active, the Bellarine Peninsula offers good **diving** and **snorkelling** opportunities. The Queenscliff Dive Centre runs diving courses and hires out equipment. On land, hire a **bike** from Queenscliff Bike Hire; take the steam train to Drysdale and cycle back along the **rail trail** – it's downhill all the way.

From Queenscliff you can catch a car/passenger ferry over the bay to **Sorrento** (p176), or continue south to **Point Lonsdale**. This laid-back little coastal town centres on its **lighthouse**, built in 1902 to help guide ships through the Heads, past the Rip and into the bay. The Rip is the turbulent passage of water leading into the bay, and is rated as one of the most dangerous seaways in the world. The **Rip View Lookout** is one vantage point where you can watch freighters and other vessels negotiating the waterway – **Point Lonsdale Pier** is another. The foreshore around the headland is a marine wonderland at low tide, when an array of rock pools and caverns become natural aquariums – bring a pair of swimming goggles. Point Lonsdale has two beaches, the calmer bay beach and the surf beach, which is patrolled by a lifesaving club over summer. The town's **cemetery** contains the graves of early pioneers, pilots, lighthouse keepers and shipwreck victims.

Barwon Heads is a pretty little resort 4km west of Ocean Grove, at the mouth of the Barwon River. The surf beaches are around the headland – **Thirteenth Beach** is one of the best.

Transport

Distance from Melbourne to Queenscliff 106km

Direction Southwest

Travel Time 1½ hours

Car Leave Melbourne across the soaring West Gate Bridge. It's a one-hour drive down the Princes Fwy (M1) to Geelong and on to the Bellarine Peninsula.

Train Regular daily services are run by V/Line (☎ 13 61 96; www.vlinepassenger.com.au) from Melbourne to Geelong ($20.40).

Bus A regular service from Geelong to Queenscliff ($6.60) is run by McHarry's (☎ 5223 2111; www.mcharrys.com.au).

Ferry A car and passenger ferry service is run on the hour from/to Sorrento (passenger $8) by **Searoad** (www.searoad.com.au).

Sights & Information

Bellarine Peninsula Railway (☎ 5258 2069; www.bpr.org.au; adult/child Queenscliff to Drysdale return $16/8 ; ☽ steam trains depart 11.15am & 2.30pm Sun, plus Tue & Thu during school holidays, daily late Dec–late Jan)

Fort Queenscliff (tours adult/child $8/4; ☽ tours 1pm daily) Tours visit the military museum, magazine, cells and Black Lighthouse.

Queenscliff Bike Hire (☎ 5258 3403; per hr incl helmet $8) Near the main pier.

Queenscliff Dive Centre (☎ 5258 1188; 37 Learmonth St, Queenscliff; 1-/2-dive trips incl equipment $100/175)

Queenscliff Historical Museum (☎ 5258 2511; Hesse St, Queenscliff; admission $2; ☽ 2-4pm) Displays various relics from the town's past.

Queenscliff Maritime Museum (☎ 5258 3440; Weeroona Pde, Queenscliff; adult/child $4/2; ☽ 10.30am-4.30pm Mon-Fri, 1.30-4.30pm Sat & Sun) A small collection of local historical maritime exhibits.

Wallington Strawberry Farm (☎ 5250 1541; 440 Wallington Rd; ☽ 9am-5pm late Sep–May)

Eating & Sleeping

Harry's (☎ 5258 3750; Princess Park, Queenscliff; mains $19-24) This legendary BYO place offers sublime seafood. And where better to enjoy food from the sea than on the foreshore in a former bathing pavilion? Bookings advised.

Queenscliff Hotel (☎ 5258 1066; www.queenscliffhotel .com.au; 16 Gellibrand St, Queenscliff; B&B $290; mains around $28) The clock stopped in the 19th century at this splendid Victorian hotel. Fortunately, the menu at the restaurants kept advancing, serving exemplary modern Australian fare.

Vue Grand Hotel (☎ 5258 1544; www.vuegrand.com.au; 46 Hesse St, Queenscliff; B&B from $240; mains around $27) Pleasing day-trippers and weekenders alike, Vue Grand offers opulent accommodation and excellent dining. The menu is international, the eye to detail is devilish and the surroundings are pure stately mansion.

GREAT OCEAN ROAD

One of the world's most spectacular coastal routes, the Great Ocean Rd ducks and weaves along the dramatic Shipwreck Coast, with long stretches of uninterrupted beach, past lush rainforest and through seaside settlements.

The eastern end is also known as the Surf Coast, and **Torquay** would be the capital. It's one of the most popular **surfing** and summer resorts on this coast, with a range of beaches for families to surfers. You can hire a board from loads of shops along the Surf Coast Hwy, or take a **lesson** with Go Ride a Wave. If you prefer cerebral surfing, head to the **Surfworld Australia Surfing Museum**.

About 7km from Torquay is the turn-off to **Bells Beach**. The powerful point break at Bells has worked its way into surfing folklore and it's here (by name only) that Keanu Reeves and Patrick Swayze battled it out in the film *Point Break*. The Bells Beach Surfing Classic (see p10), officially known as the Rip Curl Pro, is held here annually at Easter and attracts the world's top professional surfers and thousands of spectators over the five days of the contest.

Anglesea is famous for its sheer cliffs, family beach and **golf club**; its grounds are as much home to kangaroos, grazing indifferently on the fairways and greens, as they are to the golfers who pay for the privilege of using them. The next town along is **Aireys Inlet**, marked by its lighthouse. There are some great beaches and excellent bushwalks through the nearby **Angahook-Lorne State Park**.

This park covers 22,000 hectares of coast and hinterland between Aireys Inlet and Kennet River. The park has cool, temperate rainforests; blue-gum forests; waterfalls; and numerous signposted walking tracks. There is also an abundance of wildlife, and seven designated camping areas.

Lorne is the most fashionable and busiest town along this stretch of coast, attracting a mix of holiday-makers, weekenders and surfers with its great beaches, bushwalks, cafés and restaurants. Despite the summer madness, with traffic jams leading into town and a dearth of accommodation, Lorne has managed to retain much of its charm and appeal.

To go beyond here, you'll need to allow at least a few days. Perhaps the most spectacular section of the Great Ocean Rd is between Lorne and Apollo Bay, where the contrast of the ocean on one side and the forests and mountains of the **Otway Ranges** on the other is breathtaking. The Otways are an area of great natural beauty with scenic drives, walking trails, waterfalls and tiny hillside townships.

The pretty fishing town of **Apollo Bay** is a popular summer beach resort. It's a little more relaxed than Lorne, and, in addition to the fishing industry, quite a few artists and musicians live in and around the town, giving it a more alternative ambience. The **Apollo Bay Music Festival** is held over a weekend in mid-March and attracts blues, jazz, rock and folk musicians.

The **Otway National Park**, at the southernmost tip of this coast, is another natural wonderland, while further west is the small and beautiful **Melba Gully State Park**.

Transport

Distance from Melbourne to Anglesea 109km
Direction Southwest
Travel Time 2 hours
Car Leave Melbourne across the West Gate Bridge and travel down the Princes Hwy (M1) until you reach the Torquay–Surf Coast turn-off.
Train & Bus Take the V/Line (☎ 13 61 96; www.vline passenger.com.au) to Anglesea ($36.40) and Lorne ($52.40).

Sights & Information

Apollo Bay Music Festival (www.apollobaymusicfestival
.com) Held annually in March, there's a variety of music
styles, street theatre, roving performers and kids games.

Anglesea Golf Club (☎ 5263 1582; www.angleseagolf
club.com.au; Noble St, Anglesea; 18-hole round $36, club
hire $18) Dodge roos and hit birdies.

Go Ride a Wave (☎ 1300 132 441; www.gorideawave
.com.au; 2hr adult lesson $50) Spongy Malibu board and
wetsuit provided for lessons.

Surfworld Australia Surfing Museum (☎ 5261 4606;
www.surfworld.org.au; Surf City Plaza, Beach Rd, Torquay;
adult/child $7.50/4.90; ◷ 9am-5pm) 'Surf' a ball on the
mechanical wave, which explains how waves are formed
and why they break.

Eating

Kostas (☎ 5289 1883; 48 Mountjoy Pde, Lorne; mains
$22-26; ◷ breakfast, lunch & dinner) This long-lived,
loud and lively Lorne mainstay offers Greek cuisine with
a twist. The décor is refreshingly simple, with nary a
pastel starfish in sight, and it's packed from breakfast
to stumps.

Qdos Gallery & Cafe (☎ 5289 1989; 35 Allendale Rd, Lorne;
mains $17-22; ◷ breakfast & lunch Apr-Nov, breakfast,
lunch & dinner Dec-Mar, closed Wed year-round) Consume
art between courses at this restaurant-gallery amid lush
rainforest surrounds.

Reifs (☎ 5289 2366; 84 Mountjoy Pde, Lorne; mains
$17-25; ◷ breakfast, lunch & dinner Sep-Apr, dinner
Fri-Wed May-Aug) The multi-tiered decking is great for
bumper breakfasts, or a sassier evening meal.

Sleeping

Chris' Restaurant & Villas at Beacon Point (☎ 5237 6411;
www.greatoceanroad.org/christos; 280 Skenes Creek Rd,
Apollo Bay; r $125-290) Set on a cliff with sweeping coastal
views, the luxurious accommodation here is almost upstaged
by the famed restaurant, which has a Greek/Mediterranean-
inspired menu (mains $25 to $30) that lures Melbourne's
foodies down the coast.

Erskine on the Beach (☎ 5289 1209; www.erskinehouse
.com.au; Lorne; guesthouse/resort from $120/225) Right
on the beach, Erskine's accommodation options include
guesthouse rooms with shared bathrooms, and modern hotel
rooms. Facilities include a bar, dining room, games room,
tennis court, pool table and guest lounges with open fires.

DAYLESFORD & HEPBURN SPRINGS

Set amid the scenic hills, lakes and forests of the central highlands, the delightful historic
twin towns of Daylesford and Hepburn Springs are enjoying a booming revival as Victoria's
spa centre. You could come here tired and haggard, and leave feeling spiffy and renewed.

Melburnians escape from the urban rat race to indulge in the many relaxation and retreat-
style therapies available here. As well as rejuvenation centres, you'll find plenty of antique
shops, galleries, gardens, excellent cafés and restaurants, and accommodation. There's a Visitor Information Centre next to the post office with loads of information on the area.

The best route from Melbourne to Daylesford is via the **Wombat State Forest**. The countryside
around Blackwood and Trentham is worth exploring via the 50km scenic **Wombat Forest Drive**.
Just west of Blackwood, the picturesque **Garden of St Erth** has four hectares of shaded lawns
and stone paths, fragrant flowerbeds and dappled pools.

The health-giving properties of the area's mineral springs were known before gold was
discovered here, and by the 1870s Daylesford was a popular health resort, which now attracts
droves of fashionable Melburnians. The **Hepburn Spa Resort** is an impressive relaxation and rejuvenation centre, with a staggering range of health-giving services, including spas, flotation tanks,
massages and beauty treatments. Why not try a Dead Sea Mud Wrap ($95), Half-Body Fan-
tasy Tan ($30), Puffy Eye Treatment ($35),
Vanilla Milk Bath ($88) or Total Indulgence
package, with seven hours of pampering for
around $500.

Daylesford's most popular attraction is
the **Convent Gallery**, a huge 19th-century building that's now a gallery space set in sweeping
gardens. Also worth a visit are the lovely
Wombat Hill Botanic Gardens, **Lake Daylesford** and Ju-
bilee Lake, and the **Historical Society Museum.** There
are also **walking trails** in the area; some of the
best are at **Lerderderg Gorge**. Ask at the visitors
centre for details.

Transport

Distance from Melbourne 120km
Direction Northwest
Travel Time 1½ hours
Car Take the Calder Fwy from Melbourne
Train & Bus Catch the train from Melbourne to Wood-
end, from where **V/Line** (☎ 13 61 96; www.vlinepas
senger.com.au) runs buses to Daylesford; Melbourne
to Daylesford costs $29.20.

Sights & Information

Convent Gallery (☎ 5348 3211; www.conventgallery.com
.au; 7 Daly St, Daylesford; admission $5; ⏰ 10am-6pm)

Daylesford Visitor Information Centre (☎ 5348 1339;
www.visitdaylesford.com.au; Vincent St; ⏰ 9am-5pm)

Garden of St Erth (☎ 5368 6514; Simmons Reef Rd,
Blackwood; admission $7; ⏰ 10am-4pm)

Hepburn Spa Resort (☎ 5348 2034; www.hepburnspa
.com.au; Hepburn Mineral Spring Reserve) Reservations
essential.

Historical Society Museum (☎ 5348 3242; 100 Vincent
St, Daylesford; admission $3; ⏰ 1.30-4.30pm Sat, Sun &
school holidays)

Wombat Hill Botanic Gardens (Central Spring St, Daylesford; ⏰ sunrise-sunset)

Eating

Frangos & Frangos (☎ 5348 2363; 82 Vincent St, Daylesford; mains $20-28; ⏰ lunch Fri-Sun, dinner Mon, Tue, Fri
& Sat) This laid-back, cosy, communal institution is largely
responsible for bringing café culture to the spa country.
Pull up a cushion, stoke up the fire, unroll a newspaper and
indulge in some hearty Mediterranean-fuelled favourites, a
glass or two of red and a delectable dessert.

Lake House (☎ 5348 3329; King St, Daylesford; mains
$28-35; ⏰ breakfast, lunch & dinner) Lake House
combines get-away-from-it-all, lakeside accommodation
(see Sleeping p155) with some of Victoria's finest modern
Australian dining. The emphasis is on fresh local produce
that's deftly prepared and perfectly presented to please
even the pickiest of palates.

Sleeping

Lake House (☎ 5348 3329; www.lakehouse.com.au;
King St, Daylesford; r from $320) A cluster of stylish and
luxurious units near Lake Daylesford, as well as waterfront
rooms and suites. There's a guest lounge, tennis court,
spa and sauna room, and it's just a short walk from the
restaurant of the same name.

Shizuka Ryokan (☎ 5348 2030; www.shizuka.com.au;
Lakeside Dr, Hepburn Springs; r from $275) The less-is-
more principle applies here, so lovers of minimalism will
enjoy the *tatami* matting, private Japanese garden and
shoji screens. Treatments such as shiatsu are also available.

Springs Retreat (☎ 5348 2202; www.thesprings.com
.au; 124 Main Rd, Hepburn Springs; r midweek from $175)
There's a minimum two-night stay at weekends here,
which includes a meal at the hotel restaurant ($500). This
charming 1930s hotel has a range of accommodation from
traditional en-suite rooms to more modern garden suites.

YARRA VALLEY

Less than an hour's drive northeast of Melbourne, the Yarra Valley mixes great natural
beauty with a swag of attractions, including
wineries. There's also the chance to hike in
the nearby hills or bike in the valley.

The **Warrandyte State Park** is a slice of natural bush just 24km northeast of the city.
There are well-marked walking and cycling
tracks, picnic and barbecue areas, native
animals and birds, and an abundance of
wild flowers in spring. Although it's now
part of suburban Melbourne, Warrandyte
has a country-village ambience. Artists and
hippies have long been attracted to the area,
and there are galleries and potteries dotted
throughout the hills. One of the best ways
to explore the river and park is in a canoe;
several local operators hire out canoes and
equipment and organise canoeing trips.

The Yarra Valley Visitor Information

Centre in Healesville has comprehensive information on the region's sights, wineries
and accommodation – you may need a nearby pillow after all that wine. The Yarra
Valley is one of Australia's most respected wine-growing regions, with more than 30
wineries – including **De Bortoli**, **Coldstream Hills**, **Domaine Chandon**, **Fergusson**, **Yarra Burn** and **Yering
Station** – scattered among these beautiful hills and valleys. The region is particularly noted
for its pinot noir, chardonnay, cabernet sauvignon and sparkling 'methode champenoise'
wines.

Excursions – Yarra Valley

173

Healesville Wildlife Sanctuary is one of the best places to see Australian native fauna. In a natural bushland setting, walk the circular track through a series of spacious enclosures, aviaries, wetlands and display houses. The sanctuary's residents include wallabies, kangaroos, wombats, dingoes, lyrebirds, Tasmanian devils, bats, platypuses, koalas, eagles, snakes and lizards. There are regular demonstrations, such as bird-of-prey feeds, and snake shows. Ring or check the Internet for times.

A couple of kilometres north of Yarra Glen, **Gulf Station** is a National Trust–classified farm that dates back to the 1850s. With its slab-timber farmhouse, barns, stables and slaughter-house, original implements and replanted sustenance gardens and orchards, Gulf Station provides a living insight into 19th-century farm life.

Much of the valley's early history relates to the timber industry. More timber passed through Yarra Junction than any town in the world, except Seattle in the USA. Evidence of the old mills, timber tramlines and charcoal plants can still be found throughout the forests.

Powelltown, 16km southeast of Yarra Junction, was a busy timber town during the 19th century. A network of excellent **forest walks** now follows the old timber tramlines and tunnels that were built to transport the timber to the railway line. The Warburton Water Wheel & Visitor Information Centre has a leaflet entitled *Yarra State Forest: Forest Walks and Drives,* which has detailed information on these walks; pick up a copy on your way through town.

The town of **Warburton** is set in a lush, green valley by the river, with rising hills on both sides. This area was a popular health retreat in the decadent '80s, when droves of city folk came to Warburton's guesthouses to breathe the fresh mountain air and detox. It's a short drive from Warburton up to **Mt Donna Buang**, which is capped with snow in winter – the closest snow to Melbourne.

Sights & Information

De Bortoli (☎ 5965 2271; www.debortoli.com.au; Pinnacle Lane, Dixons Creek; ☺ 10am-5pm) If the wines aren't enough, there's also an excellent restaurant.

Coldstream Hills (☎ 5964 9410; www.coldstreamhills .com.au; 31 Maddens Lane, Coldstream; ☺ 10am-5pm)

Domaine Chandon (☎ 9739 1110; www.chandon .com.au; Green Point, Maroondah Hwy, Coldstream; ☺ 10.30am-4.30pm) Domaine's sparkling white will make you twinkle.

Fergusson (☎ 5965 2237; www.fergussonwinery.com.au; Wills Rd, Yarra Glen; ☺ 11am-5pm)

Gulf Station (☎ 9730 1286; Melba Hwy; adult/child $9/5; ☺ 10am-4pm Wed-Sun)

Healesville Wildlife Sanctuary (☎ 5957 2800; www .zoo.org.au; Badger Creek Rd, Healesville; adult/child $17.50/8.50; ☺ 9am-5pm)

Warburton Water Wheel & Visitor Information Centre (☎ 5966 9600; www.tourism.warburton-ranges.net.au; 3400 Warburton Hwy, Warburton; ☺ 9am-5pm)

Yarra Burn (☎ 5967 1428; www.brlhardy.com.au; 60 Settlement Rd, Yarra Junction; ☺ 10am-6pm)

Yarra Valley Visitor Information Centre (☎ 5962 2600; www.yarravalleytourism.asn.au; Harker St, Healesville; ☺ 9am-5pm)

Yering Station (☎ 9730 1107; www.yering.com; 38 Melba Hwy, Yarra Glen; ☺ 10am-5pm Mon-Fri, 10am-6pm Sat & Sun) A superb winery with an excellent restaurant to boot (see Eating below).

Eating

Eleonore's at Chateau Yering (☎ 9237 3333; www .chateau-yering.com.au; 42 Melba Hwy, Yering; mains $25-32; ☺ lunch Sat & Sun, dinner daily) The place to splurge on 19th-century grandeur and fabulous modern-European fine dining. Those on smaller budgets might like to try the neighbouring, and slightly more casual, **Sweetwater Cafe** (mains $26; ☺ 7.30am-5pm).

Yering Station (☎ 9730 1107; 38 Melba Hwy, Yering; mains $23-28; ☺ lunch) The modern Australian menu is devised to complement Yering's sublime wines, with views out to the source – the vineyards.

Sleeping

Strathvea (☎ 5962 4109; www.strathvea.com.au; Myers Creek Rd, Healesville; B&B from $150) This gourmet getaway set in English gardens and surrounded by native bushland also offers excellent dining, with a seasonal menu using local produce.

Yarra Glen Grand Hotel (☎ 9730 1230; www.yarraglen grand.com.au; 19 Bell St, Yarra Glen; r from $140) Dating back to 1888, the Yarra Glen has been lovingly restored to present one of the best country hotels in Victoria.

DANDENONG RANGES

On a clear day, you can see the Dandenong Ranges from Melbourne: Mt Dandenong, the highest point, is 633m. Despite the impact of encroaching urban sprawl and droves of visitors, the Dandenongs retain much of their appeal. Magnificent public gardens and plant nurseries, tearooms and restaurants, potteries and galleries, antique shops and markets are main attractions. There's also plenty of birdlife and native animals, plus bushwalks and picnic areas.

The Dandenong Ranges & Knox Visitor Information Centre is located just outside the Upper Ferntree Gully train station. The Parks Victoria office can supply maps of the **parks** and **walking tracks.**

The **Dandenong Ranges National Park** consists of the three largest areas of forest remaining in the Melbourne region. All three sections have barbecue areas and walking tracks. The **Ferntree Gully National Park**, named for its abundance of tree ferns, has four walking trails, each around two hours long. **Sherbrooke Forest** has a towering cover of mountain ash trees and an understorey of silver wattle, sassafras, blackwood and other exotic trees. This forest is home to numerous birds, among them rosellas, kookaburras, currawongs and honey-eaters. The **Doongalla Reserve**, on the western slopes of Mt Dandenong, is less accessible than the other two areas, so its forest areas are less crowded.

The **Mt Dandenong lookout** offers great views west over Melbourne and Port Phillip Bay.

The **William Ricketts Sanctuary** is one of the area's highlights. The sanctuary and its sculptures are the work of William Ricketts, who worked here up until his death in 1993 at the age of 94. His work was inspired by the years he spent living with Aborigines in central Australia and by their affinity with the land. His personal philosophies permeate and shape the sanctuary, which is set in damp fern gardens with trickling waterfalls and sculptures rising out of moss-covered rocks like spirits from the ground.

The high rainfall and deep volcanic soils of the Dandenongs are perfect for agriculture, and the area has long provided Melbourne's markets with much of their produce. The gardens and nurseries overflow with visitors who come to see the colourful displays of tulips, daffodils, azaleas, rhododendrons and other flora. The gardens are at their best in spring and autumn, but are worth a visit at any time.

The **National Rhododendron Gardens** have groves of cherry blossoms, oaks, maples and beeches, and over 15,000 rhododendrons and azaleas. The **Alfred Nicholas Memorial Gardens** were originally the grounds of Burnham Beeches, the country mansion of Alfred Nicholas, cofounder of Aspro and the Nicholas Pharmaceutical Company. Nearby, to the east, **George Tindale Memorial Gardens** are smaller and more intimate than the other gardens.

One of the Dandenongs' major attractions is **Puffing Billy**, a restored steam train that puffs its way through the hills and fern gullies between Belgrave and Gembrook. *Puffing Billy* is the last survivor of a series of experimental railway lines built at the end of the 19th century to link rural areas to the city. Along the way you can visit the pretty town of Emerald, with Lakeside Park and the **Emerald Lake Model Railway.**

Transport

Distance from Melbourne 35km
Direction East
Travel Time 1 hour
Car You really need your own car to explore this region properly. Take the Burwood Hwy from Melbourne to follow the Mt Dandenong Tourist Rd through the ranges.
Train The Met's suburban trains run on the Belgrave line to the foothills of the Dandenongs. From Upper Ferntree Gully train station it's a 10-minute walk to the edge of the national park. Belgrave train station is the last stop on the line and the starting point for *Puffing Billy*. It's a 15-minute walk from the train station to Sherbrooke Forest.

Sights & Information

Alfred Nicholas Memorial Gardens (☎ 13 19 63; Sherbrooke Rd, Sherbrooke; admission by donation; ☼ 10am-5pm)

Dandenong Ranges & Knox Visitor Information Centre (☎ 9758 7522; www.dandenongrangestourism.asn.au; 1211 Burwood Hwy, Upper Ferntree Gully; ☼ 9am-5pm)

Emerald Lake Model Railway (☎ 5968 3455; Lakeside Park, Emerald Park Rd; adult/child $5.50/3.50; ☼ 11.30am-3pm Tue-Sun, closed Mon-Fri Aug)

George Tindale Memorial Gardens (☎ 13 19 63; 33 Sherbrooke Rd, Sherbrooke; admission by donation; ☼ 10am-4.30pm)

Excursions – Dandenong Ranges

National Rhododendron Gardens (☎ 13 19 63; Georgian Rd, Olinda; adult/child Sep-Nov $11.65/4.45, other times $7.20/2.20; ☺ 10am-5pm year-round)

Parks Victoria office (☎ 13 19 63; Mt Dandenong Tourist Rd; Ferntree Gully; ☺ 8am-4.30pm Mon-Fri)

Puffing Billy (☎ 9754 6800; www.puffingbilly.com .au; Old Monbulk Rd, Belgrave; adult/child Gembrook return $40/20, Emerald Lakeside Park return $29.50/15; family tickets available) Puffing Billy operates up to six times every day (except Christmas Day) during holiday periods, with three or four daily services at other times. The Puffing Billy train station is a short stroll from Belgrave train station, the last stop on the Belgrave suburban line.

William Ricketts Sanctuary (☎ 13 19 63; Mt Dandenong Tourist Rd, Mt Dandenong; adult/child $5.60/2.20; ☺ 10am-5pm)

Sleeping

A Loft in the Mill (☎ 9751 1700; www.loftinthemill .com.au; 1-3 Harold St, Olinda; r from $140) This restored mill offers a wide range of accommodation, from the Calico Suite to the Cottage in the Forest.

Como Cottages (☎ 9751 2264; www.comocottages .dandenong-ranges.net.au; 1465 Mt Dandenong Tourist Rd, Olinda; cottages from $150) Canopied beds, open fireplaces and claw-foot baths are all features of these self-contained cottages.

MORNING TON PENINSULA

The boot-shaped Mornington Peninsula, which juts out between Port Phillip Bay and Western Port, is a little over an hour's drive from the city centre. Its great beaches have been a favourite summer destination for Melburnians since the 1870s, when paddle steamers carried droves of holiday-makers down to Portsea and Sorrento from the city.

The narrow spit of land at the end of the peninsula has calm beaches on Port Phillip Bay (known as the 'front beaches') and wildly rugged ocean beaches facing Bass Strait (the 'back beaches'). At the far end of the spit, Portsea has a reputation as a playground for the wealthy, while nearby Sorrento has the peninsula's best range of accommodation and restaurants.

Swimming and surfing top the list of peninsula activities, but there are also bushwalking trails through the Point Nepean National Park.

The coastal strip fronting Bass Strait is part of the Mornington Peninsula National Park, and along here you'll find rugged coastal walking tracks and some great surf beaches. There are also good swimming and surf beaches in Western Port. Inland, the peninsula is a picturesque blend of rolling hills and green pastures, terraced vineyards and dense forests.

The peninsula is also known for its fine local produce, and perhaps the best place to sample the local specialities is at one of the area's famous weekend markets. The markets at Red Hill (first Saturday morning of the month) and Mornington Racecourse (second Sunday) are the best.

The Peninsula Visitor Information Office is in Dromana.

If you're not in a hurry, turn off the Nepean Hwy at Mornington and take the slower but more scenic route that winds around the coast and rejoins the highway at Dromana, where you can take a dip in the calm waters of Safety Beach. In Mt Martha, the Briars Historic Park features wetlands, walks and barbecue areas, as well as a historic homestead.

Coolart Homestead dates back to 1895 and is surrounded by landscaped grounds. There are adjacent wetlands and a wildlife sanctuary. The grounds are the perfect spot for a picnic, with barbecues, tables and even hot water on tap.

Arthur's Seat State Park is just inland from Dromana and signposted off the Nepean Hwy. A scenic drive winds up to the summit lookout at 305m, with panoramic views of the bay and coastline. Stay for a while: use the barbecue facilities or trek the walking tracks. The Seawinds Gardens manage to combine both indigenous and European-style gardens, with stellar views and perfect picnic spots at every turn. You can also reach the summit by the Arthur's Seat Scenic Chairlift, which offers stunning views of the bay and coastline. At 40 minutes per return trip, this is Victoria's longest scenic chairlift. The chairlift has undergone extensive maintenance after experiencing mechanical difficulties in 2004.

Transport

Distance from Melbourne to Sorrento 90km
Direction South
Travel Time 1½ hours
Car Head out on the Nepean Hwy
Ferry to/from Queenscliff (see p170)

Arthur's Seat Maze has a variety of mazes, around 20 different themed gardens and a sculpture park. This is a great place to safely lose the kids, at least temporarily. Continuing the maze craze, **Ashcombe Maze & Water Garden** is the oldest hedge maze in Australia. There's also a stunning rose maze, which is made up of over 1000 scented roses. After a stroll through the 10-hectare garden rest your pegs over a drink or lunch in the licensed café.

The National Trust's **McCrae Homestead** is a timber-slab cottage built in 1846. It houses a collection of colonial furniture and the paintings and writings of pioneer Georgiana McCrae.

Historic **Sorrento** is a fashionable resort town, where South Yarra comes to the peninsula. In summer it is frenetic but in winter, sanity returns, and Sorrento is once more a sleepy seaside retreat. The town has some fine 19th-century buildings constructed from locally quarried limestone, and it boasts fine beaches (the back beach has a great rock pool for swimming at low tide), good accommodation, and plenty of cafés and restaurants. You can also take a ferry trip across to **Queenscliff** (p169).

Sorrento was the site of the first official European settlement in Victoria. The camp lasted only from October 1803 to May 1804, when the group of convicts, marines, civil officers and free settlers moved on to better-watered conditions at Hobart. The **Collins Settlement Historic Site** marks the site at Sullivan Bay, outside the Sorrento township towards Blairgowrie.

Dolphin-watching cruises in the bay are incredibly popular in season, generally October to April or May. Local operators, including Polperro Dolphin Swims and Moonraker, offer a combination of sightseeing cruises of the bay, fishing trips and dolphin-watching cruises.

Multimillion-dollar mansions are ten-a-penny in **Portsea**. The area is also a mecca for divers and diving operators and you'll more than likely be surrounded by wetsuit-clad visitors during your time here. The front beach is calm and inviting. If things get too hot, wander up to the **Portsea Hotel** and enjoy a drink in the grassy (and usually crowded) beer garden that overlooks the pier. The back beach is notoriously wild; on shore is the impressive natural rock formation **London Bridge**.

Just up from the Portsea Hotel, Dive Victoria **dives** to the locations of four WWI J-class submarines.

Sights & Information

Arthur's Seat Maze (☎ 5981 8449; www.arthursseat maze.com.au; Purves Rd, Dromana; adult/child $12/8; 🕑 10am-6pm)

Arthur's Seat Scenic Chairlift (☎ 5987 2565; Arthur's Seat Rd, Dromana; adult/child return $11/8; 🕑 11am-5pm)

Ashcombe Maze & Water Garden (☎ 5989 8387; Red Hill Rd, Shoreham; adult/child $12/7; 🕑 10am-5pm)

Briars Historic Park (☎ 5974 3686; Nepean Hwy, Mt Martha; park admission free, homestead adult/child $4/1; 🕑 9am-5pm) There's also a visitors centre, screening a free audiovisual about the area.

Collins Settlement Historic Site (Point Nepean Rd, Sorrento; admission free; 🕑 24hr)

Coolart Homestead (☎ 5983 1333; Lord Somers Rd, Somers; adult/child $6.70/3.30; 🕑 10am-5pm) There's also a visitors centre and shop here.

Dive Victoria (☎ 5984 3155; www.divevictoria.com.au; 3753 Point Nepean Rd, Portsea; 1-/2-dive trips incl equipment $115/160) It also offers dives to the locations of four WWI J-class submarines.

Moonraker (☎ 5984 4211; swimming tour $80, sightseeing $40) Dolphin- and seal-swim cruise runs for 3½ hours.

McCrae Homestead (☎ 5981 2866; 11 Beverly Rd, McCrae; adult/child $5/4; 🕑 noon-4pm daily Sep-May, Sat & Sun Jun-Aug)

Peninsula Visitor Information Office (☎ 5987 3078; Nepean Rd, Dromana; 🕑 9am-5pm)

Polperro Dolphin Swims (☎ 5988 8437; www.polperro .com.au; swimming tour $95, sightseeing $40) Dolphin cruises run for four hours.

Eating & Sleeping

Carmel B&B (☎ 5984 3512; www.carmelofsorrento .com.au; 142 Ocean Beach Rd, Sorrento; B&B $175, self-contained units $150-200) A historic limestone cottage in the centre of town, which has been tastefully restored in period style. There's a cosy guest lounge, four rooms with en suite and two self-contained units behind the main house.

Portsea Hotel (☎ 5984 2213; www.portseahotel.com.au; 3746 Point Nepean Rd, Portsea; s/d $60/105) Basic rooms with shared facilities; en-suite rooms also available.

Rubira's (☎ 5984 1888; 1 Esplanade, Sorrento; mains brasserie/restaurant $22/45; 🕑 lunch & dinner) A buzzing seafood restaurant, brasserie and takeaway. Go all out on a seafood extravaganza in the restaurant or grab some takeaway and head for the beach; either way, you're onto a winner.

Sorrento Backpackers Hostel YHA (☎ 5984 4323; sorrentoyha@primus.com.au; 3 Miranda St; dm $22) A purpose-built hostel in a bush setting.

PHILLIP ISLAND

At the entrance to Western Port, 125km southeast of Melbourne by road, is the *very* popular holiday destination of **Phillip Island**. The island itself is rugged and windswept, and there are plenty of beaches – both sheltered and with surf – a fascinating collection of wildlife and several fairly sleepy townships. Phillip Island's Penguin Parade is one of Australia's strongest tourist magnets. Tourists outnumber penguins and some visitors are disappointed by the high degree of commercialisation. The other side of the coin is that the parade and displays are educational and the money contributes to protecting the penguins' natural habitat.

There is an excellent Penguin information centre in Newhaven just after you cross the bridge to the island.

Each evening at Summerland Beach in the southwest of the island, the nesting little penguins (also called fairy or blue penguins) perform their **Penguin Parade**, emerging from the sea and waddling resolutely (and full of fish) up the beach to their nests – seemingly oblivious to the sightseers. The parade takes place like clockwork a few minutes after sunset each day. The crowds can number up to 4000 people, especially on weekends and holidays, so bookings should be made in advance. Contact the information centre at Newhaven or the **Phillip Island Nature Park**.

Transport

Distance from Melbourne 125km
Direction Southeast
Travel Time 2 hours
Car Take the Monash Fwy (M1) to the Phillip Island exit onto the South Gippsland Hwy (M420) near Dandenong.
Bus The daily bus service between Melbourne and Cowes run by **V/Line** (☎ 13 61 96) takes just over three hours ($33).

Want more Australian wildlife? A good place to see koalas is at the **Koala Conservation Centre**, with a visitor area, and elevated boardwalks running through a bush setting. Off Point Grant, the extreme southwestern tip of the island, a group of rocks called the **Nobbies** rises from the sea. Beyond these are **Seal Rocks**, home of Australia's largest colony of fur seals. Space is scarce during the breeding season from October to December, when up to 6000 seals arrive.

Phillip Island also has **mutton bird colonies**, found particularly in the sand dunes around Cape Woolamai. These birds, which are actually called shearwaters, are amazingly predictable: they arrive back on the island on 24 September each year from their migration flight from Japan and Alaska. The birds stay on the island until April. Your best chance of seeing them is at the Penguin Parade during spring and summer, as they fly in low over the sea each evening at dusk. Also try the **Forest Caves Reserve** at Woolamai Beach.

Swimming and **surfing** are popular island activities. The ocean beaches are on the south side of the island and there's a lifesaving club at Woolamai – this beach is notorious for its strong rips and currents, so swim only between the flags. If you're not a good swimmer, head for the bay beaches around Cowes, or the quieter ocean beaches such as Smith and Barry Beaches. You can also view the island from the sea with **Bay Connections Cruises**.

The walking track at rugged **Cape Woolamai** is particularly impressive; it's accessed from the Woolamai surf beach near the lifesaving club.

Sights & Information

Bay Connections Cruises (☎ 5678 3501; www.bay connections.com.au; Seal Rocks cruise adult/child $50/35) Runs a variety of cruises.

Koala Conservation Centre (☎ 5952 1307; Phillip Island Rd; adult/child $8.50/4.25; ⏱ 10am-6pm)

Phillip Island Nature Park (☎ 1300 366 422; www .penguins.org.au; Penguin Parade adult/child $16/8)

Eating & Sleeping

Carmichaels (☎ 5952 1300; 17 The Esplanade, Cowes; mains $15-32; ⏱ lunch & dinner) One of the island's best

eateries, Carmichael's offers sea views from its sun-drenched terrace, casual but on-the-ball service, and superb eats.

Castle Villa by the Sea (☎ 5952 2730; www.thecastle .com.au; 7 Steele St, Cowes; r from $250) Well-appointed suites range in style from modern designer to old-fashioned opulence. Set in a lovely garden, the Villa's facilities include spacious common areas with log fires, a bar and intimate restaurant.

Waves Apartments (☎ 5952 1351; www.thewaves .com.au; 1 The Esplanade, Cowes; apt from $275) Completely self-contained; discounts available outside high season.

Excursions – Phillip Island

Directory

Directory

TRANSPORT

AIR

You can fly into Melbourne from all the usual international points and from all over Australia. Frequent domestic flights are offered by **Qantas** (☎ 13 13 13; www.qantas.com.au) and its subsidiaries, such as **Jetstar** (☎ 13 15 38; www.jetstar.com.au), which was set up in 2004 to compete with the low fares offered by **Virgin** (☎ 13 67 89; www.virginblue.com.au).

Airports

The main airport, **Melbourne Airport** (www.melair.com.au), also known as Tullamarine, is 22km northwest of the city centre. Its international and domestic terminals are conveniently located under one roof. There are two information desks at the airport: one on the ground floor in the international arrivals area and another upstairs next to the duty-free shops.

The Tullamarine Fwy runs from the airport to Flemington, close to the city centre. The freeway transmogrifies into the CityLink tollway (opposite) en route; a 24-hour Tulla Pass can be purchased from post offices and any Shell petrol station for $3.40.

A taxi between the airport and city centre costs about $40 (including the cost of using the tollway). **Skybus** (☎ 9335 2811; www.skybus.com.au) operates a 24-hour shuttle-bus service between the airport and the city centre ($13, 20 minutes).

Avalon Airport (☎ 5227 9100; www.avalonairport.com.au) opened in mid-2004 for some Jetstar Sydney and Brisbane flights. **Sunbus** (☎ 9689 6888; www.sunbusaustralia.com.au) operates passenger transfers at Avalon Airport and travels to Franklin St in Melbourne's CBD ($12, one hour).

BICYCLE

Bicycles can be taken on suburban trains for free during off-peak times. During peak hours you'll need to buy a concession ticket for the bike. One note of caution: tram tracks can be a major hazard for cyclists in Melbourne.

See Cycling (p141) for information on bike hire.

CAR & MOTORCYCLE

You can get around Melbourne easily on the city's comprehensive tram, train and bus network. But many of Victoria's national parks, remote beaches and mountain regions are not readily accessible by public transport. So if you're planning to explore Victoria in intimate detail or just want to get off the beaten track, you'll need your own wheels.

Driving & Parking

Foreign driving licences are valid as long as they are in English or accompanied by a translation. An International Driving Permit, obtainable from your local automobile association, must be supported by your own licence, so remember to bring both with you to Australia.

In Australia, vehicles are driven on the left-hand side of the road. The speed limit in residential areas is 50km/h, rising to 75km/h or 80km/h on some main roads and dropping to 40km/h in specially designated areas such as school zones. On highways the speed limit is generally 100km/h, while on many freeways it rises to 110km/h.

The wearing of seat belts is compulsory, and small children must be belted into an approved safety seat. Motorcyclists must wear crash helmets at all times when riding. The police strictly enforce Victoria's blood-alcohol limit of 0.05% with random breath tests of drivers.

Melbourne has the peculiar road rule known as the hook turn. In central Melbourne, many intersections require that you make a right-hand turn from the left lane – so as not to obstruct tram tracks. These intersections are marked with a 'Right Turn from Left Only' sign. Affectionately known as the 'hookie', you're required to veer off to the left, joining the front of the line of traffic waiting at the red light to your left. When the traffic light turns green (for the street you're about to turn in to) hook right and complete your turn.

Parking spaces in the city are metered. Check parking signs for restrictions and times, and watch out for clearway zones that operate during peak hours. There are more than

70 car parks in the city; the Melbourne City Council produces a guide to city parking, available from the **Melbourne Visitor Information Centre** (Map pp202–04; Federation Sq). Hourly rates vary depending on the car park's location, but you'll usually pay from $3 to $6 an hour or $12 to $25 a day from Monday to Friday (less on weekends).

Hire

All the big car-hire firms operate in Melbourne. **Avis** (☎ 13 63 33; www.avis.com.au), **Budget** (☎ 1300 362 848; www.budget.com.au), **Hertz** (☎ 13 30 39; www.hertz.com) and **Thrifty** (☎ 1300 367 227; www.thrifty.com.au) have desks at the airport, and you can find plenty of others in the city. Car-hire offices tend to be at the northern end of the city centre or in North Melbourne.

The major companies all offer unlimited-kilometre rates. One-day hire rates for fully licensed drivers over 25 years of age are around $70 for a small car and $80 for a big car – obviously, the longer the hire period, the cheaper the daily rate.

Melbourne also has a number of budget operators, hiring out older vehicles at lower rates. Costs and conditions vary widely. Be sure to ask about kilometre charges, insurance, excess, and so on. Beware of distance restrictions; many companies allow you to travel only within a certain distance of the city, typically 100km. Rates start at about $35 a day; some places worth trying are: **Airport Rent-a-Car** (☎ 1800 331 220; www.airportrentacar.com.au/melbourne.htm) and **Rent-a-Bomb** (☎ 9428 0088; www.rentabomb.com.au). The **Yellow Pages** (www.yellowpages.com.au) lists lots of other firms.

If you suddenly decide you'd like to take on the undulating curves of the Great Ocean Rd on a Harley Davidson, or explore the city on a zippy 100cc, then the option is there. Victorian regulations require you to have a motorcycle licence to hire a bike. **Garner's Hire-Bikes** (☎ 9326 8676; www.garnersmotorcycles.com.au) has a large range of bikes for hire. Prices range from $99 a day for a Honda XR 100 trail bike all the way up to $275 a day for a Harley Davidson Softail Custom.

Toll Roads

Melbourne's **CityLink** (☎ 13 26 29; www.transurban.com.au) tollway road system has two main links: the southern link, using the South-eastern Fwy, which runs from the southeastern suburb of Malvern to Kings Way on the southern edge of the city centre, and the western link, which runs from the Calder Fwy intersection with the Tullamarine Fwy to the West Gate Fwy, on the western edge of the city centre.

CityLink day passes are generally the best option for visitors. A day pass for the entire system costs $9.65 and is valid for 24 hours from your first entry through a tollway. To buy a day pass, go to an Australia Post office (anywhere in Australia), a Shell service station, a CityLink customer service centre or the CityLink website. Alternatively, you can pay by credit card by telephoning CityLink.

If you accidentally find yourself on the City-Link toll road (and it's very easy to do), don't panic. Phone CityLink within 24 hours on the above number and pay the day-pass fee. If you're picking up a car from the airport, the car-hire company will be able to make arrangements for your CityLink day pass if you need one.

PUBLIC TRANSPORT

Melbourne's public transport system, also called the Met, incorporates buses, trains and trams, and operates as far as 20km out from the city centre. Tram services are relatively frequent and comprehensive in the area they cover. Buses cover routes that trams don't, while trains radiate from the city centre to the outer suburbs. All services cease around midnight.

For information on public transport, including timetables, maps, fares and zones, see the transport maps on pp217–18, or contact the **Met** (Map pp202–04; ☎ 13 16 38; www.victrip.com.au; 103 Elizabeth St, Melbourne).

Ticketing

The same ticket allows you to travel on trams, trains and buses. The most common tickets are based on a specific period of travelling time (eg two hours, one day, one week) and allow unlimited travel during that period and within the relevant zone. You must validate your ticket in the validating machine when boarding a tram or bus or entering a train station.

The metropolitan area is divided into three zones, with the price of tickets depending on which zone(s) you will be travelling in and across. Zone 1 covers the city and inner suburbs

Directory – Transport

and most travellers are unlikely to venture beyond it; adult fares follow.

Zone(s)	Two hours ($)	All day ($)	Weekly ($)
1	3.00	5.80	25.00
2 or 3	2.20	4.00	17.20
1 & 2	5.00	9.40	42.60
1, 2 & 3	7.00	12.30	52.00

There are also City Saver tickets ($2.20), which allow you to travel two sections on one continuous journey in Zone 1.

Buying a ticket is as simple as feeding your coins into a machine at the train station or on the tram, or paying the driver on a bus. Most machines are coin-only, including those on trams, so make sure you have sufficient loose change when buying your ticket. Many small businesses, such as newspaper kiosks and milk bars (corner shops), sell most tickets.

Bus

Melbourne's privatised bus network is ancillary to the trains and trams – filling in the gaps. Generally, buses continue from where the trains finish, or go to places not reached by other services, such as hospitals, universities, suburban shopping centres and the outer suburbs.

Train

Melbourne has an extensive train network that covers the city centre and suburbs (Map p217). The city service includes the underground City Loop, which is a quick way to get from one side of town to the other. Flinders Street Station is the main terminal for suburban lines.

Trains on most lines start at 5am and finish at midnight and should run every 10 minutes during peak hours, every 15 to 20 minutes at other times, and every 30 minutes after 7pm from Monday to Friday. They run approximately every 30 minutes from 5am to midnight Saturday, while it's every 30 minutes from 7am to 11.30pm Sunday.

Tram

Melbourne's trundling trams are one of the city's most distinctive features, but you might need to exercise a little patience as they're not particularly speedy and stop frequently.

Tram routes cover the city and inner suburbs extensively. The majority of routes operate as shuttle services, with the city centre acting as the hub of the wheel and the tram routes as the spokes. This makes it a good system if you want to get to somewhere from the city centre, but it's not so good if you want to travel across from one suburb to another. All tram stops are numbered out from the city centre.

Trams run along most routes about every six to eight minutes during peak hours and every 12 minutes at other times. Trams share the roads with cars and trucks, so the reality is they are often subject to delays. Services are less frequent on weekends and late at night. See the boxed text, p52, for information on the City Circle tram.

Be extremely careful when getting on and off a tram; by law, cars are supposed to stop when a tram stops to pick up and drop off passengers, but that doesn't always happen.

TAXI

Melbourne taxis are uniformly yellow. You can easily flag down a taxi: if the rooftop light is illuminated, it is available. There are plenty of taxi ranks in and around the city; the main ones are outside major hotels, as well as at Flinders Street and Southern Cross train stations.

Flagfall is $2.80, and the standard rate is $1.33 per kilometre. There is a $1 charge for telephone bookings, and another $1 is charged for service between midnight and 6am. Yellow Cabs and Silver Top have cars with wheelchair access, or phone ☎ 1300 364 050. To book a taxi, phone one of the following companies:

Black Cabs Combined (☎ 13 22 27)

Embassy Taxis (☎ 13 17 55)

Silver Top Taxis (☎ 13 10 08)

Yellow Cabs (☎ 13 19 24)

PRACTICALITIES
ACCOMMODATION

Accommodation listings in the Sleeping chapter (p156) are ordered by neighbourhood, then in alphabetical order. The majority of listings fall into the mid-range bracket, which average around $150 per night.

The **Melbourne Visitor Information Centre** (Map pp202-04; Federation Sq), a drop-in service, and **Tourism Victoria** (☎ 13 28 42) offer assistance with booking accommodation. If you're looking for last-minute discounts, try www.lastminute.com.au.

BUSINESS HOURS

Standard shop-trading hours are from 9am to 5.30pm Monday to Thursday, 9am to 9pm Friday, 9am to 5pm Saturday and 10am to 4pm Sunday. Bookshops often stay open as late as 9pm or 10pm. Milk bars are open until around 8pm, and many supermarkets stay open late. You can buy milk or cigarettes any time at numerous 24-hour convenience stores.

Most offices open from 9am to 5.30pm Monday to Friday, although some government departments close at 4.30pm or 5pm. Normal banking hours are from 9.30am to 4pm Monday to Thursday, 9.30am to 5pm Friday.

CHILDREN

The *EG* (Entertainment Guide), published in Friday's *Age,* has a 'Children's Activities' section that details what's on for children each weekend, eg pantomimes, animal nurseries and museum programmes. The free *Me!bourne Events* guide available from the **Melbourne Visitor Information Centre** (Map pp202-04; Federation Sq) also has a children's section.

See the boxed text, p51, for some of the city's favourite places for kids. Try also: Melbourne Zoo (p68), the Aquarium (p59), any of the city's public swimming pools (p142) and *Puffing Billy*, a vintage steam train that runs through the Dandenong Ranges (p175). The city's glorious parks are also great options for keeping kids amused.

The Melbourne City Council runs a **childminding centre** (Map pp202-04; ☎ 9329 9561; 104 A'Beckett St) for children up to five years old. It charges $5.50 an hour or $45 a day.

For more helpful information see Lonely Planet's *Travel with Children* by Cathy Lanigan.

CLIMATE

Melbourne has four seasons, with no great extremes. In summer average temperatures range from a high of 26°C to a low of 14°C; the average winter maximum is 13°C and the minimum 6°C; in spring and autumn average highs and lows range from around 20°C to 10°C. In Australia, summer starts in December, autumn in March, winter in June and spring in September.

Of course, averages and statistics never paint the true picture. You are just as likely to have a sunny, blue-sky day in winter and a sudden thunderstorm in summer as you are vice versa, or all four seasons will visit in one day. The saying goes that if you don't like the weather in Melbourne, just wait a couple of minutes.

Summer is the most popular time for visitors. You can expect good beach weather, particularly during late summer, and the occasional scorcher when the mercury bubbles past 40°C. The autumn months are the best time of year climatically. The days are warm and the light is staggeringly beautiful. Winters are grey, but far from freezing. And spring is typically invigorating and vital.

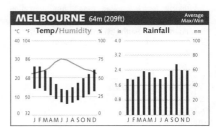

COURSES

The **CAE** (Centre for Adult Education; Map pp202-04; ☎ 9652 0611; www.cae.edu.au; 253 Flinders Lane) runs a wide variety of courses, some of possible interest to travellers. On offer is everything from languages, literature, visual arts and music to computer studies, cooking, history and philosophy. Fees vary according to the number of sessions per course, which can run from one day up to eight weeks. Course guides are available online or from the centre.

Learn how to make the perfect coffee with **Lavazza Coffee Training** (☎ 1300 307 171; www.coffeeclass.com). Courses run for three hours and are geared to the home user (Connoisseur Class $65) as well as the professional ($110).

CUSTOMS

When entering Australia you can bring in most articles free of duty, provided that **customs** (www.customs.gov.au) is satisfied they are for personal use and that you'll be taking them with you when you leave. There's the usual duty-free quota of 1L of alcohol, 250 cigarettes and dutiable goods up to the value of $400. Amounts of more than $10,000 must be declared.

With regard to prohibited goods, Australian customs has a mania about illegal drugs, and can be extremely efficient in finding any. Animal and plant quarantine is also an issue. You will be asked to declare all goods of animal or vegetable origin and to show them to an official.

DISABLED TRAVELLERS

Most of Melbourne's tourist attractions are accessible for wheelchairs. Trains and newer trams have low steps to accommodate wheelchairs and people with limited mobility. See p182 for taxi companies with wheelchair-accessible cars. There are also many car-parking spaces throughout the city allocated for disabled drivers. The excellent *Mobility Map* of Melbourne is available from the **Melbourne Visitor Information Centre** (Map pp202-04; Federation Sq) and from the **information booth** (Map pp202-04) in the Bourke St Mall. You can also view it online at the **Access Melbourne** (www.accessmelbourne.vic.gov.au) website.

Many new buildings incorporate architectural features helpful to the vision impaired, such as textured floor details at the top and bottom of stairs. Melbourne's pedestrian crossings feature sound cues.

Organisations

Access Foundation (www.accessibility.com.au/melbourne) City guide to Melbourne's accessible sites.

National Information Communication and Awareness Network (Nican; ☎ 1800 806 769; www.nican.com.au) An Australia-wide directory providing information on access issues, accommodation, sporting and recreational activities, transport and specialist tour operators.

Royal Victorian Institute for the Blind (RVIB; ☎ 9522 5222; www.rvib.org.au)

RTA (☎ 13 11 74; www.vicroads.vic.gov.au) Supplies temporary parking permits for disabled international drivers.

Traveller's Aid (Map pp202-04; ☎ 9654 2600; level 2, 169 Swanston St) A helpful and friendly independent organisation catering to travellers, particularly with special needs. It has loads of information, a lounge, café, wheelchair-accessible toilets, showers and lockers. There is also a disability access service offering minor repairs to wheelchairs and battery recharge, as well personal care attendance. It has a second location at **Southern Cross Station** (Map pp202-04; ☎ 9670 2873; Spencer St) next to Platform 1.

Victorian Deaf Society (☎ 9657 8111; www.vicdeaf.com.au)

ELECTRICITY

Power supply is 240V 50Hz, and the plugs are three-pin, but not the same as British three-pin plugs (which are larger). Universal adaptors are available from shops selling outdoor supplies, as well as from luggage shops, some hardware shops and chemists.

EMBASSIES

Most foreign embassies are in Canberra but some countries have diplomatic representation in Melbourne. Their opening hours are generally from 8.30am to 12.30pm and 1pm to 4.30pm Monday to Friday. Embassies or consulates in Melbourne include the following:

Canada (Map pp202-04; ☎ 9653 9674; www.canada.org.au; Level 50, 101 Collins St, Melbourne, 3000)

Germany (Map pp214-15; ☎ 9828 6888; 480 Punt Rd, South Yarra, 3141)

Indonesia (Map pp214-15; ☎ 9525 2755; 72 Queens Rd, Melbourne, 3004)

Japan (Map pp202-04; ☎ 9639 3244; 360 Elizabeth St, Melbourne, 3000)

Malaysia (Map pp214-15; ☎ 9867 5339; 492 St Kilda Rd, Melbourne, 3004)

UK (Map pp202-04; ☎ 9650 4155; www.ukemb.gov.au; Level 17, 90 Collins St, Melbourne, 3000)

USA (Map pp214-15; ☎ 9526 5900; http://usembassy-australia.state.gov/melbourne/; 553 St Kilda Rd, Melbourne, 3004)

EMERGENCY

In the case of a life-threatening emergency, dial ☎ 000. This call is free from any phone, and the operator will connect you to either the police, ambulance or fire brigade.

Other useful numbers in an emergency:

Lifeline Counselling (☎ 13 11 14) A 24-hour service available in six languages.

Poisons Information Centre (☎ 13 11 26)

Police (Map pp202-04; ☎ 9247 5347; 228-232 Flinders Lane)

RACV Emergency Roadside Service (☎ 13 11 11)

Translating & Interpreting Service (☎ 13 14 50) Available 24 hours.

GAY & LESBIAN TRAVELLERS

The gay scene is an integral part of city life; however, there are exclusively gay venues and accommodation options. Up-to-date listings can be found in the local gay street press, such as *Melbourne Star,* **MCV** (www.mcv.net.au), **Bnews** (www.bnews.net.au), and **Lesbiana** (www.lesbiana.com.au). All are free and available from cafés, bars and clubs. The **ALSO Foundation** (☎ 9827 4999; www.also.org.au) is Victoria's premier gay and lesbian community-based organisation. The website contains a services directory, which is also published in print and available at **Hares & Hyenas Bookshop** (Map p212; ☎ 9824 0110; 135 Commercial Rd, South Yarra).

Melbourne's first gay-focused radio station, Joy FM, was founded in 1993. The city's festival calendar includes gay events, such as the **Midsumma Festival** (☎ 9415 9819; www.midsumma.org.au) held each January/February. See p9 for more details. The Midsumma organisation showcases a wide range of theatrical, musical, artistic and sporting events, such as the Midsumma Carnival Street Party in Commercial Rd, Prahran; the Pride March down Fitzroy St, St Kilda; and Red Raw, a dance party held on the Saturday of Australia Day weekend. If you're visiting towards the end of March, check out the **Melbourne Queer Film & Video Festival** (www.melbournequeerfilm.com.au), which showcases the best of queer cinema from Australia and overseas.

HOLIDAYS
Public Holidays
On public holidays, government departments, banks, offices, large stores and post offices close. About the only shops you will find open are the 24-hour convenience stores.

Victoria observes the following nine public holidays:

New Year's Day 1 January

Australia Day 26 January

Labour Day First or second Monday in March

Easter Good Friday and Easter Monday in March/April

Anzac Day 25 April

Queen's Birthday Second Monday in June

Melbourne Cup Day First Tuesday in November

Christmas Day 25 December

Boxing Day 26 December

When a public holiday falls on a weekend, the following Monday is declared a holiday (with the exception of Anzac Day and Australia Day).

School Holidays
The school year is divided into four terms. Holidays are generally as follows: the longest break is the Christmas holiday from mid-December until the end of January, then there are three two-week holiday periods which vary from year to year, but fall approximately from late March to mid-April, late June to mid-July and mid-September to early October.

INTERNET ACCESS
Most hotels have phone jacks in the room that allow you to use your laptop to access email and the Internet. All you need are dial-in numbers, which are provided by your ISP.

If you don't have a laptop, most backpacker hostels have a terminal or two where you can access the Internet. All public libraries have limited access (you may need to book), or there are loads of Internet cafés with super-fast connections. Access charges range from $4 to $9 an hour. Some Internet cafés include:

e:fifty five (Map pp202-04; ☎ 9620 3899; downstairs, 55 Elizabeth St; per hr $4, 40 min free if you buy a beer; ☾ 10am-1am Mon-Fri, noon-3am Sat & Sun)

Net City (Map p213; ☎ 9525 3411; 7/63 Fitzroy St, St Kilda; per hr $4.50; ☾ 9.30am-11pm)

World Wide Wash (Map pp206-08; ☎ 9419 8214; 361 Brunswick St, Fitzroy; per hr $6; ☾ 9.30am-10pm) Here you can do your washing, check your emails and have coffee.

MAPS
The **Melbourne Visitor Information Centre** (Map pp202-04; Federation Sq) and **information booth** (Map pp202-04; Bourke St Mall) hand out the free *Melbourne Visitors Map,* which covers the city and inner suburbs. For more comprehensive coverage, Lonely Planet publishes the *Melbourne City Map.*

Comprehensive street directories are produced by Melway, UBD and Gregory's, and are available at bookshops and newsagents. The *Melway Greater Melbourne Street Directory* is such a Melbourne institution that places often give their location by simply stating the relevant Melway page and grid reference.

Map Land (Map pp202-04; ☎ 9670 4383; 372 Little Bourke St) is the city's best source for a wide range of maps.

MEDICAL SERVICES
Visitors from Finland, Italy, Malta, the Netherlands, New Zealand, Sweden and the UK have reciprocal health rights and can register at any **Medicare office** (☎ 13 20 11; www.hic.gov.au).

Clinics
Carlisle Contemporary Health Practice (Map p213; ☎ 9537 3600; 30 Carlisle St, St Kilda) General practitioners; bookings advised, though that's no guarantee you won't be kept waiting.

Travellers' Medical & Vaccination Centre (TMVC; Map pp202-04; ☎ 9602 5788; www.traveldoctor.com.au; 2nd fl, 393 Little Bourke St) Specialists in travel-related medical advice such as inoculations.

Emergency Rooms

Public hospitals with 24-hour accident and emergency departments (generally known as 'casualty wards') include:

Alfred Hospital (Map pp214-15; ☎ 9276 2000; Commercial Rd, Prahran)

Royal Melbourne Hospital (Map p209; ☎ 9342 7000; Grattan St, Parkville)

St Vincent's Hospital (Map pp206-08; ☎ 9288 2211; 41 Victoria Pde, Fitzroy)

MONEY

Australia uses the decimal system of dollars and cents (100 cents to the dollar). There are $100, $50, $20, $10 and $5 notes, as well as $2, $1, 50¢, 20¢, 10¢ and 5¢ coins. Although 5¢ is the smallest coin in circulation, prices are often still marked to the single cent. Shops should round prices to the nearest 5¢ on your *total* bill, not on individual items.

ATMs

Most bank branches have 24-hour ATMs and will accept debit cards that are linked to international network systems, such as Cirrus, Maestro, Barclays Connect and Solo. There is a limit on the daily withdrawal amount, which is usually around $1000. Almost all retail outlets have Eftpos, which allows you to pay for purchases electronically.

Changing Money

Changing foreign currency or travellers cheques is no problem at most banks. There are foreign-exchange booths at Melbourne Airport's international terminal, which are open to meet all arriving flights. Most large hotels will also change currency or travellers cheques for their guests but the rate might not be as good as from other outlets.

The Australian dollar tends to fluctuate a bit against the greenback (US dollar). In recent years it has generally been pretty weak, until mid-2004 when it peaked at US80¢. For an approximate guide to the exchange rate see Quick Reference on the inside front cover of this guidebook.

Credit Cards

The most commonly accepted credit cards are Visa, MasterCard, American Express and, to a lesser extent, Diners Club. For lost or stolen card services call:

American Express ☎ 1300 132 639

Diners Club ☎ 1300 360 060

MasterCard ☎ 1800 120 113

Visa ☎ 1800 450 346

Travellers Cheques

American Express, Thomas Cook and other well-known international brands of travellers cheques are all accepted throughout Victoria. **Thomas Cook** (Map pp202-04; ☎ 9654 4222; 261 Bourke St) and **American Express** (Map pp202-04; ☎ 9633 6712; 233 Collins St) have city offices.

NEWSPAPERS & MAGAZINES

Melbourne has two major daily newspapers. The **Age** (www.theage.com.au) gives excellent local coverage of local issues, with reasonable coverage of international news. The Saturday and Sunday editions have review sections and magazines with plenty of weekend reading; there are other interesting pull-out sections during the week. The **Herald Sun** (www .heraldsun.com.au) is a tabloid-style paper published in several editions throughout the day. The **Australian** (www.theaustralian.news.com), a national daily, is also widely available.

Big newsagents and bookshops stock magazines suited to all interests and hobbies, from pet grooming to sewing. **McGills** (Map pp202-04; ☎ 9602 5566; 187 Elizabeth St), **Readings** (Map pp206-08; ☎ 9347 6633; www.readings.com .au; 309 Lygon St, Carlton) and **Borders** (Map p212; ☎ 9824 2299; 500 Chapel St, South Yarra) have a staggering array of titles. Readings has the best alternative local selection; Borders and McGills stock all the glossies.

Melbourne Magazine (www.melbournemag .com) is a glossy monthly with city-specific content, available from most newsagents. You'll probably encounter a street vendor selling the **Big Issue** (www.bigissue.org.au). This quality weekly magazine supports the homeless and gives an alternative spin on topical issues.

POST

Australia's postal services are efficient and inexpensive. It costs 50¢ to send a standard letter or postcard within Australia. Australia Post has divided international destinations into two zones: Asia Pacific and the Rest of the World. Airmail letters cost $1 and $1.50 respectively. Postage for postcards and aerograms is the same to any country: $1 and 80¢ respectively.

Generally, post offices are open from 9am to 5pm Monday to Friday. You can buy stamps from most newsagents.

The **Melbourne GPO** (Map pp202-04; ☎ 13 13 18; cnr Little Bourke & Elizabeth Sts; ☺ 8.30am-5.30pm Mon-Fri, 9am-4pm Sat, 10am-4pm Sun) offers a poste restante service. You'll need to provide some form of photo ID to collect your mail.

RADIO

Melbourne has loads of radio stations broadcasting everything from hits-and-memories to talkback. Following is a selection:

ABC Classic FM (105.9FM) Classical music.

News Radio (1026AM) Nonstop news and proceedings of federal parliament.

Nova (100.3FM) Old and new music targeting the thirty-somethings.

Radio National (621AM) A diversity of topics covered, with fascinating features. Has a 10-minute world-news service every hour on the hour.

Radio for the Print Handicapped (1179AM) Readings of daily newspapers; between 11.05pm and 6am broadcasts the BBC World Service.

3AW (1278AM) Top-rating commercial talkback station.

3CR (855AM) Noncommercial community radio station.

3JJJ (107.5FM) The Australian Broadcasting Commission's national youth network. Specialises in alternative music and young people's issues.

3LO (774AM) Regular talkback programmes, an excellent news service on the hour and a world-news feature at 12.10pm every weekday.

3MBS (103.5FM) Classical music.

3PBS (106.7FM) Independent subscriber-based station, with alternative music programmes.

3RRR (102.7FM; www.rrr.org.au) Excellent subscriber-based station featuring independent music, current affairs and talk-show programmes; streaming online.

3SBS (93.1FM) Multilingual station.

3ZZZ (92.3) Multilingual station.

TAXES & REFUNDS

There is a 10% goods and services tax (GST) automatically added to almost anything you purchase, although some fresh-food items are exempt. If you purchase goods with a total minimum value of $300 from any one supplier up to 30 days before your departure from Australia, you are entitled to a refund of any GST paid. You can organise your refund at the designated booth at Melbourne Airport, or contact the **Australian Customs Service** (☎ 1300 363 263; www.customs.gov.au) for more details.

TELEPHONE

The area code for Melbourne (and Victoria) is ☎ 03 and the country code for dialling into Australia is ☎ 61. Toll-free numbers start with the prefix ☎ 1800, while numbers that start with ☎ 1300 charge the cost of a local call no matter where you're calling from.

Local calls from public phones cost 40¢, while most local calls from private phones cost 25¢. In both cases you can talk for an unlimited amount of time. Calls to mobile phones attract higher rates and are timed.

Mobile Phones

Mobile-phone numbers generally have 10 digits, with four-digit prefixes beginning with ☎ 04. Australia's digital network is compatible with GSM 900 and 1800 (used in Europe and NZ), but generally not compatible with systems used in the USA and Japan. Most mobiles brought from other Australian states can be used in the Melbourne area, but check roaming charges with your carrier.

Phonecards

There's a wide range of local and international phonecards available from most newsagents and post offices for a fixed dollar value (usually $10, $20, $30 etc). These can be used with any public or private phone by dialling a toll-free access number and then the PIN number on the card.

TELEVISION

Melbourne has six free-to-air TV stations. The three commercial networks – Channels Seven, Nine and Ten – are just like commercial channels anywhere, with a varied but not particularly adventurous diet of sport, soap operas, lightweight news and sensationalised current affairs, plus plenty of sitcoms (mainly American). Of the three, Channel Ten differentiates itself by producing youth-oriented programmes. See p32 for a rundown on locally produced shows.

Channel Two is the government-funded, commercial-free ABC station. It produces some excellent current affairs shows, documentaries and a more informed news service, and screens its fair share of sport and sitcoms (mainly British). The ABC also has a knack for making good comedy and drama that receives critical acclaim but low ratings.

The best international news service is at 6.30pm daily on the publicly funded Special Broadcasting Service (SBS, Channel 28, UHF). SBS is a multicultural channel that has some of the most diverse programmes shown on TV, including current affairs, documentaries, Spanish soap operas, and films (with English subtitles when necessary).

For something completely different tune into community-based Channel 31 (UHF), which pays its bills by broadcasting horse racing but also produces some quirky, amateur and interesting local programmes.

TIME

Victoria (along with Tasmania, NSW and Queensland) keeps Eastern Standard Time, which is 10 hours ahead of GMT/UTC. That means that when it's noon in Melbourne it's 9pm the previous day in New York, 2am in London and 11am in Tokyo.

Daylight-saving time, when the clocks are put forward an hour, is between the last Sunday in October and the last Sunday in March.

TIPPING

In Australia tipping is fairly entrenched, although the practice is not as essential as it is in the USA, perhaps because Australian workers are protected by a more generous minimum wage. As in the UK and most of continental Europe, it's customary, but not compulsory, to tip in restaurants and cafés: tip if you think the service warranted it, and 10% of the bill is usually enough. If you want to tip your hotel porter, $2 to $5 is an appropriate amount. Taxi drivers don't expect tips as such but many do expect you to round up to the nearest dollar and may fuss over the handing out of change if you don't offer.

TOURIST INFORMATION

The government-run **Melbourne Visitor Information Centre** (Map pp202-04; Federation Sq; 9am-6pm) is your one-stop-shop for tourist information. The centre is a drop-in service providing multilingual services, Internet access

and an accommodation and tour service. An **information booth** (Map pp202-04; Bourke St Mall; daily) also offers tourist information. The phone service and website of **Tourism Victoria** (☎ 13 28 42; www.visitvictoria.com.au) are excellent sources of information to get you up to speed before you arrive. The international terminal at Melbourne Airport also has a tourist information booth open daily.

Visitor information centres carry the free information guides *Melbourne Events* and *Melbourne: Official Visitors Guide*. These have all sorts of helpful information, including a calendar of events, transport maps, attraction and accommodation listings.

Another good resource for visitors is **Information Victoria** (Map pp202-04; ☎ 1300 366 356; 356 Collins St), a government-run bookshop that stocks a wide variety of publications and maps about Melbourne and Victoria.

Parks Victoria (☎ 13 19 63; www.parkweb.vic .gov.au) has an information service and will mail out brochures; its website is loaded with useful information on state and national parks.

VISAS

All visitors need a visa. Only NZ nationals are exempt, and even they receive a 'special category' visa on arrival. The type of visa you require depends on the reason for your visit.

For information on visas, as well as on customs and health issues, check the website of the **Department of Immigration & Multicultural & Indigenous Affairs** (www.immi.gov.au). Visa application forms are available on this website, or from Australian diplomatic missions overseas or travel agents, and you can apply by mail or in person.

WOMEN TRAVELLERS

Melbourne is generally a safe place for women travellers, although you should avoid walking alone late at night. Aussie male culture does have its sexist elements, and sexual harassment does occur. If you do encounter infantile sexism from drunken louts, best you leave and choose a better place.

The following organisations offer advice and services for women:

Royal Women's Hospital Health Information Service (☎ 9344 2007)

Royal Women's Hospital Sexual Assault Unit (☎ 9344 2201)

Women's Health Information Service (☎ 1800 133 321)

WORK

If you come to Australia on a 12-month 'working holiday' visa you can officially work for the entire 12 months, but you can only stay with any one employer for a maximum of three months. On the other hand, working on a regular tourist visa is strictly prohibited.

To receive wages you must have a Tax File Number (TFN), issued by the Australian Taxation Office. Application forms are available at all post offices, and you are required to show your passport and visa. Finding work may take some time and effort. Short-term job opportunities usually exist in factories, the hospitality industry, fruit picking, nannying, telephone sales and collecting for charities. Saturday's *Age* has extensive employment listings, or try online at www.mycareer.com.au.

Doing Business

Tourism Victoria (www.visitvic.com.au) has a corporate section of use to people in Melbourne on business. The *Age* has a daily pull-out section dealing with business issues. Business- and finance-specific publications to look out for include the *Australian Financial Review* and *Business Review Weekly* (BRW).

Volunteer Work

Good Company (www.goodcompany.com.au) is a not-for-profit organisation that matches professionals, skilled in all areas, with community organisations needing short-term projects fulfilled on a pro-rata basis. Otherwise, you may have some luck contacting your preferred organisation directly while you're in town.

Directory – Practicalities

Behind the Scenes

THE LONELY PLANET STORY

The story begins with a classic travel adventure: Tony and Maureen Wheeler's 1972 journey across Europe and Asia to Australia. There was no useful information about the overland trail then, so Tony and Maureen published the first Lonely Planet guidebook to meet a growing need.

From a kitchen table, Lonely Planet has grown to become the largest independent travel publisher in the world, with offices in Melbourne (Australia), Oakland (USA), London (UK) and Paris (France).

Today Lonely Planet guidebooks cover the globe. There is an ever-growing list of books and information in a variety of media. Some things haven't changed. The main aim is still to make it possible for adventurous travellers to get out there – to explore and better understand the world.

At Lonely Planet we believe travellers can make a positive contribution to the countries they visit – if they respect their host communities and spend their money wisely.

THIS BOOK

This 5th edition of *Melbourne* was researched and written by Simone Egger. Simone was helped by contributions from Geraldine Barlow, Jeff Sparrow, Meredith Badger and Tony Macvean. The two previous editions were written by David McClymont and the 1st and 2nd editions by Mark Armstrong. The guide was commissioned right here in Lonely Planet's home-town office and developed by:

Commissioning Editors Errol Hunt, Kalya Ryan
Coordinating Editor Andrea Baster
Coordinating Cartographer Simon Tillema
Coordinating Layout Designer Indra Kilfoyle
Editors Andrew Bain
Proofreader Suzannah Shwer
Index Andrea Baster, Indra Kilfoyle
Cover Designer Nic Lehman
Series Designer Nic Lehman
Series Design Concept Nic Lehman & Andrew Weatherill
Managing Cartographer Corinne Waddell
Mapping Development Paul Piaia
Project Manager Rachel Imeson
Regional Publishing Managers Kate Cody, Virginia Maxwell
Series Publishing Manager Gabrielle Green

Thanks to Dan Caleo, Piotr Czajkowski, Adriana Mammarella, Kate McDonald, Stephanie Pearson, Andrew Weatherill

Cover photographs by Lonely Planet Images: Palm tree shadows, Catani Gardens, St Kilda, Regis Martin (top); Architectural feature, Federation Square, Juliet Coombe (bottom); Orange, Prahran, James Braund (back).

Internal photographs by James Braund/Lonely Planet Images except for the following: p2 (#2) Richard I'Anson/Lonely Planet Images; p2 (#5) John Banagan/Lonely Planet Images. All images are the copyright of the photographers unless otherwise indicated. Many of the images in this guide are available for licensing from Lonely Planet Images: www.lonelyplanetimages.com.

ACKNOWLEDGMENTS

Many thanks to Metlink Victoria Pty Ltd for the use of the Melbourne transport network maps.

THANKS
SIMONE EGGER

We have John Cope-Williams to thank for that hangover. Tony Macvean, Kate Cawley, Meredith Badger, Lisa Richardson, Alisa Gwinner and Hilary Badger all provided expert advice on shopping, eating and entertainment. Big thanks to Jeff Sparrow and Geraldine Barlow for their contributions to the text. Thanks also to Paul Mathis and

SEND US YOUR FEEDBACK

We love to hear from travellers – your comments keep us on our toes and help make our books better. Our well-travelled team reads every word on what you loved or loathed about this book. Although we cannot reply individually to postal submissions, we always guarantee that your feedback goes straight to the appropriate authors, in time for the next edition. Each person who sends us information is thanked in the next edition – and the most useful submissions are rewarded with a free book.

To send us your updates – and find out about LP events, newsletters and travel news – visit our award-winning website: www.lonelyplanet.com.

Note: We may edit, reproduce and incorporate your comments in Lonely Planet products such as guidebooks, websites and digital products, so let us know if you don't want your comments reproduced or your name acknowledged. For a copy of our privacy policy visit www.lonelyplanet.com/privacy.

Liz Jones for their time and contributions. In the Lonely Planet house, bucketloads of thanks to editors Andrea Baster and Andrew Bain, to Errol Hunt, Kalya Ryan, and to David McClymont (for last edition's text). Matthew Saville, thanks for taking my photo – the world's least-willing subject. I've saved the best till last: Simon King, Ruthie Davis, Mum (and her frozen blueberries), and my ever-resourceful brother Warren Egger – thank you.

OUR READERS

Many thanks to the travellers who used the last edition and wrote to us with helpful hints, useful advice and interesting anecdotes. Your names follow:

Olivia Astorino, Jim Banks, Laura Brown, Stephanie Carr, Jeni Charter, Marie Colfer, Alison Coll, D Collins, Ari den Boer, Danielle Derks, Tim Dowdall, Sandra Eastern, Roger Paul Edmonds, Paul Eldridge, Anne Glazier, Rakesh Goel, Dorte Gollek, Annette Hagen, Bels Hillard, Geoff & Carol Hodgson, Caroline Hurd, Anna Illner, Stephen Ireland, Andrea Jones, Maayke & Erik Kazemier, Deborah Koch, Varry Lavin, Howard Lee, Michelle Lee, Alan Lewis, Dawn Lindsay, Beth Marsh, Michaela Matross, Connor McLaughlin, Theresa Mun Yi Leong, Jennifer Mundy, Kate Nielsen, Siobhan Noel, Sara Pike, Mark Pinan, Spencer Plaitin, Rick Pratley, Laura Proietti, Abe Remmo, Dan Richards, Jeff Robbins, Grace Rowland, Bettina Short, David Sinclair, Sanjay Sinha, Mark Smalley, Michael Smith, Darren Sugrue, Natalie Surrey, Matty Taylor, Linda Tighe, Terry Varcoe, Adrian Warren, Anthony Warren, Jeroen van der Weijden, Mae Wong, James Wood, Eoin Wrenn

Notes

Index

See also separate indexes for Eating (p197), Drinking (p197), Shopping (p198) and Sleeping (p198).

000 map pages
000 photographs

Index

197

MAP LEGEND

ROUTES
Tollway
Freeway
Primary Road
Secondary Road
Tertiary Road
Lane
Track
One-Way Street
Unsealed Road
Mall/Steps
Tunnel
Walking Tour
Walking Trail
Walking Path

TRANSPORT
Ferry
Metro
Tram
Rail
Rail (Underground)

HYDROGRAPHY
River, Creek
Water

AREA FEATURES
Area of Interest
Beach, Desert
Building, Featured
Building, Information
Building, Other
Building, Transport
Land
Mall
Park
Sports
Cemetery, Christian

POPULATION
CAPITAL (NATIONAL)
Large City
Small City
CAPITAL (STATE)
Medium City
Town, Village

SYMBOLS

Sights/Activities
Beach
Christian
Islamic
Jewish
Monument
Museum, Gallery
Ruin
Swimming Pool
Trail Head
Zoo, Bird Sanctuary

Eating
Eating

Drinking
Drinking

Entertainment
Entertainment

Shopping
Shopping

Sleeping
Sleeping
Camping

Transport
Airport, Airfield
Bus Station
Cycling, Bicycle Path
Parking Area
Taxi Rank

Other
Picnic Area

Information
Bank, ATM
Embassy/Consulate
Hospital, Medical
Information
Internet Facilities
Police Station
Post Office, GPO
Toilets

Geographic
Lighthouse
Lookout
Mountain, Volcano
National Park
Waterfall

Map Section

Moonee Ponds

A

B

C

D

Medway Golf Club

Highpoint Shopping Centre

Fairbairn Park

Maribyrnong Rd

Ascot Vale

See Parkville & North Melbourne Map (p209)

CityLink

1 Braybrook

Hampstead Rd

Pipemakers Park

Ascot Vale

Brunswick Rd

Western Hwy

Maidstone

Rosamond Rd

Gordon St

Riverside Golf Course

Mt Alexander Rd

Ballarat Rd

Maribyrnong

Showgrounds 11

Newmarket

Flemington Bridge

Royal Park

South Rd

Footscray Park

Flemington Racecourse 3

Smithfield Rd

Racecourse Rd

Flemington Rd

Barkly St

Ballarat Rd

Kensington 7

Kensington

Macaulay

2 Tottenham

Tottenham

West Footscray

Footscray

12

South Kensington

Macaulay Rd

Sunshine Rd

5 Footscray

North Melbourne

Geelong Rd

Middle Footscray

Whitehall St

Hyde St

4

8

Dynon Rd

Footscray Rd

North Melbourne

To Princes Fwy

Williamstown Rd

Seddon

Coode Island

West Melbourne

16

Somerville Rd

15

Dudley St
New Quay Prm

Telstra Dome

3 Francis St

Yarraville 20

Anderson St

Hyde St

Yarra River

Bolte Bridge

Victoria Harbour

Docklands

Brooklyn

McIvor Reserve

Yarraville 13

18 Ballarat St

Westgate Golf Course

Stony Creek

Lorimer St

CityLink

Altona North

West Gate Fwy

Yarraville

West Gate Bridge

Westgate Park

Todd Rd

Simon St

Fishermans Bend

West Gate Fwy

See South Melbourne & Albert Park Map (pp214–15)

Blackshaws Rd

Hudsons Rd
Spotswood

Hall St

10

Spotswood

Williamstown Rd

Port Melbourne

Albert Park

4

Newport Lakes Park

Mason St

Maddox Rd

Challis St

Newport

Sandridge Beach

Bay St

North Rd

Newport Park

Webb Dock

Greenwich Bay

Princes Pier

Beacon Cove

Lagoon Pier

Beaconsfield Pde

Beach

Pier

Altona Lakes Public Golf Course

Melbourne Rd

Douglas Pde

The Strand

Station Pier

Williamstown North

Champion Rd

Williamstown Cemetery

Kororoit Creek Rd

North Williamstown

Ferguson St

Bay Cruises

Hobsons Bay

Altona Coastal Park

5

Victoria St

Williamstown Beach

Osborne St

Williamstown

Williamstown

Jawbone Conservation Reserve

Williamstown Beach

Esplanade

Altona Bay

6

Port Phillip Bay

SIGHTS & ACTIVITIES (pp49–82)
Fairfield Amphitheatre.................1 G2
Fairfield Boathouse & Tea Gardens..2 G2
Flemington Racecourse................3 C2
Footscray Community Arts Centre..4 C2
Footscray Market......................5 C2
Harold Holt Swim Centre.............6 H5
Living Museum..........................7 C2
Maribyrnong River Cruises..........8 C2
Melbourne Planetarium...........(see 10)
RPS – the Board Store...............9 F6
Scienceworks.........................10 B4
Showgrounds.........................11 C1

EATING (pp99–116)
Bo De Trai.............................12 B2
Cafe Fidama..........................13 B3
Carlisle Wine Bar....................14 F6
Gravy Train...........................15 B3
Livebait...............................16 D3
Wall Two 80...........................17 F6
Yarraville Hotel......................18 B3

ENTERTAINMENT (pp125–136)
Red Stitch............................19 F5
Sun Theatre..........................20 B3

CENTRAL MELBOURNE

Eades Park

Queen Victoria Market

A
B
C
D

West Melbourne

Hawke St
Roden St
Spencer St
Rosslyn St
Walsh St
Milton St
William St
Peel St
Queen St

1

Adderley St
Stanley St

P
Carpark

117
37

Anthony St

Railway Pl

Dudley St

Batman St

Jeffcott St

Flagstaff Gardens

8

Singers La
Wills St

Australian Federal Police Headquarters

2

Adderley St

King St

Flagstaff Commonwealth Law Courts

Little Lonsdale St

La Trobe St

William Angliss Institute of TAFE

106

Supreme Court

3

86, City Circle

Wurundjeri Way

Melbourne City Mail Centre

The Age

City Power Station

Little Bourke St

58
124
113

Crombie La
Gresham St

Church St

4

Harbour Esp

City Circle

35
Telstra Dome

Southern Cross (Spencer St)

Godfrey St

86,95,96

121

129

Spencer St

Francis St

Collins St

Australian Stock Exchange

28

122

Highlander La

5

Docklands

11,31,42

107

119

114
112

Flinders La

Downie St

17

Flinders St

North Wharf Rd

48

Wurundjeri Way

96,109,112

6

South Wharf Rd

26

Melbourne Exhibition Centre

19

6
Crown Entertainment Complex

Claredon St
Whiteman St

202

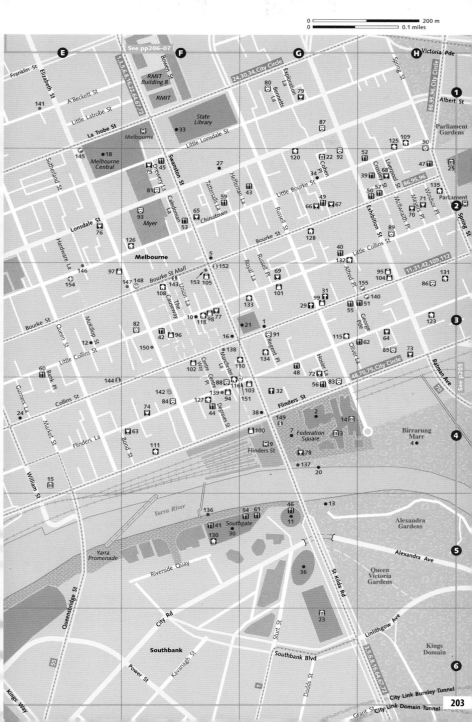

EAST MELBOURNE

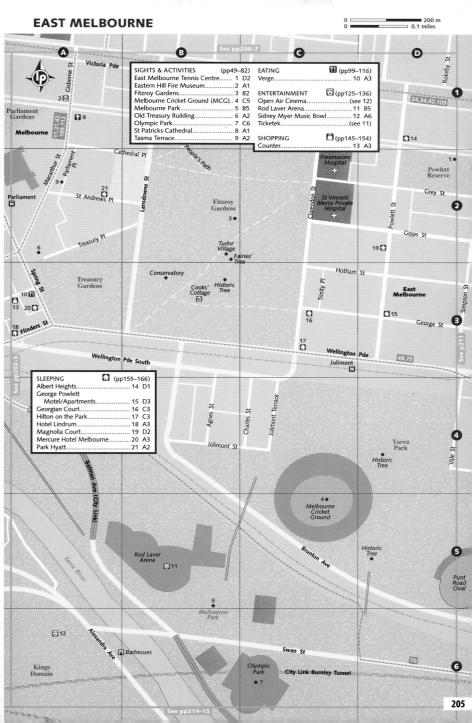

0   200 m
0   0.1 miles

SIGHTS & ACTIVITIES (pp49–82)
East Melbourne Tennis Centre....... 1 D2
Eastern Hill Fire Museum................ 2 A1
Fitzroy Gardens.............................. 3 B2
Melbourne Cricket Ground (MCG).. 4 C5
Melbourne Park............................. 5 B5
Old Treasury Building..................... 6 A2
Olympic Park................................. 7 C6
St Patricks Cathedral...................... 8 A1
Tasma Terrace................................ 9 A2

EATING (pp99–116)
Verge.. 10 A3

ENTERTAINMENT (pp125–136)
Open Air Cinema...........................(see 12)
Rod Laver Arena............................ 11 B5
Sidney Myer Music Bowl................ 12 A6
Ticketek.......................................(see 11)

SHOPPING (pp145–154)
Counter... 13 A3

SLEEPING (pp155–166)
Albert Heights................................ 14 D1
George Powlett
  Motel/Apartments...................... 15 D3
Georgian Court.............................. 16 C3
Hilton on the Park......................... 17 C3
Hotel Lindrum............................... 18 A3
Magnolia Court.............................. 19 D2
Mercure Hotel Melbourne............. 20 A3
Park Hyatt...................................... 21 A2

CARLTON & FITZROY

College Cres

A **B** **C** Davis St **D**

Melbourne
General
Cemetery

Princes St

1

Cemetery Rd East

Victoria Pl

Lygon St 122

Lytton St

Neill St

Parkville

Keppel St

Kay St

Palmerston St

Pitt St

Station St

Canning St

2

Swanston St

Cardigan St

Palmerston St

Union Rd

Tin Al

65

Spencer Rd

University
of
Melbourne

8 122

23 74

Elgin St

Drummond St

70 32 46

17

Macarthur Pl North

Macarthur
Square

Monash Rd

85 20

Wilson Ave

3

1,3,5,6,8,16,
22,64,67,72

50 31

Faraday St

Royal
Womens
Hospital

Dorrit St

University St

Barkly St

Murchison St

Murchison
Square

Owen St

Nicholson St

Grattan St

Carlton St

See p209

4

Lincoln Sq
North

82

Rathdowne St

Carlton

Carlton
Gardens
North

78

Argyle Pl North

Lygon St

Lincoln
Square

Pelham St

Argyle
Square

Lincoln Sq
South

Argyle Pl South

80

Bouverie St

Cardigan St

Drummond St

Melbourne
Museum

49 11

96

5

Queensberry St

13

Royal
Exhibition
Building

81

86

77

76

Earl St

Carlton
Gardens
South

Nicholson St

6

Melbourne

10

Victoria St

86,96

83

12

Mackenzie St

1,3,5,6,8,16,
22,64,67,72

Franklin St

Swanston St

RMIT

24,30,34

PARKVILLE & NORTH MELBOURNE

0		500 m
0		0.25 miles

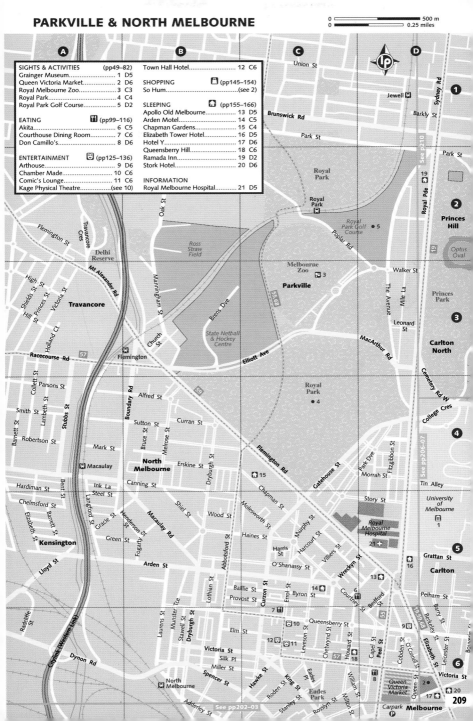

Union St

Jewell

Brunswick Rd

Park St

Royal Park

Royal Park

Royal Park Golf Course ● 5

Poplar Rd

Melbourne Zoo ● 3

Parkville

Walker St

The Avenue

Mile La

Leonard St

MacArthur Rd

Sydney Rd

Barkly St

Park St

Princes Hill

Optus Oval

Princes Park

Carlton North

Flemington St
Travancore Cres

Delhi Reserve

Mt Alexander Rd

Oak St

Ross Straw Field

Manningham St

Church St

Travancore

High St
Shields St
Victoria St
Hill Princes St
Holland Ct

Racecourse Rd

Flemington

Brens Dve

State Netball & Hockey Centre

Elliott Ave

Royal Park
● 4

Cemetery Rd W

College Cres

Collett St
Parsons St
Smith St
Lambeth St
Barnett St
Robertson St

Stubbs St

Mark St

Boundary Rd

Alfred St

Sutton St
Bruce St
Melrose St

Curran St

Macaulay

North Melbourne

Erskine St

Dryburgh St

Flemington Rd

Gatehouse St

Park Dve

Morrah St

Fitzgibbon St

Tin Alley

University of Melbourne

Hardiman St
Bent St
Chelmsford St

Ink La
Steel La
Langford St
Gracie St
Henderson St
Fogarty St

Canning St

Shiel St

Wood St

Macaulay Rd

Green St

Kensington

Elizabeth St
Barrett St

Arden St

Lloyd St

Abbotsford St

Lothian St

Molesworth St

Haines St

Harris St

O'Shanassy St

Murphy St

Harcourt St

Villiers St

Wreckyn St

Courtney St

Story St

Royal Melbourne Hospital
21 ✚

Grattan St

Carlton

Radcliffe St

Citylink Western Link

Dynon Rd

Laurens St
Munster Tce
Stawell St
Dryburgh St

Elm St

Victoria St
Silk Pl
Miller St

Spencer St

Hawke St

North Melbourne

Adderley St

Baillie St

Provost St

Curzon St

Errol St

Byron St

Queensberry St

Leveson St

Chetwynd St

Howard St

Roden St

King St

Eades Pl

Stanley St

Rosslyn St

Capel St

Peel St

Cobden St

William St

Milton St

O'Connell St

Berkeley St

Barry St

Pelham St

Leicester St

Elizabeth St

Victoria St

Queen Victoria Market

Carpark Melbourne

See pp202–03

209

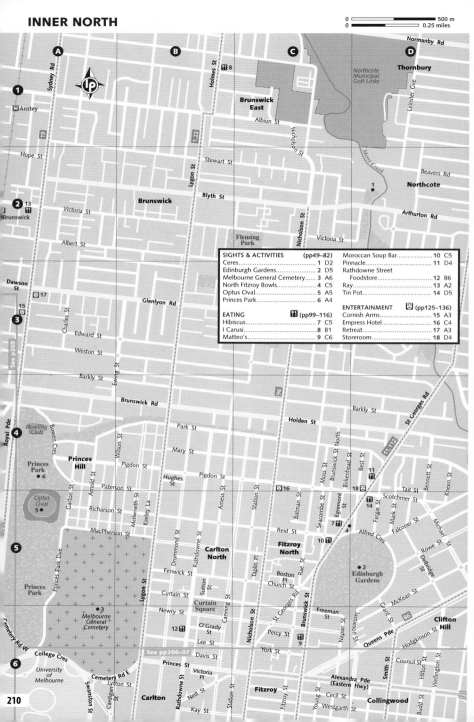

SIGHTS & ACTIVITIES	(pp49–82)
Ceres	1 D2
Edinburgh Gardens	2 D5
Melbourne General Cemetery	3 A6
North Fitzroy Bowls	4 C5
Optus Oval	5 A5
Princes Park	6 A4

EATING	(pp99–116)
Hibiscus	7 C5
I Carusi	8 B1
Matteo's	9 C6

Moroccan Soup Bar	10 C5
Pinnacle	11 D4
Rathdowne Street Foodstore	12 B6
Ray	13 A2
Tin Pot	14 D5

ENTERTAINMENT	(pp125–136)
Cornish Arms	15 A3
Empress Hotel	16 C4
Retreat	17 A3
Storeroom	18 D4

ABBOTSFORD & RICHMOND

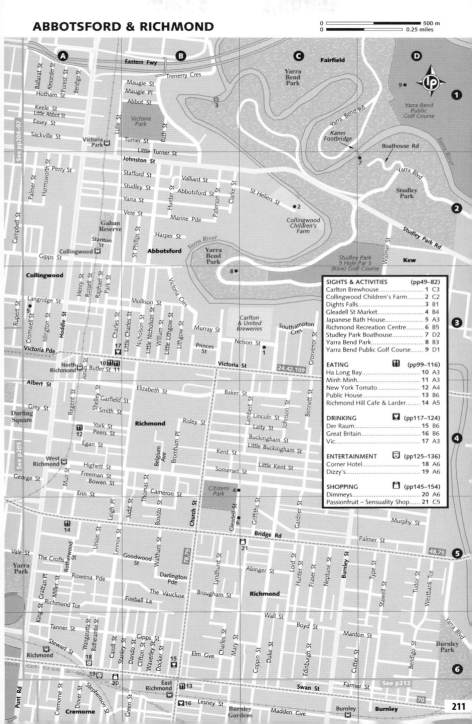

0 _____ 500 m
0 _____ 0.25 miles

SIGHTS & ACTIVITIES	(pp49–82)
Carlton Brewhouse	1 C3
Collingwood Children's Farm	2 C2
Dights Falls	3 B1
Gleadell St Market	4 B4
Japanese Bath House	5 A3
Richmond Recreation Centre	6 B5
Studley Park Boathouse	7 D2
Yarra Bend Park	8 B3
Yarra Bend Public Golf Course	9 D1

EATING	(pp99–116)
Ha Long Bay	10 A3
Minh Minh	11 A3
New York Tomato	12 A4
Public House	13 B6
Richmond Hill Cafe & Larder	14 A5

DRINKING	(pp117–124)
Der Raum	15 B6
Great Britain	16 B6
Vic	17 A3

ENTERTAINMENT	(pp125–136)
Corner Hotel	18 A6
Dizzy's	19 A6

SHOPPING	(pp145–154)
Dimmeys	20 A6
Passionfruit – Sensuality Shop	21 C5

211

SOUTH YARRA, TOORAK & PRAHRAN

0 ————————————— 500 m
0 ————————————— 0.3 mi

SIGHTS & ACTIVITIES (pp49–82)
Como House..............................1 C3
Essential Ingredient Cooking
    School.................................2 A4
Fitness First.............................3 B2
Herring Island..........................4 C2
Prahran Aquatic Centre.............5 B5
Prahran Market........................6 A5

EATING (pp99–116)
Blakes Cafeteria......................7 A5
Da Noi....................................8 A3
David's...................................9 A5
Jacques Reymond...................10 C6
Orange..................................11 A5
Pearl.....................................12 B2
Windsor Castle.......................13 A6

DRINKING (pp117–124)
Back Bar................................14 A6
Blue Bar.................................15 A5
Borsch Vodka & Tears.............16 A6
Candy Bar..............................17 A5
DaDa Bar..........................(see 17)
Greville Bar............................18 A5
La La Land.............................19 A6

ENTERTAINMENT (pp125–136)
Boutique.................................20 A5
Cinema Europa.......................21 B4
Commercial Lounge.................22 A5
Duke of Windsor.....................23 A6
OneSixOne.............................24 A5
Q Bar.....................................25 B3
Revolver.................................26 A5
Viper Room............................27 A4

SHOPPING (pp145–154)
Chapel Bazaar........................28 A5
Collette Dinnigan....................29 B4
Dinosaur Designs....................30 B3
Ellin Ambe.............................31 A5
Fat 272..................................32 A5
Handworks.............................33 A5
Kill City............................(see 33)
Owl.......................................34 A5
RG Madden.............................35 B2

SLEEPING (pp155–166)
Claremont Accommodation......36 A3
Como....................................37 B3
Toorak Manor.........................38 C4

INFORMATION
Borders..............................(see 21)
Hares & Hyenas Bookshop.......39 A5

212

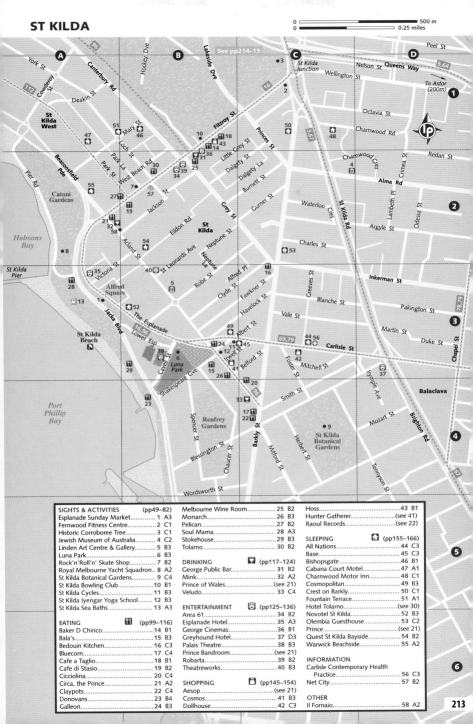

0 _____ 500 m
0 _____ 0.25 miles

See pp214–15

SIGHTS & ACTIVITIES	(pp49–82)
Esplanade Sunday Market	1 A3
Fernwood Fitness Centre	2 C1
Historic Corroboree Tree	3 C1
Jewish Museum of Australia	4 C2
Linden Art Centre & Gallery	5 B3
Luna Park	6 B3
Rock'n'Roll'n' Skate Shop	7 B2
Royal Melbourne Yacht Squadron	8 A2
St Kilda Botanical Gardens	9 C4
St Kilda Bowling Club	10 B1
St Kilda Cycles	11 B3
St Kilda Iyengar Yoga School	12 B3
St Kilda Sea Baths	13 A3

EATING	(pp99–116)
Baker D Chirico	14 B1
Bala's	15 B3
Bedouin Kitchen	16 C3
Bluecorn	17 C4
Cafe a Taglio	18 B1
Cafe di Stasio	19 B3
Cicciolina	20 C4
Circa, the Prince	21 A2
Claypots	22 C4
Donovans	23 B3
Galleon	24 B3

Melbourne Wine Room	25 B2
Monarch	26 B3
Pelican	27 B2
Soul Mama	28 A3
Stokehouse	29 A3
Tolarno	30 B2

DRINKING	(pp117–124)
George Public Bar	31 B2
Mink	32 A2
Prince of Wales	(see 21)
Veludo	33 C4

ENTERTAINMENT	(pp125–136)
Area 61	34 B2
Esplanade Hotel	35 A3
George Cinemas	36 B1
Greyhound Hotel	37 D3
Palais Theatre	38 B3
Prince Bandroom	(see 21)
Robarta	39 B3
Theatreworks	40 B3

SHOPPING	(pp145–154)
Aesop	(see 21)
Cosmos	41 B3
Dollhouse	42 C3

Hoss	43 B1
Hunter Gatherer	(see 41)
Raoul Records	(see 22)

SLEEPING	(pp155–166)
All Nations	44 C3
Base	45 C3
Bishopsgate	46 B1
Cabana Court Motel	47 A1
Charnwood Motor Inn	48 C1
Cosmopolitan	49 B3
Crest on Barkly	50 C1
Fountain Terrace	51 A1
Hotel Tolarno	(see 30)
Novotel St Kilda	52 B3
Olembia Guesthouse	53 C2
Prince	(see 21)
Quest St Kilda Bayside	54 B2
Warwick Beachside	55 A2

INFORMATION	
Carlisle Contemporary Health	
Practice	56 C3
Net City	57 B2

OTHER	
Il Fornaio	58 A2

SOUTH MELBOURNE & ALBERT PARK

0 _____ 500 m
0 _____ 0.25 miles

E

Power St

Sturt St

Grant St

23

4

6

Dodds St

Wells St

Miles St

Wells Pl

Tope St

Little Bank St

5 17

Park St

Napier St

Cobden St

Thomson St

Eastern Rd

Palmerston Cres

F

City Link Burnley Tunnel

City Link Domain Tunnel

St Kilda Rd

Government House Dve

Middleton La

3,5,6,8,16,
64,67,73

13

Birdwood Ave

9

15

Dallas Brooks Dve

**Kings
Domain**

**Kings
Domain**

8

24

Albert Rd

Bowen La

Kings Way

34

Bromby St

Arnold St

Adams St

Domain St

Hope St

Millswyn St

Park St

36

28

Toorak Rd

G

Olympic
Park

Alexandra Ave

Barbecues

Melbourne
Park

Yarra River

H

See p205

Punt Rd

Kelso St

Cremorne

City Link (Monash Fwy)

1

Clowes St

12

**Royal
Botanic
Gardens**

Anderson St

Punt Rd

2

16

Domain Rd

32

Leopold St

Marne St

Walsh St

**South
Yarra**

Caroline St

Avoca St

38

3

Ralston St

Caroline St S

Macfarlan St

Powell St

Alexandra St

Lang St

Fawkner St

Nicholson St

Albion St

Pasley St

See p212

Albert Rd

Albert Rd Dve

Lakeside Dve

31

Arthur St

Queens Rd

Queens La

10

Aquatic Dve

**Gunn
Island**

3

**Albert Park
Lake**

1

**Albert Park Golf
Course**

Louise St

40

Hanna St

41

Alfred La

7

**Fawkner
Park**

Moffat St

Affleck St

Margaret St

Argo St

Moore St

72

4

Commercial Rd

**Alfred
Hospital**

37

Baker La

Athol St

Moss St

Prahran

Greville St

Alfred St

Donald St

Perth St

Charles St

5

Beatrice St

Roy St

29

30

Lorne St

Moubray St

**Wesley
College**

**Victorian
School for
Deaf Children**

Punt Rd

High St

6

Andrew St

Raleigh St

Gladstone St

Upton Rd

Windsor

6

Canterbury Rd

Armstrong St

McGregor St

Lakeside Park Rd

Canterbury Pl

York St

112

39

Lakeside Dve

Queens La

Queens Rd

Union St

3,5,16,64,67

Henry St

Peel St

Queens Way

Nelson St

Ashworth St

Patterson St

Park St

Longmore St

**St Kilda
West**

Hockey Dve

Village Green Dve

Cowderoy St

See p213

WILLIAMSTOWN

0 ————— 500 m
0 ————— 0.3 mi

A   **B**   **C**   **D**

1   **2**   **3**   **4**   **5**   **6**

Yarra River

To Southbank

Howe Pde Extension

Williamstown Rd

Hall St
Drake St
Burleigh St
Home Rd
Collingwood St
Newport
North Rd
Peel St
Wilkins St
Oakbank St
Alma Tce
Paine St
Latrobe St
Bunbury St
Douglas Pde
Yarra St
White St
Chandler St
Thomas St
Douch St
Princes St
Melbourne Rd
Albert St
Queen St
Braw St
Power St
Clis St
Federal St
Russell Pl
John St
Champion Rd
Freyer St
Burgoyne St
Hosking St
Macquarie St
Mariner St
North Williamstown
Stevedore St
College St
Wellington Pde
Haslam St
Dover Rd
Clark St
Kororoit Creek Rd
Station St
Ferguson St
Lyons St
Maclean St
James St
Verdon St
Electra St
Charles St
Victoria St
Perry St
Pasco St
Hannan St
Knight St
Laverton St
Railway Cres
Stewart St
Williamstown Beach
Railway Pl
Parker St
Cecil St
Cole St
Aitken St
Nelson Pl
Ann St
Little Osbourne St
Forster St
Coogee La
Osbourne St
Hanmer St
Williamstown
Kanowna St
Bayview St
Gellibrand St
Garden St
Williamstown Botanic Gardens
Twyford St
Thompson St
Williamstown
Railway Tce
Timeball Tower
Gloucester Reserve
Sadler Reserve
Fearon Reserve
St Giliians St
Illawarra St
Fort Gellibrand
Point Gellibrand Coastal Heritage Park
Williamstown Beach
Hatt Reserve
Esplanade
Morris St
Battery Rd
Williamstown Cricket Ground
Cyril Curtain Reserve

Greenwich Bay

Hobsons Bay

The Strand

Bay Cruises

Commonwealth Reserve

Port Phillip Bay

🏛 4
🏛 1
5 🍴
8 🍴
6 🍴
7 🍴
2 ●
3 ●
🚃 North Williamstown
🚃 Williamstown Beach
🚃 Williamstown
🏊 Williamstown Beach

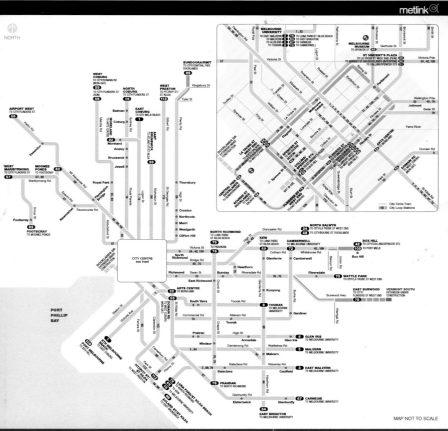

NORTH

MAP NOT TO SCALE

Information

Ticketing Zones

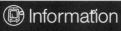

City Saver Zone 1 Zone 2 Zone 3 Nearest Train Station Connecting Bus Tram Terminus Park-Ride

Routes: 1, 3, 5, 6, 8, 16, 19, 22, 24, 30, 31, 42, 48, 55, 57, 59
64, 67, 68, 69, 70, 72, 75, 78, 79, 82, 86, 95, 96, 109, 112

For train, tram and bus information call 131 638 / (TTY) 9619 2727
(6am–10pm daily) or visit www.metlinkmelbourne.com.au

For Yarra Trams customer feedback and lost property call
1800 800 166 (6am–10pm daily) or visit www.yarratrams.com.au

To find your closest Metcard retail outlet or to have
your tickets home delivered call the Metcard Helpline
on (TTY) 1800 652 313 (8am–6pm Monday–Friday,
9am–1pm Saturday)

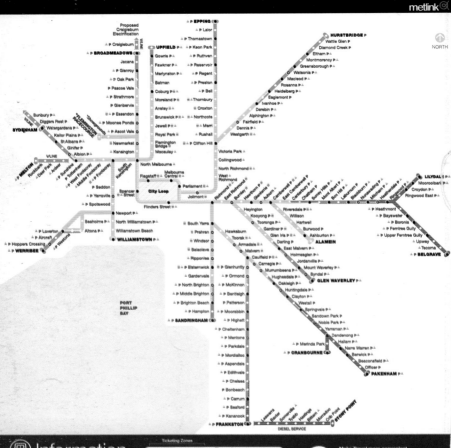

Melbourne Train Network